recipes FROM THE heart

FROM THE HEARTS AND KITCHEN... .S. FOODSERVICE™ ASSOCIATES

FULLPLATES
FULLLIVES™

THIS COOKBOOK IS PART OF U.S. FOODSERVICE'S FULL PLATES, FULL LIVES INITIATIVE.
WWW.FULLPLATESFULLLIVES.COM

NET PROCEEDS FROM THE SALE OF THIS COOKBOOK WILL BENEFIT
AMERICA'S SECOND HARVEST – THE NATION'S FOOD BANK NETWORK

APPETIZERS

BREADS

BREAKFAST & BRUNCH

ENTRÉES

VEGETABLES & SIDE DISHES

SALADS

SOUPS

DESSERTS

CONTENTS

RECIPES FROM THE HEART

recipes

> AMERICA'S SECOND HARVEST, THE LARGEST DOMESTIC HUNGER-RELIEF ORGANIZATION IN THE UNITED STATES, DISTRIBUTES MORE THAN 2 BILLION POUNDS OF FOOD EACH YEAR THROUGH ITS NETWORK OF MORE THAN 200 FOOD BANKS THROUGHOUT THE COUNTRY.

> EVERY DOLLAR DONATED TO AMERICA'S SECOND HARVEST HELPS PROVIDE 20 POUNDS OF FOOD AND GROCERY PRODUCTS TO MEN, WOMEN, AND CHILDREN FACING HUNGER IN THE UNITED STATES.

recipes FROM THE heart

FROM THE HEARTS AND KITCHENS OF U.S. FOODSERVICE® ASSOCIATES

foreword by PAULA DEEN

proceeds will benefit

AMERICA'S SECOND HARVEST – THE NATION'S FOOD BANK NETWORK

US FOODSERVICE®
Your partner beyond the plate.™

R
Th

of fi

d
na
or ir
or
rom t
rpose

n this bc
service
ized ar
d Tra
s menti
egis

FOREWORD

HEY Y'ALL

The American dream is alive and well, and I'm livin' proof. I started a restaurant when I hadn't much more than a dime to my name. But what I did have was even more important – the support and love of family and friends, and the generosity of strangers who took a chance and helped me.

The people helped by America's Second Harvest – The Nation's Food Bank Network are no different than you and me; they're just goin' through a rough patch. They need people to have faith in them like the good folks at U.S. Foodservice are showin' with this book. And, when folks are given a helping hand, a hearty meal and a chance to learn, they will make their dreams a reality. The soul of this cookbook is in the circle of giving made possible by America's Second Harvest and local food banks across the country.

At the heart of the cookbook – well, it's all about the food! In my neck of the woods, food connects us all. In the South, people spend a whole lot of time in the kitchen sharing recipes and passing down traditions. For me, it began in my Grandmomma Paul's kitchen, something always smelled good in there. Her cooking came from within. It was how she showed her love, her compassion, her neighborliness.

Food brings everyone to the table. Try the tasty treats in here, contributed by the good folks at U.S. Foodservice, who are sharing their recipes as well as their cherished mealtime memories. I'm honored to be part of this amazing, kindhearted effort. Whether you're a fancy chef type or just a plain ol' cook who's puttin' down three squares a day for the kids, there are recipes you'll enjoy making as much as your family and guests will enjoy eating them.

Most of all, as you look at the bounty you're able to put on your table every night, I know you'll feel good that you've just helped others enjoy a full plate too. Thank y'all for helping.

> PAULA DEEN, QUEEN OF SOUTHERN AND HOMESTYLE COOKING AND HOST OF THE FOOD NETWORK'S *PAULA'S HOME COOKING*, LEARNED THE SECRETS OF SOUTHERN COOKING FROM HER GRANDMOTHER SOME 30 YEARS AGO.

PAULA'S RESTAURANT IN SAVANNAH GEORGIA, THE LADY AND SONS, HAS GATHERED ACCOLADES FROM CRITICS AND, MORE IMPORTANTLY, FROM HER CUSTOMERS WHO RETURN AGAIN AND AGAIN.

PAULA HAS APPEARED ON THE *OPRAH WINFREY SHOW*, AND HAS WRITTEN A NUMBER OF COOKBOOKS. ALSO POPULAR IS HER MAGAZINE, *COOKING WITH PAULA DEEN*.

FULL PLATES

HEARTFELT GREETINGS

Thank you for purchasing *Recipes from the Heart* in support of America's Second Harvest – The Nation's Food Bank Network. We hope that these recipes and stories will help bring life to the meals you share with family and friends. This cookbook comes from the heart of U.S. Foodservice, its associates, and reflects our dedication to help those in our community who are not getting enough to eat.

As people in the food business, we understand the bounty that food brings to one's life. Having access to healthy food marks the difference between thriving and merely existing. We also recognize that family recipes and traditions create a personal tapestry of mealtime memories, bringing food to life, and we are delighted to share some of our personal stories with you.

This cookbook is a result of our passion for fighting hunger in America, and for enriching lives with human compassion. The 27,000 associates of U.S. Foodservice, as well as many generous business partners, are engaged in the Full Plates, Full Lives™ campaign. Our goal: to raise funds to support the critical efforts of America's Second Harvest to put nutritious food on the plates of those who need it. We'll pursue our goal through fundraising efforts such as the sale of this cookbook and other elements of our Full Plates, Full Lives™ campaign.

Please use this book often, share it with family and friends and encourage them to purchase it for themselves and others. Think about the comfort you find in a good meal and the bonds you make when you share a meal; the associates of U.S. Foodservice have done so by sharing some of the personal stories that bring their recipes to life. At the end of this book of homemade favorites, you will also find stories that will take you to the heart of hunger and how America's Second Harvest makes a significant difference in peoples' lives – one by one.

With great thanksgivings,
Bob Aiken
President and Chief Executive Officer > U.S. Foodservice

> AN ESTIMATED 35.5 MILLION AMERICANS ARE FOOD INSECURE, MEANING THEIR ACCESS TO ENOUGH FOOD IS LIMITED BY A LACK OF MONEY AND OTHER RESOURCES.

> OVER 12.6 MILLION CHILDREN LIVE IN FOOD INSECURE HOUSEHOLDS.

FULL LIVES

ON A THANKFUL NOTE

Our mission at America's Second Harvest – The Nation's Food Bank Network is to feed America's hungry through a nationwide network of member food banks and to engage the country in the fight to end hunger. If you let yourself think about it, the magnitude of hunger in America is staggering. More than 25 million Americans count on our assistance, and so many more go uncounted and unfed.

Each year, our network of food banks and food-rescue organizations distributes more than two billion pounds of food and grocery products to millions of hungry Americans. We maintain a highly sophisticated network of food collection and distribution centers and work with hundreds of food partners on a regular basis. U.S. Foodservice is one of our valued partners, helping us ensure that the shelves in our nation's food banks and the kitchens of our food bank agencies are full.

We believe that every single person can do something to aid in the fight against hunger in America. By purchasing this cookbook, you have already helped by contributing to U.S. Foodservice's Full Plates, Full Lives™ campaign. Please consider lending your hands and your hearts to help America's hungry. At the end of the cookbook you will find resources on how you can help.

With gratitude,
The Staff and Volunteers of America's Second Harvest –
The Nation's Food Bank Network
www.secondharvest.org

> AMERICA'S SECOND HARVEST RECEIVED A CHARITABLE COMMITMENT RATING OF 98 PERCENT FROM *FORBES* MAGAZINE, MEANING 98 PERCENT OF ALL PRODUCT AND FINANCIAL DONATIONS RECEIVED BY AMERICA'S SECOND HARVEST GO DIRECTLY TOWARD FEEDING HUNGRY PEOPLE.

> MORE THAN 25 MILLION AMERICANS ARE HELPED BY THE AMERICA'S SECOND HARVEST NETWORK EACH YEAR.

> THE USDA ESTIMATES 96 BILLION
POUNDS OF FOOD ARE WASTED
EACH YEAR IN THE UNITED STATES.

A PARTNERSHIP THAT WORKS

AMERICA'S SECOND HARVEST – THE NATION'S FOOD BANK NETWORK AND U.S. FOODSERVICE, AN INDUSTRY LEADER IN FOOD DISTRIBUTION UNITE TO COMBAT HUNGER

At U.S. Foodservice, we answer the call to end hunger in several ways: by supporting and encouraging our associates to act locally to fight hunger, and, as a national partner of America's Second Harvest, by helping to put food in the hands of those who need it most. U.S. Foodservice and its associates regularly donate food to America's Second Harvest.

Every day, U.S. Foodservice moves hundreds of tons of food through more than 70 distribution centers across America to over 250,000 customers, including your favorite neighborhood restaurants, hospitals, hotels and schools. With those kinds of numbers and ever-changing marketplace demands, we take the opportunity to share high quality products that may otherwise be wasted. America's Second Harvest makes it possible to efficiently distribute those high quality food products to member food banks.

ACROSS AMERICA: U.S. FOODSERVICE ACTING LOCALLY WITH NATIONAL IMPACT

As an organization, we at U.S. Foodservice are committed to living our values. These shared values guide the way we work with customers, the food industry, our communities, and our partners. We emphasize integrity, safety, and quality as the foundation of our values. We operate with responsibility, accountability, partnership, innovation, openness, respect and diversity. We weave these principles into everything we do.

Living these values in the workplace comes easily to our associates. We are proud of their citizenry within their own neighborhoods. The more than 27,000 associates across the country have always worked to make their communities better. In 2006, the 70-plus U.S. Foodservice locations contributed more than $2.2 million in products to local causes and events in addition to thousands more raised for food banks across the country.

The first step in fighting hunger is awareness and education, and this cookbook is loaded with inspirational ingredients for community action. Stories of need are answered by the caring spirit of America's Second Harvest programs and volunteers.

FOOD CREATES OPPORTUNITIES

Food creates possibilities in a person's life; food insecurity threatens a person's ability to thrive. Hunger can devastate in so many ways: the ability to function in school and at work, the risk of failing physical and emotional health, and even the erosion of community stability. From this notion has risen the Full Plates, Full Lives™ campaign between U.S. Foodservice and America's Second Harvest. This cookbook represents one of a number of activities taking place through this campaign, locally and nationally, to fight hunger.

The America's Second Harvest network of food banks provides a lifeline of support in hundreds of communities. It starts with putting good food on plates, but that is only the beginning. America's Second Harvest and its partners create communities of service. Educating Americans and engaging their help creates a blanket of support and a tapestry of care to lift up the hungry, provide them with opportunities and help them thrive.

A staggering fact is that one out of every ten people live with constant uncertainty about the source of their next meal – what the U.S. Food and Drug Administration (USDA) calls "food insecurity." The nationwide network of food banks

> THE CONCEPT OF FOOD BANKING BEGAN IN 1967; AMERICA'S SECOND HARVEST WAS ESTABLISHED IN 1979. THE NAME IS BASED ON THE BIBLICAL REFERENCE THAT APPEALS TO FARMERS AND LANDOWNERS TO LEAVE A SECOND HARVEST FOR THE POOR AND STRANGERS IN THEIR MIDST.

> IN FY 2007, 11.9 MILLION POUNDS OR 542 TRUCKLOADS OF DONATED FOOD WERE DISTRIBUTED FREE OF CHARGE TO 153 FOOD BANKS THROUGH RELIEF FLEET.

maintained by America's Second Harvest helps people from all walks of life and all backgrounds, when they fall on hard times. America's Second Harvest understands that people who are hungry and need help often feel a deep sense of shame because they are unable to provide for themselves and their families. Therefore, America's Second Harvest programs and food bank volunteers work hard to create a sense of welcome and support so people in need are comfortable asking for help, and accepting it. Many come back as volunteers, extending the circle of care.

The America's Second Harvest network is an oasis for people to comfortably find help, be helped, and help others. From providing a safe haven for school children to have a meal or snack, to providing groceries and assistance to seniors, and opportunities to learn self-sufficiency, America's Second Harvest supports seven innovative community programs:

- BackPack™ Program. The BackPack™ Program is designed to meet the needs of hungry children at times when free or reduced-priced lunches are not available, such as weekends and school vacations. The BackPack™ Program discreetly sends backpacks filled with nutritious, child-friendly snacks and food home with children for the weekend.

- Community Kitchen.® The Community Kitchen® program provides job training to low-income adults to prepare them for careers in the food service industry. As part of their training, students also develop valuable professional and life skills including interviewing skills, supervising techniques and conflict management. As the students work through the program, they serve their communities by preparing hundreds of nutritious meals for a variety of social service agencies. The program is an innovative way to feed the hungry, train the unemployed and support individuals who are making the transition to sustained self-sufficiency.

> MORE THAN ONE-THIRD (36 PERCENT) OF ALL CLIENT HOUSEHOLDS SERVED BY THE AMERICA'S SECOND HARVEST NETWORK HAVE ONE OR MORE ADULTS EMPLOYED.

> MORE THAN 9 MILLION CHILDREN ARE SERVED BY THE AMERICA'S SECOND HARVEST NETWORK, OF WHICH MORE THAN 2 MILLION ARE AGE 5 AND UNDER – THIS REPRESENTS MORE THAN 72 PERCENT OF ALL CHILDREN IN POVERTY.

- **Disaster Relief.** When disaster strikes, America's Second Harvest provides food and relief supplies to emergency feeding centers serving victims through a network of more than 200 member food banks and food-rescue organizations.

- **National Produce Program.** To increase the network's capacity to handle fresh foods, America's Second Harvest has established the National Produce Program. This program offers a comprehensive array of services built around securing and distributing fresh produce throughout the America's Second Harvest network.

- **Kids Cafe.** Partnering with local community service groups like Boys & Girls Clubs, America's Second Harvest supports Kids Cafe to provide low income children with a warm meal, snacks, and a safe place to learn, socialize or play.

- **Relief Fleet.** America's Second Harvest has created an active network of transportation companies who provide deeply discounted or complimentary trailer space to help transport donated food to food banks.

- **Seafood Initiative.** Supported by the seafood industry, this program brings highly nutritious, protein-rich foods to the food bank tables in useable portions.

HUNGRY FOR MORE?

The intent of this cookbook is to inspire as well as create memorable mealtimes. Use these recipes to share a meal with new friends and neighbors. Donate fresh, nutritious food to a local food bank. Share a story of America's Second Harvest with someone and suggest they make a donation. Help make meals at a local food bank. Volunteer to mentor at a Kids Cafe. There are so many ways to make a difference in the fight against hunger. *Buy this book for a friend.*

Use this cookbook as a resource and a call to action. You'll find pages in the back of the cookbook to help you find a local food bank or to learn more about America's Second Harvest and its network of food banks.

> FOR EVERY DOLLAR SAVED ON TRANSPORTATION, THE AMERICA'S SECOND HARVEST NETWORK CAN PROVIDE FIVE MEALS TO A NEEDY FAMILY OF FOUR. LAST YEAR, THE NETWORK SAVED NEARLY $596,000 IN TRANSPORTATION COSTS, ENABLING THOSE FUNDS TO BE PUT BACK INTO PROGRAMS THAT FEED THE HUNGRY.

GIVING BACK

GIVING BACK TO THE COMMUNITIES WE LIVE AND WORK IN IS MORE THAN THE RIGHT THING TO DO; IT CONNECTS US ALL AND CREATES A LEGACY IN WHICH WE CAN ALL TAKE PRIDE.

Integrity, safety, and quality are the basis for everything U.S. Foodservice does. These values shape the way we do business, how we treat our associates, and demonstrate our commitment to responsible corporate citizenship. In 2006, U.S. Foodservice divisions and locations contributed more than $2.2 million in products and money to 350 local causes and events. Here are some of the ways we live our values every day.

- During the southern California fires of 2007, the U.S. Foodservice San Diego division stayed fully operational, providing uninterrupted service to fire-fighters, fire kitchens, emergency centers, healthcare facilities and military bases, as well as donating products by the truckload to community organizations in need.

- U.S. Foodservice is a committed expert on food safety and delivers the National Restaurants Association's food safety training and certification program at cost to its customers.

- During Thanksgiving 2007, the Inter-Faith Food Shuttle in Raleigh, North Carolina, partnered with the local U.S. Foodservice division to ensure a bountiful feast for the community's needy. U.S. Foodservice and Sara Lee donated 500 foil-wrapped turkeys and family sized packages of vegetables. To ensure food safety, coolers and ice were also provided to transport the food safely back to the agencies.

- In Oklahoma City, U.S. Foodservice associates hold a monthly cook-off with the proceeds donated to a local charity.

- Mentoring youth through the "Beating the Odds" Foundation has been a focus for the Altoona/Greensburg, Pennsylvania division of U.S. Foodservice for years. Those efforts have motivated hundreds of children to make the right choices in their lives. In 2007 the division received the Leigh Steinberg Beating the Odds Quarterbacks of Life Award for its outstanding work.

> IN 2007, 62 PERCENT OF AMERICANS RESPONDING TO A SURVEY COMMISSIONED BY AMERICA'S SECOND HARVEST CONSIDERED HUNGER A MAJOR PROBLEM IN OUR COUNTRY; 41 PERCENT SAID THAT THE PROBLEM HAS GOTTEN WORSE.

appetizers

apple dip

Susan Borkowicz > *Mesa, Arizona*

Serves 6 to 8

INGREDIENTS

1 (8-ounce) **brick cream cheese, softened**
1 (8-ounce) **container Cool Whip, thawed**
1 jar caramel ice cream topping
6 Granny Smith or Red Delicious apples
2 cups ginger ale

PREPARATION

Mix the cream cheese, Cool Whip, and ice cream topping together. Place in a serving bowl. Cut the apples in slices and put them in the ginger ale—this will keep them from turning brown and give them a delicious flavor. Chill. At serving time, drain the apples and serve with the dip.

bean dip

Kelli Greer > *Shawnee, Kansas*

Serves 10 to 15

INGREDIENTS

1/2 pound ground beef
1 can refried beans
1 cup sour cream
1 (8-ounce) **package cream cheese, softened**
1 cup chopped onion
1 package taco seasoning
1 (4-ounce) **can sliced black olives**
1 cup cheddar cheese, shredded

PREPARATION

Preheat oven to 325ºF. Sauté and drain the ground beef. Mix in all ingredients except the cheddar cheese. Bake for 30 minutes or until warm. Sprinkle with cheddar cheese. Continue to bake until the cheese is melted. Serve with tortilla chips.

BREADS

BREAKFAST & BRUNCH

ENTRÉES

VEGETABLES & SIDE DISHES

SALADS

SOUPS

DESSERTS

bruschetta

Michael Koenen > *Plymouth, Minnesota*

Serves 8 to 10

INGREDIENTS

8 Roma tomatoes, seeded, cored, and chopped
1 ounce fresh basil
1/4 red onion, diced
2 teaspoons garlic, peeled and minced
1/4 teaspoon salt
1/4 teaspoon ground pepper (mixed peppercorns)
1 tablespoon olive oil
1 tablespoon balsamic vinegar
2 baguettes
Garlic olive oil (spray pump variety)

PREPARATION

Wash and prepare the tomatoes. Leave at room temperature. Chop the basil into 1/4-inch pieces. In a large bowl, combine the tomatoes, onion, garlic, salt, pepper, olive oil, balsamic vinegar, and basil; mix well. Cut bread into 1/2-inch slices. Lay slices on baking sheet and spritz with olive oil. Bake at 350ºF for 5 minutes or until lightly crisped. Top each piece of bread with bruschetta mixture and serve.

cheese crispies

Ginger Catoe > *Lugoff, South Carolina*

Serves 8 to 10

INGREDIENTS

1 1/2 cups (3 sticks) margarine, softened
2 cups extra-sharp cheese, grated
2 cups crispy rice cereal
1/2 teaspoon lemon juice
1/2 teaspoon tabasco sauce
1/2 teaspoon salt
2 cups all-purpose flour

PREPARATION

Preheat oven to 350ºF. Combine all of the ingredients in the order listed, mixing flour in last. Roll into small balls and press with your thumb. Bake for 15 to 20 minutes. For a spicier taste, add more tabasco.

> " I LIKE TO MAKE THESE SNACKS FOR TAILGATE PARTIES AT UNIVERSITY OF SOUTH CAROLINA FOOTBALL GAMES. WE USUALLY SERVE THEM WITH A HOT BOWL OF CHILI. "
>
> > Ginger

confetti squares

Larry Chavanne > *Buffalo, New York*

Serves 15 to 20

INGREDIENTS

2 packages refrigerated crescent rolls
2 (8-ounce) **packages cream cheese, softened**
3 tablespoons mayonnaise
1/2 teaspoon dried basil leaves, crushed
1/3 teaspoon garlic powder
2 cups finely chopped vegetables (use a variety: broccoli florets, olives, red onion, red and green peppers)
Salad Supreme seasoning

PREPARATION

Heat oven to 350ºF. Press the crescent rolls into a 15 by 10 by 1-inch baking sheet to form a single piece of dough. Bake 12 to 15 minutes, until the crust is golden brown. Remove from the oven and cool completely; set aside. Combine the cream cheese, mayonnaise, basil, and garlic powder. Mix well. Spread the mixture thinly over the cooled crust. Top with the chopped vegetables and sprinkle generously with the Salad Supreme. Cut into squares. Refrigerate until ready to serve.

BREADS

BREAKFAST & BRUNCH

ENTRÉES

VEGETABLES & SIDE DISHES

SALADS

SOUPS

DESSERTS

chesapeake bay crab cake

Bryan Corsini > *Atlanta, Georgia*

Serves 8 to 10

INGREDIENTS

1 (16-ounce) **can crab claw meat**
1 (16-ounce) **can crab special meat**
2 eggs
1 egg yolk
1 1/2 cup breadcrumbs
1 tablespoon Dijon mustard
3/4 cup mayonnaise
Old Bay seasoning

PREPARATION

Combine all the ingredients (use Old Bay seasoning to taste) and form into 4-ounce patties. Sauté in butter, broil, or bake until golden brown. Optional: Sauté green onions and chopped yellow and red peppers. Cool and serve on top of crab cakes.

crab dip

Patricia Ferguson > *St. Charles, Missouri*

Serves 4

INGREDIENTS

2 pounds backfin crabmeat
12 green onions
3 cloves garlic
1 (8-ounce) **package cream cheese, softened**
1 cup heavy sour cream
1 cup mayonnaise
2 dashes hot sauce
2 dashes Worcestershire sauce
Juice from 1/2 lemon
Pinch of pepper

PREPARATION

Drain the crabmeat. Chop the green onions with stems and set aside. Crush the garlic cloves. Mix all of the ingredients in a large bowl, using an electric mixer.

> "I MAKE THIS CRAB DIP EVERY CHRISTMAS IN HONOR OF MY FATHER. IT WAS HIS FAVORITE DIP. ONCE YOU TAKE THIS DIP TO A PARTY, PEOPLE WILL EXPECT YOU TO BRING IT EVERY TIME."
>
> > Patricia

crab fluffs

Israel Arnove > *Parkville, Maryland*

Serves 12

INGREDIENTS FOR CRAB MIXTURE

1 pound crabmeat
1/2 cup Italian seasoned breadcrumbs
1 large egg
1/4 cup mayonnaise
1 teaspoon Worcestershire sauce
1 teaspoon dry mustard
1/2 teaspoon salt
1/4 teaspoon pepper

INGREDIENTS FOR BATTER

1 1/2 cups all-purpose flour
2 teaspoons baking powder
1 teaspoon Old Bay seasoning
1/2 teaspoon salt
1/4 teaspoon celery seed
1/2 teaspoon lemon-pepper seasoning
2 eggs
2 teaspoons mayonnaise
1/4 teaspoon prepared mustard
1 cup milk
Margarine, butter, or oil for frying

PREPARATION FOR CRAB MIXTURE

Remove all cartilage from the crabmeat and place the crabmeat in a bowl. In another bowl, mix the breadcrumbs, egg, mayonnaise, Worcestershire sauce, dry mustard, salt, and pepper. Pour the mixture over the crabmeat and mix gently but not thoroughly. If the mixture is too dry, add a little more mayonnaise. Shape into 12 balls. Set aside.

PREPARATION FOR BATTER

In a large bowl, mix the flour, baking powder, Old Bay seasoning, celery seed, and lemon-pepper seasoning. In a small bowl, beat the eggs; mix in the mayonnaise and mustard. Add the egg mixture to the flour mixture. Slowly stir in the milk until the batter is the consistency of medium pancake batter. Coat crab balls one at a time with the batter and drop gently into hot fat (350°F). Cook until browned, then remove and drain. Coat balls again, cook in fat again until golden brown on all sides. Remove and drain. Serve immediately.

> **THIS RECIPE HAS BEEN IN MY WIFE'S FAMILY FOR GENERATIONS. MY MOTHER-IN-LAW PASSED IT DOWN TO MY WIFE. IT'S A CROWD FAVORITE, ESPECIALLY IN MARYLAND, THE HOME OF OLD BAY SEASONING.**
>
> > Israel

BREADS

BREAKFAST & BRUNCH

ENTRÉES

VEGETABLES & SIDE DISHES

SALADS

SOUPS

DESSERTS

crabmeat muffins

Janice Simonian > *Newnan, Georgia*

Serves 15 to 20

INGREDIENTS

1/2 cup (4 ounces/1 stick) **salted butter, softened**
1 (8-ounce) **jar Cheese Whiz**
2 teaspoons mayonnaise
1/2 teaspoon garlic powder
1 (6 1/2-ounce) **can crabmeat, drained**
8 to 10 English muffins

PREPARATION

Combine the butter, Cheese Whiz, mayonnaise, and garlic powder. Add the crabmeat and mix together. Split the English muffins and spread with the crabmeat mixture. Place on a cookie sheet, cover, and chill until the mixture has hardened. Broil muffins until the tops are brown and bubbly. Cut in halves or quarters to serve. Muffins freeze well for up to 6 months.

> "WHEN WE LIVED IN GERMANY FOR FIVE YEARS, OUR FRIENDS WERE OUR FAMILY. DURING THE HOLIDAYS, WE ALL GOT TOGETHER AND EXCHANGED RECIPES; THIS WAS ONE OF THE FAVORITES."
>
> > Janice

caramel apple dip

Catherine Schouviller > *Princeton, Minnesota*

Serves 10

INGREDIENTS

1 (8-ounce) **package cream cheese**
3 tablespoons brown sugar
1 jar butterscotch caramel topping
1 cup Heath Baking Bits (not chocolate-covered)
6 apples (Granny Smith works well)

PREPARATION

Blend the cream cheese and brown sugar, and spread the mixture in the bottom of a decorative pie plate. Drizzle the caramel topping over the mixture and top with the Heath Bits. Chill and serve with sliced apples.

> "I HAVE SERVED THIS AT MANY GATHERINGS IN THE FALL APPLE SEASON IN MINNESOTA. EVERYONE RAVES ABOUT HOW GOOD IT IS."
>
> > Catherine

deviled eggs
new england style

Tom Egan > *Peabody, Massachusetts*

Serves 6

INGREDIENTS

1 dozen jumbo eggs
1 tablespoon white vinegar
3/4 cup regular mayonnaise
3/4 cup Miracle Whip
2 ounces Philadelphia cream cheese
1 teaspoon kosher salt or sea salt
2 teaspoons cracked black pepper, plus additional for topping
1/2 teaspoon dried chives
1/2 teaspoon Spanish paprika
1 jar of pimento-stuffed green olives

PREPARATION

Carefully place the eggs into a large pot and fill with cold water halfway to the top. Add the white vinegar to the water (helps in shell-removal process). Bring to a boil and cook 10 to 15 minutes, until eggs are hard-boiled. Remove eggs from the water and let cool. Shell eggs. Cut them in half lengthwise and scoop the cooked yolks into a mixing bowl.

Mash the yolks, then add the mayonnaise, Miracle Whip, cream cheese, olives, salt, and cracked pepper. Mix until smooth. Transfer the mixture into a pastry bag and slowly fill the cut egg whites. The yolk mixture should overfill the hole and cover most of the egg white. (Note: If you do not have a pastry bag, use a teaspoon.)

Place the deviled eggs on a serving tray. Sprinkle with dried chives and dust with paprika. A pinch of cracked pepper adds a nice flavor.

> WHEN I WAS GROWING UP, THESE DEVILED EGGS WERE ALWAYS ON THE TABLE AT THANKSGIVING, CHRISTMAS, AND NEW YEAR'S. I AM NOW OFFICIALLY IN CHARGE OF THE DEVILED EGGS DURING THE HOLIDAY SEASON (PROBABLY BECAUSE NO ONE ELSE WANTS TO SHELL FOUR DOZEN EGGS).
>
> > Tom

BREADS

BREAKFAST & BRUNCH

ENTRÉES

VEGETABLES & SIDE DISHES

SALADS

SOUPS

DESSERTS

feed the neighborhood salsa

Cheryl Humphreys > *Prospect, Kentucky*

Serves 30

INGREDIENTS

6 Roma tomatoes
1 yellow tomato
1 orange tomato
1 green pepper
1 red pepper
1 orange pepper
1 yellow pepper
2 small cans sliced black olives
2 cans white shoepeg corn
2 cans black-eyed peas
Fresh cilantro
1 bottle Robusto Italian dressing
Pinch of garlic salt
2 teaspoons lime juice
1/2 teaspoon granulated sugar
1 jar chopped jalapeños (optional)
Tortilla chips

PREPARATION

Seed and chop all peppers and tomatoes. (Note: If yellow and orange tomatoes are not available, add a few extra Roma tomatoes.) Transfer to a large bowl. Drain the olives and add to the tomatoes and peppers. Add the corn and black-eyed peas (undrained). Chop fresh cilantro to taste and add to the bowl. Add the Italian dressing, garlic salt, lime juice, sugar, and jalapeños. Serve with the tortilla chips. Leftover salsa is great served with eggs, fish, chicken, or burritos.

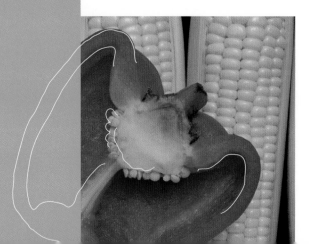

jeanne's meatballs

Mike Bloms > *St. Michael, Minnesota*

Serves 6 to 7

INGREDIENTS FOR MEATBALLS

1 pound hamburger
1/3 cup onion, finely chopped
1 egg
1/2 cup breadcrumbs
1/4 cup milk
1 teaspoon salt
4 teaspoons Worcestershire sauce

INGREDIENTS FOR SAUCE

1/2 cup ketchup
1/2 cup onion, finely chopped
1/3 cup granulated sugar
1/3 cup white vinegar
2 tablespoons Worcestershire sauce
1/8 teaspoon pepper

PREPARATION

Preheat oven to 350ºF. Mix all the ingredients for meatballs together. Shape mixture into 1-inch balls. Bake on a cookie sheet approximately 30 minutes until done. Mix all the ingredients for the sauce together. Place meatballs in a crock-pot. Pour the sauce over the meatballs. Cook for 2 to 3 hours at 155ºF until meatballs are cooked through.

APPETIZERS

BREADS

BREAKFAST & BRUNCH

ENTRÉES

VEGETABLES & SIDE DISHES

SALADS

SOUPS

DESSERTS

jalapeño bacon wraps

Kristina Mendoza > *Houston, Texas*

Serves 8 to 10

INGREDIENTS

1 pound fresh whole jalapeños
1 (8-ounce) package Philadelphia cream cheese
1 package Lit'l Smokies sausage
1 pound bacon
1 package of toothpicks

PREPARATION

Preheat oven to 350ºF. Slice the jalapeños lengthwise. Remove stems and scrape the insides of the jalapeños with a teaspoon to remove seeds. Spread some of the cream cheese inside each jalapeño. Place a sausage on top of the cream cheese. Wrap each jalapeño with a strip of bacon. Stick a toothpick all the way through the center of the jalapeño. Lay on baking pan and place in oven for 15 to 20 minutes or until bacon is brown and cooked.

jalapeño hot hams

Mike Palmer > *Allentown, Pennsylvania*

Serves 8 to 10

INGREDIENTS

2 (8-ounce) bricks cream cheese (do not use low fat)
6 to 8 fresh or canned jalapeño peppers
1 medium onion
1 pound thin-sliced deli ham

PREPARATION

Let the cream cheese soften for an hour at room temperature. Finely dice the peppers and onions and mix with the cream cheese in a bowl. Spread the mixture (about 1/8-inch thick) onto each slice of deli ham and roll it up. Chill rolls in the refrigerator. Cut rolls into bite-sized pieces. The longer they sit after preparation, the spicier (hotter) they will get. Canned jalapeños are hotter than fresh ones, and you can use the juice from the can to thin the cream cheese when you mix ingredients.

lumpia (filipino egg roll)

Anthony Sauler > *Livermore, California*

Serves 15

INGREDIENTS

1 tablespoon sesame oil
3 cloves garlic, crushed
1/2 cup finely chopped onion
1 pound ground pork or ground turkey
1 cup minced carrots
1/2 cup chopped green onions
1 cup thinly sliced green cabbage
1 teaspoon ground black pepper
1 teaspoon salt
1 teaspoon garlic powder
1 tablespoon soy sauce
30 lumpia wrappers
4 cups vegetable oil for frying (amount will vary depending on the wok or skillet used)

PREPARATION

Place a wok or large skillet over medium heat, and pour in the sesame oil. Add the garlic and onion and sauté for 3 to 4 minutes until the onions are translucent. Add the ground pork or turkey. Stir frequently until no pink is visible in the meat. Stir in the carrots, green onions, and cabbage, and cook for another 2 minutes. Season with the pepper, salt, garlic powder, and soy sauce. Remove from heat and spread the mixture on a cookie sheet to cool.

Place 2 heaping tablespoons of the filling near one corner of each wrapper, leaving a 1 1/2-inch space on each side. Roll the wrapper tightly over the filling, tucking in the sides as you go. (Loose rolls can come apart in the hot oil.) Moisten the outside of the wrapper with water to seal the edges. Cover the rolls with plastic wrap to retain moisture.

Heat a heavy skillet to medium heat, add the vegetable oil to 1/2-inch depth, and continue heating for 5 minutes. To make sure the oil is hot enough, dip the back of a wooden spoon into the oil. If tiny bubbles appear, the oil is hot enough. Slide 3 or 4 lumpia at a time into the oil. Fry the rolls for 1 to 2 minutes, or until all sides are evenly golden brown. Drain on paper towels. Serve immediately.

> "LUMPIA ARE A DELECTABLE TREAT FROM THE PHILIPPINES. THEY ARE LIKE EGG ROLLS FILLED WITH GROUND MEAT AND/OR FINELY CHOPPED VEGETABLES. MAKING AND EATING LUMPIA WERE IMPORTANT IN MY CHILDHOOD. I ALWAYS KNEW A BIG EVENT WAS HAPPENING WHEN MY MOTHER, GRANDMOTHER, AND AUNTS WOULD SIT AROUND A TABLE, ROLLING LUMPIA QUICKLY AND METICULOUSLY, AND SHARING THE LATEST FAMILY GOSSIP."
>
> > Anthony

BREADS

BREAKFAST & BRUNCH

ENTRÉES

VEGETABLES & SIDE DISHES

SALADS

SOUPS

DESSERTS

mop's famous pimento cheese

Mike Arrowood > *Chicago, Illinois*

Serves 10 to 15

INGREDIENTS

1 pound pepper jack cheese, grated
1 (16-ounce) container sour cream
2 cups four-cheese finely grated pack
3 tablespoons mayonnaise
1 (4-ounce) jar red pimentos
1 (4-ounce) jar diced green chilies (optional)

PREPARATION

Mix all the ingredients in a large bowl. Serve with any type of cracker or bread. Also makes delicious sandwiches.

easy summer sausage

Kate Clemmons > *Tecumseh, Kansas*

Serves 8 to 10

INGREDIENTS

2 pounds lean ground beef
2 tablespoons quick-cure salt
1 teaspoon garlic salt or garlic powder
1 teaspoon onion salt or onion powder
1 cup water
2 teaspoons liquid smoke
1 tablespoon mustard seed

PREPARATION

Mix all of the ingredients well. Divide into 2 balls, and roll each ball into a log shape. Wrap in foil. Refrigerate overnight. Bake the next day in a 350ºF oven for 1 1/2 hours. Unwrap during the last half hour for better color. Serve hot or cold with cheese and crackers. If there's any left, wrap in new foil for freezing.

> "MY PARENTS WORKED FOR HOURS EVERY CHRISTMAS TO MAKE THIS SAUSAGE FOR FRIENDS AND FAMILY, AND I'VE CONTINUED THE TRADITION. IN FACT, I USUALLY MAKE 20 LOAVES AT A TIME. IT'S SO EASY TO GRAB ONE FROM THE FREEZER WHENEVER I NEED A QUICK SNACK OR APPETIZER. THIS IS AN EASY RECIPE TO DOUBLE OR TRIPLE."
>
> > Kate

mirza ghasemi

Mahvash Howell > *Anaheim Hills, California*

Serves 4 to 6

INGREDIENTS

4 medium eggplants
6 to 7 medium tomatoes
7 tablespoons olive oil
5 cloves garlic, finely chopped
2 teaspoons turmeric
Salt and pepper
5 eggs (or 8 egg whites)
1 teaspoon cinnamon

PREPARATION

Wash the eggplants and tomatoes. Grill the eggplants until the skin is dark brown and roasted. (Leave stems on while grilling.) Let the eggplants cool, then remove the skin and cut them into small pieces. Chop the tomatoes into 1-inch cubes and set aside.

Heat 2 tablespoons of olive oil in a deep pan, add the garlic, and sauté with 1 teaspoon of turmeric and salt to taste until golden brown. Add the eggs and stir a few times until they are cooked. Remove from the pan and set aside.

Sauté the tomatoes in 2 tablespoons of olive oil, adding salt and pepper to taste. Cook until tomatoes are soft and the juice is reduced to one-third. Add the eggplant, 3 more tablespoons of olive oil, and the cinnamon. Stir until the eggplant and tomatoes are completely mixed and the juice from the tomatoes is absorbed into the eggplant. Cook for 20 minutes, stirring from time to time. Add the garlic/egg mixture and cook for another 15 minutes.

Serve with bread as an appetizer, or with rice as a main dish.

> " MY FOUR SIBLINGS AND I LOVED TO WATCH MY MOM COOK THIS DISH. WHEN SHE PEELED THE SKIN OFF THE GRILLED EGGPLANT, SHE ALWAYS LEFT A LITTLE BIT OF EGGPLANT ON THE STEM AND GAVE IT TO US. WE WOULD ADD SALT AND EAT IT. "
>
> > Mahvash

BREADS

BREAKFAST & BRUNCH

ENTRÉES

VEGETABLES & SIDE DISHES

SALADS

SOUPS

DESSERTS

mississippi-sin cheese dip

Kevin Edmonds > *Jackson, Mississippi*

Serves 8 to 10

INGREDIENTS

1 loaf French bread
1 (6-ounce) package sharp cheddar cheese
1 (8-ounce) package cream cheese, softened
1 (8-ounce) container sour cream
1/2 cup green onions, chopped
1 teaspoon Worcestershire sauce
2 (4-ounce) cans chopped green chilies
1 cup chopped ham

PREPARATION

Dig out the center of the French bread and cube what is removed to use for dipping. Set aside. Combine the remaining ingredients in a large mixing bowl. Transfer the mixture into the hollowed-out bread "bowl" and bake at 350ºF for 1 hour. Place baked bread bowl in the center of a serving dish with cubed bread around the outside for dipping.

pumpkin pie dip

Bob Weaver > *Altoona, Pennsylvania*

Yields 4 cups

INGREDIENTS

1 (8-ounce) package cream cheese, softened
2 cups confectioners' sugar
1 cup canned pumpkin
1/2 cup sour cream
1 teaspoon ground cinnamon
1 teaspoon pumpkin pie spice
1/2 teaspoon ground ginger
Gingersnap cookies

PREPARATION

In a large bowl, mix the cream cheese and sugar until smooth. Add the pumpkin, sour cream, cinnamon, pumpkin pie spice, and ginger. Stir until blended. Serve with the gingersnaps.

game-time dip

Opal Mae Lowrance > *Montgomery, Alabama*

Serves 10

INGREDIENTS

2 (11-ounce) **cans white shoepeg corn**
2 (15.5-ounce) **cans black-eyed peas**
1 bunch **green onions**
2 (10-ounce) **cans Ro-Tel diced tomatoes and green chilies**
1 (8-ounce) **bottle Kraft Italian dressing**
1 teaspoon **garlic powder**
Frito Scoops, for serving

PREPARATION

Drain the white shoepeg corn and black-eyed peas. Chop the onions. Mix all the ingredients in a large bowl. Chill overnight. Serve with Frito Scoops.

rumaki

Sharon Kouba > *Grand Forks, North Dakota*

Serves 15 to 20

INGREDIENTS

2 cups **ketchup**
2 cups **brown sugar**
5 cans **whole water chestnuts**
3 pounds **thin-sliced bacon**

PREPARATION

To make the sauce, mix ketchup and brown sugar and warm in the microwave. Set aside. Drain the water chestnuts. If any are larger than a mouthful, cut them in half. Cut the bacon strips in thirds. Wrap a strip of bacon around each chestnut and secure with a toothpick. Place on a cookie sheet. Bake at 350°F for about 30 minutes or until the bacon is done. Drain on paper towels. Place in a crockpot. Cover with sauce and keep warm.

> "THIS RECIPE CAME FROM MY LATE UNCLE, WHO WAS A HUGE ALABAMA FAN, AN AWESOME HUNTER, AND A GREAT COOK. IF YOU'VE EVER BEEN TO ALABAMA IN THE FALL, YOU KNOW THAT MEN WILL BE IN ONE OF THREE PLACES: AT WORK, IN THE WOODS, OR WATCHING FOOTBALL ON TV. THIS RECIPE IS INCREDIBLY EASY TO PREPARE — IT ONLY TAKES 10 MINUTES. STICK IT IN THE REFRIGERATOR OVERNIGHT, INVITE YOUR BUDDIES OVER, GRAB A BAG OF FRITO SCOOPS, AND TURN ON THE GAME."
>
> > Opal

> "I MAKE THIS RECIPE OFTEN TO SHARE WITH FAMILY AND FRIENDS. IF YOU WANT SOME FOR YOURSELF, GET IT BEFORE COMPANY ARRIVES. I HAVE NEVER HAD LEFTOVERS!"
>
> > Sharon

APPETIZERS

BREADS

BREAKFAST & BRUNCH

ENTRÉES

VEGETABLES & SIDE DISHES

SALADS

SOUPS

DESSERTS

roasted eggplant dip

Julie Kellam > *Eldersburg, Maryland*

Serves 4 to 6

INGREDIENTS

1 medium eggplant, peeled
1 medium red onion
1 medium red pepper
4 cloves garlic, minced
1 teaspoon coarse or kosher salt
1 tablespoon olive oil
1 tablespoon tomato paste

PREPARATION

Preheat oven to 400ºF. Cut the eggplant, onion, and pepper into bite-sized pieces and place in a large roasting pan, such as an 11 by 17-inch jellyroll pan. Sprinkle the garlic, salt, and olive oil over the veggies, cover with foil, and roast for about 1 hour, until the veggies are tender. Stir once or twice during roasting. Remove from oven and transfer to a blender or food processor. Add the tomato paste and blend until smooth. Serve with pita bread or crackers.

shrimp mold

Laurie Kennedy > *Denver, Colorado*

Serves 5

INGREDIENTS

1 (10 3/4-ounce) **can condensed tomato soup**
2 (1/4-ounce) **envelopes unflavored gelatin**
1/2 cup cold water
6 ounces cream cheese, softened
1 cup mayonnaise or Miracle Whip
1 pound canned or steamed shrimp, coarsely chopped
1/2 cup celery, minced
1/2 cup green onions, minced
Green olives, for garnish
1 box Ritz crackers

PREPARATION

Heat the soup in a small saucepan or microwave. In a medium bowl, stir the gelatin into the cold water. Add the hot tomato soup. In a medium bowl, combine the cream cheese and mayonnaise. Add the soup mixture and mix well. Add the shrimp, celery, and green onions. Transfer the mixture into a 1-quart mold and refrigerate for at least 1 hour but preferably overnight. Unmold onto a serving plate and garnish with green olives. Serve with the Ritz crackers.

" MY MOM GAVE ME THIS RECIPE ABOUT 30 YEARS AGO. WHENEVER I TAKE IT TO A POTLUCK, IT DISAPPEARS FAST. YOU CAN EXPERIMENT WITH DIFFERENT HERBS AND SPICES. DILL WEED IS GOOD, OR ADD A LITTLE MINCED GARLIC, A COUPLE SHOTS OF TABASCO, OR A DASH OF CHILI POWDER. "

> Laurie

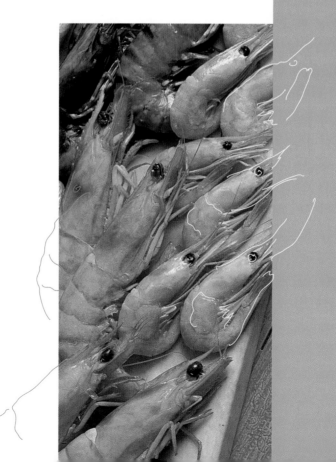

BREADS

BREAKFAST & BRUNCH

ENTRÉES

VEGETABLES & SIDE DISHES

SALADS

SOUPS

DESSERTS

spinach balls

Kimber Tschida > *Plymouth, Minnesota*

Serves 40

INGREDIENTS

2 boxes frozen spinach, chopped
2 cups breadcrumbs
4 eggs, beaten
3/4 cup (6 ounces/1 1/2 sticks) **salted butter or margarine, melted**
1 large onion, chopped fine
Salt and pepper
3 ounces Romano cheese

PREPARATION

Thaw and drain the spinach. (Do not cook.) Mix the spinach with the breadcrumbs, eggs, butter, onion, and salt and pepper. Chill in the refrigerator. When mixture is cold, form into 1-inch balls and place on an ungreased cookie sheet. Bake at 375ºF for about 20 minutes. Drain on paper towels. Roll hot balls in the Romano cheese.

spinach rolls

Melissa Miller > *Greenville, South Carolina*

Serves 8 to 10

INGREDIENTS

1 (8-ounce) **package cream cheese, softened**
1/2 cup sour cream
1/2 cup mayonnaise
1 envelope Ranch Dip mix
4 green onions, chopped
1 jar bacon bits or 1 cup crumbled bacon
2 (10-ounce) **packages chopped spinach, thawed, drained, and squeezed dry in paper towels**
1 package 8 to 10-inch flour tortillas

PREPARATION

In a medium mixing bowl, combine the cream cheese, sour cream, and mayonnaise. Beat in dip mix. Add the green onion, bacon bits, and spinach (broken into small clumps). Mix thoroughly. Spread the mixture onto the tortillas, leaving a 1/2-inch space around the edge. Roll up each tortilla tightly and wrap each in plastic wrap. Chill for several hours or overnight. To serve, cut off ends and cut into 1/2-inch slices.

sweet and sour meatballs

Rich Friedman > *Longmont, Colorado*

Yields 40 meatballs

INGREDIENTS

3 eggs (room temperature)
2 pounds ground beef (room temperature)
1 medium yellow or white onion, finely chopped
2 tablespoons parsley, finely chopped
12 graham cracker squares, finely chopped
4 saltines, finely chopped
1 (16-ounce) can cranberry sauce
1 cup plain sauerkraut, drained
1 (16-ounce) jar chili sauce
2 cups water
1 cup brown sugar

PREPARATION

Preheat oven to 325°F. In a large bowl, crack the eggs and whisk slightly. Add the ground beef, onion, parsley, graham crackers, and saltines. Mix by hand and form into balls (slightly smaller than a golf ball). Place on an ungreased cookie sheet and bake for 30 minutes.

Discard meat juice and put the meatballs in a 4-quart pan or crockpot. In a large bowl, combine the cranberry sauce, sauerkraut, chili sauce, water, and brown sugar. Stir together and add to the meatballs. Heat the mixture thoroughly and simmer for 30 minutes, or leave in a crockpot on high for at least an hour. Serve with small bowls and spoons.

> **MY WIFE HAS BEEN MAKING THIS DISH FOR YEARS. IT IS ABSOLUTELY DELICIOUS AND IS USUALLY ONE OF THE FIRST DISHES TO GO AT A PARTY. IT'S FUN TO SURPRISE YOUR GUESTS WITH THE UNUSUAL COMBINATION OF INGREDIENTS. IT REHEATS WELL AND TASTES BETTER AS IT STANDS.**
>
> > Rich

BREADS

BREAKFAST & BRUNCH

ENTRÉES

VEGETABLES & SIDE DISHES

SALADS

SOUPS

DESSERTS

walnut shrimp

Denia Wong > *Las Vegas, Nevada*

" BEFORE I MOVED TO LAS VEGAS, I TAUGHT CHINESE COOKING IN UTAH FOR SIX YEARS. THIS WAS ALWAYS A POPULAR DISH. "

> Denia

Serves 4 to 6

INGREDIENTS

1 pound medium shrimp, peeled, deveined, and towel-dried
Pinch of salt
1/4 teaspoon white ground pepper
1 teaspoon egg white, beaten
1 teaspoon potato starch
1 teaspoon sesame seeds
1/2 cup walnuts
Oil for deep-frying
1 tablespoon honey
1/3 cup Miracle Whip
2 tablespoons unsweetened pineapple juice
1 tablespoon granulated sugar

PREPARATION

Mix the shrimp with the salt and white pepper. Add the egg white, then the potato starch. Toast the sesame seeds in a pan over very low heat, shaking constantly for even browning. Drop the walnuts into boiling water and boil for about a minute, then drain and dry. Deep-fry the walnuts in medium-hot oil until golden, then remove. Drizzle the honey over the walnuts and sprinkle with the toasted sesame seeds. Deep-fry the shrimp in very hot oil briefly, until just cooked. Remove the shrimp and drain oil. Mix the Miracle Whip, pineapple juice, and sugar in a pan over low heat until smooth. Return the shrimp to the pan and toss until the shrimp are coated with the sauce. Sprinkle the walnuts over the shrimp.

baked chicken salad dip

Betsy Taylor > *Raleigh, North Carolina*

Serves 8 to 10

INGREDIENTS

2 tablespoons margarine
1 cup sliced celery
1/2 cup chopped onion
1/2 cup mayonnaise
1/2 cup sour cream
1 tablespoon lemon juice
1/2 teaspoon salt
1/8 teaspoon pepper
2 cups cooked chicken, cubed
1/2 cup slivered almonds, toasted
1 (6-ounce) can sliced mushrooms, drained
1/4 cup crushed potato chips
Crackers

PREPARATION

In a large skillet, melt the margarine over medium heat. Add the celery and onion, and cook about 4 minutes, or until tender. Remove from heat. Stir in the mayonnaise, sour cream, lemon juice, salt, and pepper. Add the chicken, almonds, and mushrooms, and toss to coat well. Transfer into a 1 1/2-quart casserole dish and sprinkle with the crushed potato chips. Bake in a 325ºF oven for 25 to 30 minutes, or until hot. Serve with crackers.

BREADS

BREAKFAST & BRUNCH

ENTRÉES

VEGETABLES & SIDE DISHES

SALADS

SOUPS

DESSERTS

easter pie

Rose Hildreth > *Bay Point, California*

Serves 8

INGREDIENTS

15 ounces ricotta cheese
2 hard-boiled eggs
1/4 pound pepperoni
1/3 pound prosciutto
12 ounces mozzarella cheese
1/3 pound boiled ham
3 beaten eggs
1/4 cup grated parmesan cheese
1 teaspoon black pepper
2 (9-inch) **frozen pie shells**

PREPARATION

Preheat oven to 350ºF. Cut up the ricotta cheese, hard-boiled eggs, pepperoni, prosciutto, mozzarella, and ham. Mix together in a large bowl. Add the beaten eggs, parmesan cheese, and black pepper and mix everything together. Transfer to one pie shell. Cover with the second shell and prick the top with a fork. Bake for 1 hour and 15 minutes, or until a toothpick comes out dry when inserted into center of the pie.

" EVERY EASTER, WHILE OTHER KIDS WERE ON EASTER EGG HUNTS, I MADE SURE I WAS AT HOME TO EAT THIS PIE RIGHT OUT OF THE OVEN. MY MOM ALWAYS HAD TO MAKE TWO OF THEM SO EVERYONE COULD GET THEIR FILL. NOW I MAKE IT FOR EASTER, AND I MAKE AN EXTRA ONE SO MY SON GETS ENOUGH FOR HIMSELF! "

> Rose

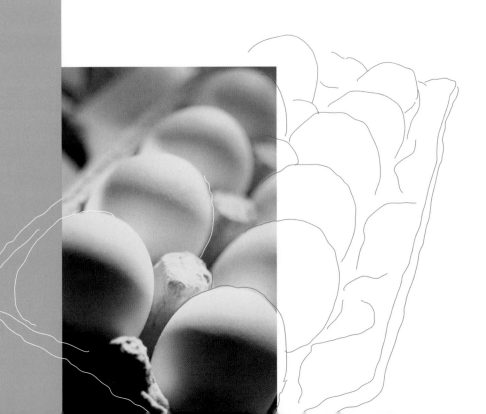

hot onion dip

Matt Hutchinson > *Jackson, Mississippi*

Serves 8

INGREDIENTS

1 (16-ounce) **bag diced onions**
1 **bag shredded parmesan cheese**
1/2 **cup mayonnaise**
3 (8-ounce) **packages cream cheese, softened**

PREPARATION

Preheat oven to 350ºF. Blend all of the ingredients together. Place in a baking dish sprayed with Pam. Bake until bubbly and browned on top, usually 45 minutes.

irish sharp ale cheese

Jim Schaffer > *Yardley, Pennsylvania*

Serves 12 to 14

INGREDIENTS

1/2 **pound grated sharp cheddar cheese**
4 **ounces cream cheese** (room temperature)
1 **tablespoon Dijon mustard**
1 **tablespoon celery seed**
1/2 to 2/3 **cup dark ale** (Guinness, of course)
Pinch of paprika

PREPARATION

Blend all of the ingredients except the paprika in a food processor. Place in a serving bowl and sprinkle with the paprika. Serve with crackers, breadsticks, or crudités.

> WE CELEBRATE ST. PATRICK'S DAY WITH ALL THINGS IRISH. WHAT COULD BE BETTER THAN SHARP CHEESE AND GUINNESS?
>
> > Jim

APPETIZERS

BREADS

BREAKFAST & BRUNCH

ENTRÉES

VEGETABLES & SIDE DISHES

SALADS

SOUPS

DESSERTS

mango salsa

Robin Hopper > *Greenville, South Carolina*

Serves 4 to 6

INGREDIENTS

3 large tomatoes
1 medium purple onion
2 jalapeño peppers
12 sprigs cilantro
4 fresh mangoes

PREPARATION

Chop the tomatoes, onion, and jalapeño peppers into small chunks. Pull the leaves from each sprig of cilantro and chop into very tiny pieces. Peel the mangoes and chop into chunks slightly larger than the tomatoes. Mix all ingredients. The salsa is better if refrigerated overnight. It can be as chunky or as fine as you want.

south austin ceviche

Sone Monteverdi > *Austin, Texas*

Serves 12

INGREDIENTS

4 pounds shrimp, cooked and chopped
6 large limes, juiced
1 large lemon, juiced
1 small white onion, chopped
1 cucumber, peeled and chopped
1 large tomato, coarsely chopped
1 jalapeño pepper, chopped
1 bunch cilantro
1 tablespoon kosher salt
Ground black pepper

PREPARATION

In a large glass or ceramic bowl, gently toss the shrimp with the lime juice and lemon juice. Mix in the onion, cucumber, tomato, jalapeño, cilantro, salt, and pepper. Cover bowl and chill 1 hour in the refrigerator. Serve with water crackers or as a fish topping.

spinach-artichoke dip

Rachel Rogers > *Vernon, Connecticut*

Serves 8 to 10

INGREDIENTS

1 box frozen spinach
1 (14.75-ounce) can of artichoke hearts
1 cup shredded cheddar cheese
1 cup shredded Swiss cheese
1 teaspoon garlic powder
1 tablespoon dehydrated onion
1/4 cup parmesan cheese
1/2 cup mayonnaise

PREPARATION

Preheat over to 350ºF. Cook the spinach as directed on the package. Drain. Drain the artichoke hearts and chop into bite-sized pieces. Mix all of the ingredients in a shallow baking dish. Add more mayonnaise if needed to make it spreadable. Bake for 20 minutes or until cheese is melted and the mixture is bubbly. Serve with toasted pita chips, nacho chips, crackers, or bread.

BREADS

BREAKFAST & BRUNCH

ENTRÉES

VEGETABLES & SIDE DISHES

SALADS

SOUPS

DESSERTS

stuffed grape leaves

Charles Aboyoun > *Columbia, Maryland*

Serves 6

INGREDIENTS FOR MEAT STUFFING

1/2 cup uncooked rice
1 pound ground beef
3 tablespoons allspice
2 teaspoons salt
1/3 cup water

INGREDIENTS FOR GRAPE LEAF WRAPPING

1 jar (50 to 60) grape leaves
8 cloves garlic, peeled
3/4 cup lemon juice
2 1/2 cups water
1 tablespoon salt
1/2 cup olive oil

PREPARATION

For the meat stuffing, rinse and drain the rice. Mix the rice, meat, allspice, salt, and water in a bowl. To assemble, spread out each leaf, glossy side down, and cut off the stem. Put 1 tablespoon of the meat mixture in the middle of the leaf and roll it like a cigar. When all leaves are rolled, stack them in a 2-quart saucepan. Sprinkle in garlic cloves. Lay a heavy plate on top of the leaves so they won't loosen during cooking. Add the lemon juice, water, salt, and olive oil. Cover and bring to a boil. Reduce heat and cook for 30 minutes. Drain juice and let cool for 5 minutes. Serve with pita bread and hummus.

> "MY SYRIAN GRANDMOTHER PASSED THIS RECIPE DOWN TO MY WIFE AT HER BRIDAL SHOWER. SHE SAID, 'THIS IS HIS GRANDFATHER'S, HIS FATHER'S, AND HIS FAVORITE MEAL. KEEP IT THAT WAY.' MY WIFE HAS MAINTAINED THIS TRADITION FOR ME AND FOR MY FATHER."

> Charles

BREADS

BREAKFAST & BRUNCH

ENTRÉES

VEGETABLES & SIDE DISHES

SALADS

SOUPS

DESSERTS

swedish meatballs

Ginny Birkett > *Ormond, Florida*

Yields 5 dozen meatballs

INGREDIENTS FOR MEATBALLS

1 pound ground beef
1/2 cup dry breadcrumbs
1/3 cup minced onion
1/4 cup milk
1 egg, slightly beaten
1 tablespoon parsley flakes
1 teaspoon salt
1/8 teaspoon pepper
1/2 teaspoon Worcestershire sauce

INGREDIENTS FOR SAUCE

1 (12-ounce) **bottle chili sauce**
1 (10-ounce) **jar grape jelly**
2 teaspoons red wine vinegar

PREPARATION

Mix all the ingredients for the meatballs together and shape into 1-inch balls. Brown the meatballs in a medium-hot skillet, lightly coated with olive oil. When meatballs are browned, pour off fat. Heat the chili sauce, then add the jelly and vinegar. Pour over the meatballs. Keep meatballs warm in a crockpot set on low.

" I GOT THIS RECIPE FROM MY BELOVED AUNT NELLIE, WHO WAS LIKE A SECOND MOTHER TO ME. I CAN REMEMBER HER MAKING THESE MEATBALLS YEARS AGO—PEOPLE WERE ALWAYS SHOCKED TO HEAR ABOUT THE GRAPE JELLY. MY FAMILY ENJOYS THESE MEATBALLS AS AN APPETIZER EVERY TIME WE HAVE A BIG GATHERING. "

> Ginny

tortilla pinwheels

Amy Elwood > *Clearfield, Utah*

Serves 8 to 10

INGREDIENTS

1 (8-ounce) **package sour cream**
1 (8-ounce) **package cream cheese, softened**
1 (4-ounce) **can diced green chiles, drained**
1 (4-ounce) **can chopped black olives, drained**
1 cup grated cheddar cheese
1/2 cup chopped green onions
Garlic salt and seasoned salt
5 flour tortillas
1 to 2 jars of salsa

PREPARATION

Mix together the sour cream, cream cheese, chiles, olives, cheddar cheese, and onions. Season to taste with the garlic salt and seasoned salt. Divide and spread evenly over the tortillas. Roll tortillas and cover tightly with plastic wrap. Refrigerate for several hours. To serve, unwrap tortilla rolls and cut into 1/2 to 3/4-inch-thick slices. Lay pinwheels flat on a plate with a dish of salsa in the center for dipping.

breads

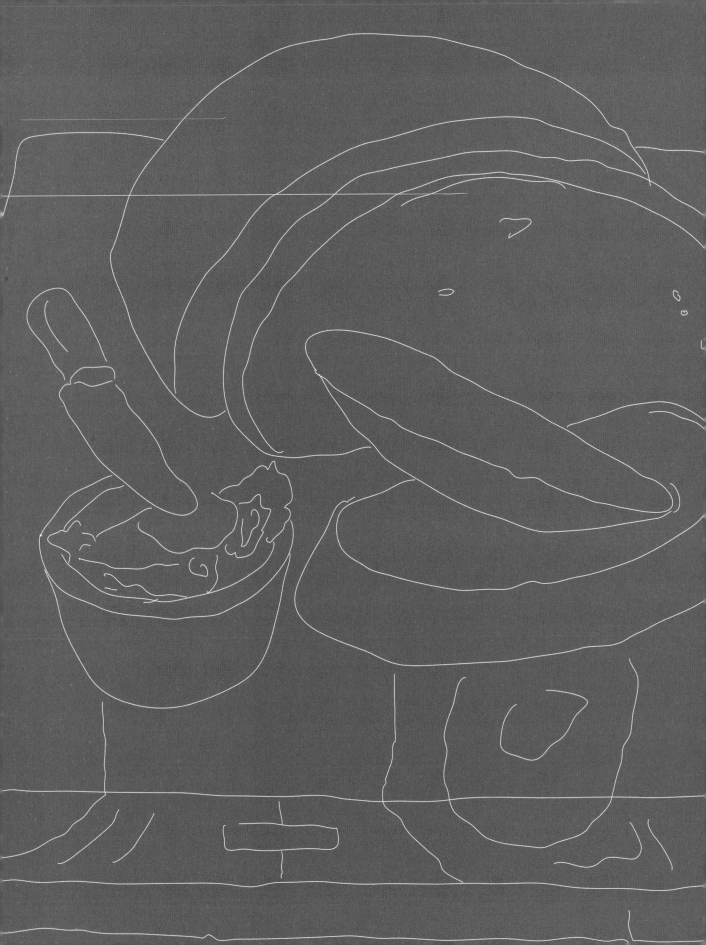

biscuits

Michelle Dry > *Austin, Texas*

Yields 18 biscuits

INGREDIENTS

1/4 cup (2 ounces/1/2 stick) **plus 1/4 cup** (2 ounces/1/2 stick) **cold margarine**
2 cups all-purpose flour, plus additional for dredging
Pinch of salt
1 tablespoon baking powder
1 cup milk

PREPARATION

Preheat oven to 400ºF. Melt 1/4 cup of the margarine in the bottom of a baking pan. In a large bowl, combine the flour, salt, and baking powder; cut the remaining margarine into the mixture until crumbly. Mix in the milk until all the flour is incorporated.

Spoon out a small amount of dough and drop into a small bowl of flour to coat. Transfer to the baking pan and dredge through melted margarine and toss to coat.

Bake for 15 minutes, flip biscuits in pan, and bake for another 8 to 10 minutes until golden brown.

> "MY FAMILY LOVES THESE BISCUITS! MY HUSBAND'S GRANDMOTHER ALWAYS FLIPPED HER BISCUITS TO BROWN BOTH SIDES. DREDGING THE DOUGH THROUGH THE MELTED MARGARINE ENHANCES THE FLAVOR AND HELPS WITH THE BROWNING. I WOULD GET TOSSED OUT IF I TRIED TO SERVE ANY OTHER BISCUIT TO MY FAMILY."
>
> > Michelle

APPETIZERS

BREADS

BREAKFAST & BRUNCH

ENTRÉES

VEGETABLES & SIDE DISHES

SALADS

SOUPS

DESSERTS

boston brown bread

Pamela Welch > *Phoenix, Arizona*

Yields 2 loaves

INGREDIENTS

1 cup raisins
2 cups buttermilk
1 1/4 cups wheat flour
1 cup yellow cornmeal
1 cup all-purpose flour
2 teaspoons baking powder
1 cup molasses
1/4 cup nuts (optional)

PREPARATION

In a small bowl, add the raisins to the buttermilk to plump; set aside. Combine the wheat flour, cornmeal, all-purpose flour, and baking powder in a large mixing bowl and blend together with a wire whisk. Add the molasses to the buttermilk and raisins and mix thoroughly. Stir the buttermilk mixture into the dry ingredients until well blended.

Grease 2 1-pound coffee cans and fill each two-thirds full with the bread mixture. Cover with aluminum foil (do *not* use rubber bands to hold foil in place). Place the coffee cans in a large pot and fill with warm water halfway up the cans. Cover the pot and bring the water to a simmer. Steam for 3 hours. Check the water level from time to time; if necessary, replenish with hot water to maintain the water level at the halfway point.

The loaves are done when a metal skewer or knife blade inserted in the center comes out clean. Take cans out of the pot and turn them upside down, allowing the loaves to slide out. Place loaves on their sides on a wire rack to cool. Serve with butter or cream cheese. Wrap loaves in foil if not served immediately; refrigeration is not needed.

> " FOR SEVERAL YEARS, I MADE THIS DURING THE HOLIDAY SEASON. ONE YEAR I GAVE A LOAF TO MY BEST FRIEND, NOT KNOWING THAT SHE DIDN'T LIKE MOLASSES. I ASSURED HER THAT IF SHE GAVE IT TO HER MOM, SHE'D BE THE STAR OF THE EVENING — AND, OF COURSE, SHE WAS. "
>
> > Pamela

APPETIZERS

BREADS

BREAKFAST &
BRUNCH

ENTRÉES

VEGETABLES &
SIDE DISHES

SALADS

SOUPS

DESSERTS

cardamom orange braid

Dennis Anderson > *Monongahela, Pennsylvania*

Yields 2 loaves

INGREDIENTS FOR BREAD BRAID

2 packages active dry yeast
5 1/2 to 6 cups all-purpose flour
1/2 teaspoon ground cardamom
1 cup milk
1/2 cup granulated sugar
1 teaspoon salt
1/2 cup (4 ounces/1 stick) salted
    butter or margarine
1 1/2 tablespoons grated orange rind
1/3 cup orange juice
2 eggs, whole
1 egg yolk, beaten
1 tablespoon milk

INGREDIENTS FOR WHIPPED
ORANGE BUTTER

1/2 cup (4 ounces/1 stick) salted
    butter, softened
2 tablespoons orange juice
    concentrate
2 tablespoons powdered sugar
1 1/2 tablespoons finely grated
    orange rind

PREPARATION FOR BREAD BRAID

In a large mixing bowl, combine the yeast, 2 cups of the flour, and the cardamom. In a 1-quart saucepan, heat the milk, sugar, salt, and butter to a temperature of 110ºF to 115ºF degrees on a candy thermometer. Stir to melt the butter. Add the milk mixture to the dry ingredients, beating on low speed with an electric mixer until blended. Add the orange rind, orange juice, and whole eggs.

Continue beating on low speed for 30 seconds, and then increase mixer speed to high and beat an additional 3 minutes. Add 3 more cups of flour by hand and mix well. Turn dough out onto a floured board and work in another 1/2 cup of flour. Knead 5 to 8 minutes until dough is smooth and elastic. Put in a greased bowl, turning dough to grease all sides. Cover with a damp cloth and let rise in a warm place until double in size (about 1 hour). Punch dough down and divide into 6 equal-size balls. Cover and let rest for 10 minutes. Roll each ball into a rope about 18 to 20 inches in length.

On a well-greased baking sheet, form each loaf by taking 3 ropes of dough and braiding them, pinching ends securely. Cover and let rise 30 minutes more. To bake, preheat the oven to 350ºF. Whisk together the egg yolk and milk. Just before baking, brush braided dough with the egg yolk mixture. Bake for 20 to 30 minutes or until golden. Serve with orange butter.

PREPARATION FOR WHIPPED ORANGE BUTTER

Combine all the ingredients in a food processor; process until smooth. Transfer the butter mixture to a small serving bowl and chill until ready to serve.

circle bread

Lisa Gilbert > *Montgomery, Alabama*

Yields 12 Servings

INGREDIENTS

2 cups biscuit baking mix
1/2 cup water, cold
1/4 teaspoon garlic powder
1/4 cup parmesan cheese, grated
2 tablespoons salted butter, melted
2 tablespoons sesame seeds
2 tablespoons salted sunflower seeds

PREPARATION

Preheat the oven to 425ºF. In a large bowl, mix the biscuit baking mix, water, and garlic powder until a soft dough forms. On an ungreased pizza pan, pat the dough with floured hands into a 10-inch circle. Brush the dough with the butter. Sprinkle with the parmesan cheese. Sprinkle with the sesame seeds and sunflower seeds; press into dough. Cut the circle into 12 wedges. Bake 15 to 20 minutes, until top is golden brown.

yeast rolls

Jennifer Rice > *Lenexa, Kansas*

Yields 16 rolls

INGREDIENTS

2 packages dry yeast
2 cups water, lukewarm
2 eggs
1 cup oil
1 cup granulated sugar
6 cups all-purpose flour
1 teaspoon salt

PREPARATION

Dissolve the yeast in the lukewarm water. Beat the eggs in a large bowl, add the oil and sugar, and mix well. Add the flour and salt, mix in the yeast, and stir well. Cover and store in the refrigerator for at least 4 hours.

When ready to use, preheat oven to 425ºF and grease a baking pan. Roll out the dough and cut to desired size. Put the rolls in the greased pan. Let rolls rise until doubled in size. Bake for 15 minutes.

cranberry orange
corn bread

Megan Vayette > *Hatteras Island, North Carolina*

Yields 1 loaf

INGREDIENTS

1/2 cup (4 ounces/1 stick) salted butter
1 cup granulated sugar
2 eggs
1 1/2 cups all-purpose flour
1 cup yellow cornmeal
2 tablespoons baking powder
1/2 teaspoon salt
1 1/2 cups buttermilk
1 cup fresh cranberries, sliced in half
1 large orange (for zest)

PREPARATION

Preheat oven to 375ºF and grease 9 by 9-inch pan. Cream the butter and sugar together. Add the eggs to the creamed mixture and blend until fully combined. In separate bowl, mix together flour, cornmeal, baking powder, and salt.

Pour one third of the buttermilk into the flour mixture and stir by hand. Alternate mixing the rest of the buttermilk and creamed butter into the flour, stirring by hand until fully combined. Zest 1 large orange into the batter and add the cranberries, stirring until combined. Pour the batter into the greased pan. Bake for 40 to 45 minutes.

> "THIS BREAD HAS BECOME A HOLIDAY STAPLE FOR MY FAMILY. BE SURE TO MAKE EXTRAS BECAUSE IT TASTES EVEN YUMMIER THE DAY AFTER!"
>
> > Megan

APPETIZERS

BREADS

BREAKFAST & BRUNCH

ENTRÉES

VEGETABLES & SIDE DISHES

SALADS

SOUPS

DESSERTS

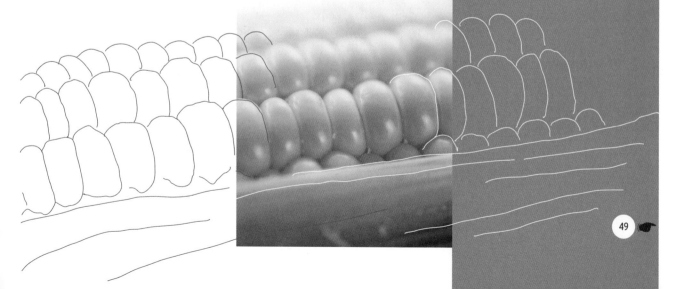

easy breakfast rolls

Jeanette Russell > *Salem, Missouri*

Serves 4 to 6

INGREDIENTS

1/2 cup chopped pecans
1 package frozen Parker House rolls
1 package regular butterscotch pudding (not instant)
6 tablespoons (6 ounces/3/4 stick) **margarine, melted**
3/4 teaspoon cinnamon
1/2 cup brown sugar

PREPARATION

Grease a Bundt pan. Spread the pecans evenly in the bottom of the pan. Cut the frozen rolls into quarters and put in the pan. Sprinkle the dry pudding mix over rolls. Combine the margarine, cinnamon, and brown sugar. Pour over top of the rolls. Let rise for 9 to 10 hours at room temperature.

Preheat oven to 350ºF. Bake rolls for 30 minutes. Turn bundt pan upside down while warm; let cool before eating.

special corn bread

Lisa Arrasmith > *Cincinnati, Ohio*

Serves 6 to 8

INGREDIENTS

1/2 cup (4 ounces/1 stick) **salted butter**
8 ounces sour cream
1 (8-ounce) **can creamed corn**
2 teaspoons granulated sugar
2 eggs, beaten
1 cup self-rising cornmeal

PREPARATION

Preheat oven to 400ºF. Melt the butter in a cast-iron skillet. Mix the sour cream, creamed corn, sugar, eggs, and cornmeal together with the butter in the skillet. Place skillet in the oven; bake for 20 to 25 minutes. Do *not* use cornbread mix; must use self-rising cornmeal.

ellie's herb bread

De Carter > *Brooklyn Park, Minnesota*

Serves 4 to 6

INGREDIENTS

1 loaf Italian bread, whole
1/2 cup (4 ounces/1 stick) salted butter, at room temperature
1 teaspoon parsley flakes, plus additional for topping
1/4 teaspoon dill weed
1/2 teaspoon garlic powder
1/4 teaspoon oregano
Parmesan cheese

PREPARATION

Preheat oven to 400°F. Slice the bread to desired thickness and set aside. Blend the butter, parsley, dill, garlic, and oregano together and spread mixture on one side of each slice of bread. Put the pieces back together on a piece of aluminum foil and make a "boat" (leave the top of the foil open). Sprinkle with parmesan cheese and parsley, also sprinkling parmesan cheese between the slices of bread if desired. Bake for 10 minutes or until heated thoroughly.

> "THIS IS THE FIRST THING THAT'S GONE WHEN I MAKE IT. FRIENDS REQUEST IT WHEN WE'RE INVITED TO POTLUCK EVENTS. THE DILL GIVES THIS A LITTLE EXTRA BOOST."
>
> > De

sunday morning sticky buns

Teresa Mills > *Glen Burnie, Maryland*

Serves 4

INGREDIENTS

1 package of Pillsbury original biscuits (8 per can)
2 cups (1 pound/4 sticks) unsalted butter
Cinnamon sugar, to taste
Large marshmallows

PREPARATION

Preheat oven to 350°F. Lightly grease muffin tins; open the biscuits and roll each one a little larger and thinner. Melt the butter in glass dish. Place the cinnamon sugar in a small bowl.

Roll the marshmallows in the melted butter and then dip into cinnamon sugar.

Place each marshmallow (standing on end) on top of a biscuit. Bring sides of the biscuit up and around the marshmallow and twist; place twisted side down in muffin tin and bake 15 to 20 minutes.

> "THIS IS A RECIPE I LEARNED IN GIRL SCOUTS MANY YEARS AGO IN INDIANA. IT WAS QUITE EASY SO MY MOM WOULD TURN ME LOOSE IN THE KITCHEN, WITH A LITTLE SUPERVISION OF COURSE! I WOULD PUT THESE TOGETHER FOR MOM AND DAD, AND BETWEEN THE SMELL OF FRESH COFFEE BREWING AND THESE IN THE OVEN, DADDY WAS QUICK OUT OF BED ON SUNDAY MORNINGS."
>
> > Teresa

grandma johnston's yeast rolls

James Littlemyer Jr. > *Brookport, Illinois*

Yields 16 rolls

INGREDIENTS

2 packages active dry yeast
1 cup water, lukewarm
4 tablespoons vegetable oil
4 tablespoons granulated sugar
1/4 teaspoon salt
2 large eggs
3 to 4 cups all-purpose flour

PREPARATION

Preheat oven to 350ºF. Spray bottom and sides of a 9 by 13-inch cake pan evenly with cooking spray and set aside. In a large glass or plastic bowl (do not use metal) combine the yeast, water, oil, sugar, salt, and eggs. Use a wooden or plastic spoon (do not use metal) and mix ingredients thoroughly. Cover with a towel or plastic wrap and put the bowl in a warm place for 15 minutes. Uncover and gradually mix in 2 cups of the flour until well incorporated. Cover again with a towel or plastic and set aside for a further 15 minutes. (The mixture should be almost double in size and spongy.)

Add enough of the remaining flour to form a dough. Knead dough, then form dough into balls about 2 inches in diameter and place balls in the prepared cake pan. Set the pan in a warm place for about 25 minutes to let the dough rise. Place in the preheated oven and bake for 15 minutes or until golden brown.

mama doris's oatmeal bread

Rachel Rogers > *Vernon, Connecticut*

Serves 12

INGREDIENTS

1 cup old-fashioned oats
2 cups water, boiling
1/2 cup molasses
1 teaspoon salt
1 tablespoon shortening
1/4 cup water, lukewarm
1 package dry yeast
4 cups all-purpose flour
1 tablespoon vegetable oil

PREPARATION

Measure the oats into a large bowl. Pour the boiling water over the oats; add the molasses, salt, and shortening. Stir and let cool to lukewarm. Meanwhile, stir the yeast and the 1/4 cup lukewarm water together in a small bowl. Let the yeast mixture sit until foamy (about 10 minutes). Add the yeast mixture to the cooled oat mixture.

Add the flour, 1 cup at a time, stirring well, to form a soft dough. Turn dough out onto a lightly floured board and knead for 10 minutes, adding more flour a tablespoon at a time to prevent sticking.

Use the oil to coat the sides and bottom of a large bowl. Place the dough into the bowl and turn over to coat sides and top with oil. Cover with plastic wrap or a dry dishtowel and let rise in a warm place until doubled in size (approximately 1 hour). Punch dough down. Turn out onto floured board again; gently knead for 1 minute, then cut in half and shape each half into a loaf. Place each loaf into a greased loaf pan. Cover with plastic wrap/towel again and let rise until almost doubled and dough has risen above the edge of the pans.

Preheat oven to 375ºF. Bake bread for 40 minutes. (Bottom of loaves should make a hollow sound when tapped.) Turn out of pans to cool on wire racks. Let cool for 10 to 15 minutes before eating.

> "I NEVER KNEW MY GRANDMOTHER DORIS MERRITT – 'MAMA DORIS.' BUT WHEN I STARTED MAKING HOMEMADE BREAD 12 YEARS AGO I FOUND THIS RECIPE, IN AN ABBREVIATED FORM, IN HER RECIPE BOX. AFTER A LITTLE EXPERIMENTATION, THE FAMILY AGREED IT WAS A WINNER."
>
> > Rachel

APPETIZERS

BREADS

BREAKFAST & BRUNCH

ENTRÉES

VEGETABLES & SIDE DISHES

SALADS

SOUPS

DESSERTS

ma's irish scones

Kevin McConville > *Trevor, Wisconsin*

Yields approximately 3 dozen

INGREDIENTS

1 cup raisins
4 cups all-purpose flour
1 teaspoon baking soda
1 1/2 teaspoons baking powder
1/4 teaspoon salt
1/2 cup granulated sugar
1/2 cup (4 ounces/1 stick) **salted butter**
1 egg
1 1/2 cups buttermilk

PREPARATION

Preheat oven to 400ºF. Soak the raisins in a small amount of water to soften. Sift the flour, baking soda, baking powder, salt, and sugar together in a large mixing bowl; cut in the butter. Add the raisins, set aside.

Beat the egg and buttermilk together in a separate mixing bowl. Add to dry mixture, stir with a wooden spoon. Knead 5 times. Turn out onto a lightly floured board. Roll dough until it is 3/4-inch thick. Cut into rounds with a lightly floured cutter or a small water glass. Place on an ungreased cookie sheet. Bake for 10 minutes or until scones are lightly browned. Cool slightly, split and serve with butter, jam, and/or honey.

These freeze well. Just defrost and eat at room temperature or reheat in the oven.

night owl sweet rolls

Judy L. Fongheiser > *Bethlehem, Pennsylvania*

Yields 1 pan of rolls

INGREDIENTS

1/2 cup (4 ounces/1 stick) **salted butter or margarine**
1 small package pecans, halved or chopped (optional)
1 bag frozen bread rolls
1 package regular butterscotch pudding (not instant)
1/2 cup light brown sugar

PREPARATION

Grease sides and bottom of a baking pan with the butter or margarine. Set aside the remaining butter or margarine.

Spread the pecans across the bottom of the pan and place the frozen rolls on top. Sprinkle the dry pudding mix over the rolls, then sprinkle with the light brown sugar. Cut up the remaining butter or margarine, sprinkle over the rolls. Cover the pan loosely with foil and leave out overnight (rolls will rise overnight).

To bake, preheat oven to 350°F. Bake for approximately 35 minutes. When the rolls are finished baking, take the pan out of the oven and run a knife around the edges of the baking pan. Place a serving tray over the pan, hold the tray down tightly over the baking dish, and flip it over. (Be careful when flipping the rolls, because the liquid in the pan is hot.)

"EVEN THOUGH MY DAD WAS A PASTRY CHEF WHO MADE ELEGANT PASTRIES, HE ALWAYS LOVED WHEN I MADE THESE SIMPLE SWEET ROLLS FOR HIM. WE ENJOYED THEM WITH COFFEE AND FAMILY CONVERSATION."

> Judy

APPETIZERS

BREADS

BREAKFAST & BRUNCH

ENTRÉES

VEGETABLES & SIDE DISHES

SALADS

SOUPS

DESSERTS

pumpkin bread or muffins

Ellen Blevins > *Virginia Beach, Virginia*

Yields 2 loaves or numerous mini muffins

INGREDIENTS

3 1/3 cups all-purpose flour, sifted
2 teaspoons baking soda
1 1/2 teaspoons salt
1 teaspoon cinnamon
1 teaspoon nutmeg
3 cups granulated sugar
4 eggs
1 1/2 cups canned pumpkin
1 cup vegetable oil
2/3 cup water

INGREDIENTS FOR TOPPING

2 tablespoons salted butter, melted
2 tablespoons granulated sugar
1/2 teaspoon cinnamon

PREPARATION

Preheat oven to 350ºF. Stir the flour, baking soda, salt, cinnamon, nutmeg, and sugar together in the workbowl of a mixer or a mixing bowl. Quickly add eggs, pumpkin, oil, and water. Mix with a dough hook (or by hand) until dry ingredients are just moistened. Put mixture into 2 greased loaf pans (or mini muffin pans); bake for 1 hour. Let cool 5 minutes, then transfer from pans to a wire rack. While loaves are still warm, brush on the melted butter and then sprinkle with the sugar and cinnamon.

breakfast & brunch

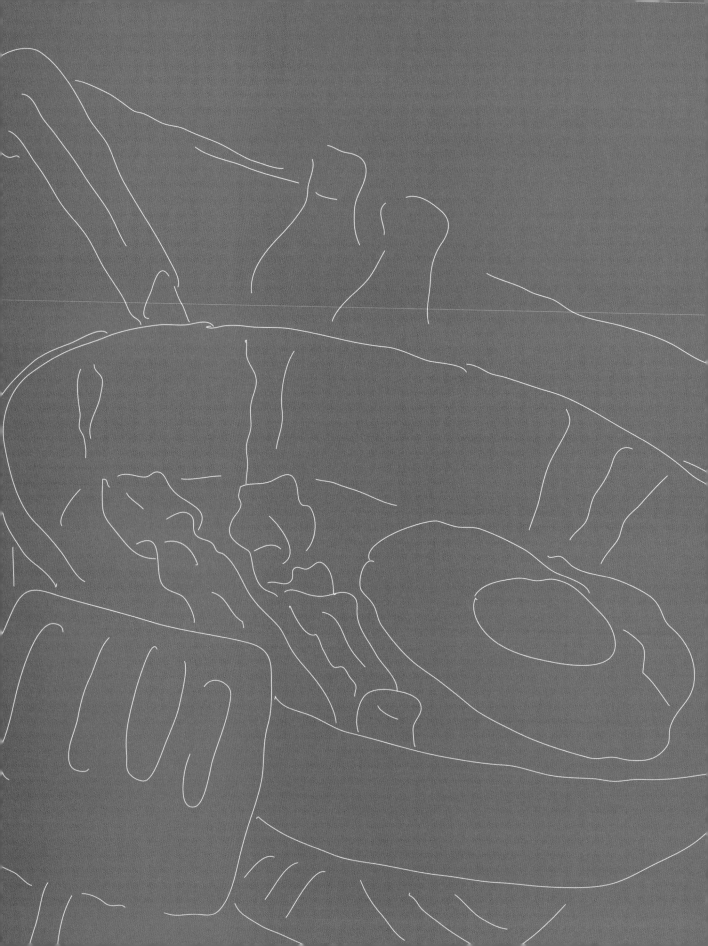

a heart-healthier omelet

Carol Gasiorek > *Norridge, Illinois*

Yields 1 omelet

INGREDIENTS

1 teaspoon zero transfat margarine alternative
1/4 teaspoon freeze-dried chives
1/4 cup fresh baby bella mushrooms, sliced
1/2 teaspoon imitation bacon bits
1/4 cup egg substitute
Pepper, to taste
1 slice fat-free American cheese

PREPARATION

In a nonstick omelet pan, melt the margarine alternative. Add the chives, mushrooms, and bacon bits. Sauté for 1 minute over medium heat. Evenly distribute ingredients in the pan. Add the egg substitute, pouring evenly to cover all ingredients and bottom of pan. Add pepper to taste. Cook until bottom side is lightly browned. Flip omelet over. Tear the cheese slice in half and use cheese slice halves to cover half of omelet. When cheese is slightly melted and bottom of omelet is golden brown, fold omelet in half. Cook for an additional 30 seconds. Turn omelet out onto a plate. Garnish with slices of fresh fruit (optional).

APPETIZERS

BREADS

BREAKFAST & BRUNCH

ENTRÉES

VEGETABLES & SIDE DISHES

SALADS

SOUPS

DESSERTS

breakfast casserole

Marilyn Cuber > *Darien, Illinois*

Yields 1 casserole

INGREDIENTS

2 1/2 cups dried bread croutons
2 cups cheddar cheese, shredded
1 1/2 pounds pork sausage, browned and well drained
4 eggs
2 cups plus 1/4 cup of milk
3/4 teaspoons dry mustard
1 (10-ounce) **can cream of mushroom soup**

PREPARATION

Mix the croutons, cheese, and browned sausage together and put into a greased 9 by 13-inch pan. Mix eggs, 2 cups of milk, and mustard together and pour into pan over crouton mixture. Cover with foil and refrigerate overnight.

When ready to bake, preheat oven to 350ºF. Mix the cream of mushroom soup with the remaining 1/4 cup milk and spread over top of casserole. Bake for 1 hour or until casserole is bubbly in the center.

breakfast quiche

Chad Krockover > *West Lafayette, Indiana*

Serves 6 to 10

INGREDIENTS

24 ounces hash browns
1/3 cup margarine, melted
4 ounces pepper jack cheese, sliced
6 eggs
1 1/2 cups milk
2 cups diced ham
1 1/2 cups mozzarella cheese, shredded
Salt and freshly ground black pepper

PREPARATION

Preheat oven to 350ºF. Press the hash browns into a greased 9 by 13-inch pan; pour the melted margarine over hash browns. Bake for 20 minutes. Lay slices of the pepper jack cheese over the hot hash browns. Whisk together the eggs and milk, pour over hash browns. Sprinkle with the diced ham. Top with the shredded mozzarella and salt and pepper to taste. Bake for a further 35 to 40 minutes until the egg mixture is firm.

cheese and sausage quiche (a.k.a. hot dog pie)

Jody Hollister > *Rosemont, Illinois*

Yields 1 quiche

INGREDIENTS FOR FILLING

3/4 cup sausage links
1/2 cup onion, chopped
1/2 cup green pepper, chopped
1 1/2 cup cheddar cheese, grated
1 tablespoon flour
1 baked pie shell
2 large eggs, beaten
1 cup evaporated milk
1 tablespoon dried parsley
3/4 teaspoon salt
1/4 teaspoon garlic
1/4 teaspoon pepper

INGREDIENTS FOR PIE SHELL

2 cups flour, sifted
1/2 teaspoon salt
1/2 cup (4 ounces/1 stick) plus
    2 tablespoons salted butter
    or margarine, sliced
1 large egg
1 to 2 tablespoons water, cold

PREPARATIONS FOR PIE SHELL

In a food processor with a chopping blade, add flour, salt, and butter. Process until butter is the size of cornmeal, about 5 to 10 seconds. Add the egg and 1 tablespoon of the water. Process until mixture forms a ball. Add a little more water if mixture is too dry and doesn't form a ball. Chill at least 30 minutes. To bake, preheat oven to 400ºF. Roll out pastry on a floured surface and place in pie tins. Bake for 8 minutes or until golden brown. Cool before adding filling. Yields 2 pie shells.

PREPARATIONS FOR FILLING

Fry the sausage until brown. Remove from pan, drain on paper towels, and cool. If using fresh sausage, drain a little of the drippings if there is a lot of grease; leave about 1 tablespoon in the pan to sauté the onion and green pepper. Sauté the onion and green pepper in drippings until cooked. Slice cooled sausage into bite-size pieces. In a bowl, combine sliced sausage pieces and cooked onion and green pepper and set aside.

Preheat oven to 375ºF. In a separate bowl, combine the grated cheese and flour and toss to mix. When the sausage mixture has cooled to room temperature, stir the mixture into the cheese. Put combined mixtures into a pie shell. Mix the eggs, evaporated milk, parsley, salt, garlic, and pepper and pour over the mixture in the pie shell. Bake 35 to 40 minutes. Crust will be nicely browned.

> "WHEN QUICHE FIRST BECAME POPULAR, IT WAS A FOREIGN WORD TO MY CHILDREN (AND TO SOME ADULTS TOO). SO, IN ORDER TO TEMPT MY CHILDREN TO TRY IT, WE DUBBED IT 'HOT DOG PIE,' AND IT WAS AN INSTANT HIT."
>
> > Jody

APPETIZERS

BREADS

BREAKFAST & BRUNCH

ENTRÉES

VEGETABLES & SIDE DISHES

SALADS

SOUPS

DESSERTS

egg and sausage casserole

Wanda Odum > *Fairburn, Georgia*

Serves 12

INGREDIENTS

6 eggs
2 cups milk
1 cup cheddar cheese, grated
6 slices of bread, cubed
1 pound sausage, browned and drained
1 teaspoon salt
1 teaspoon pepper
1 teaspoon Worcestershire sauce

PREPARATION

Grease two 13 by 9-inch pans. Combine the eggs and milk in a large bowl and beat until well blended. Add the cheese, bread, sausage, salt, pepper, and Worcestershire sauce and mix well. Pour into the prepared pans. Cover and refrigerate overnight. To bake, preheat oven to 350ºF and bake uncovered for 45 minutes. Serve hot or cold.

grandma's breakfast

Sharon Schuler > *Lubbock, Texas*

Serves 6

INGREDIENTS

2 cans of biscuit dough
1 small package of sausage
1 small can of diced green chilies, drained
1 cup shredded cheddar cheese
1/4 cup (2 ounces/1/2 stick) **salted butter, melted**
1 bunch of green onions, chopped

PREPARATION

Preheat oven to 400ºF. Spray a Bundt pan with non-stick spray. Quarter the raw biscuits. Crumble the sausage and fry until done. Mix the biscuits, sausage, chilies, cheese, melted butter, and onions; pour into prepared pan. Bake for 20 minutes or until a toothpick inserted comes out clean. Turn out onto plate and serve warm.

hearty apple spice pancakes

Richard Karsh > *Peoria, Arizona*

Serves 8

INGREDIENTS

2 cups all-purpose flour
3/4 cup granulated sugar
3 tablespoons baking powder
1/4 cup oil
3 eggs
2 individual packages apple-cinnamon instant oatmeal

PREPARATION

Grease and preheat a griddle to 375ºF. Combine all the ingredients in a bowl; mix with an electric mixer on low until smooth (about 2 minutes). Pour silver-dollar-sized pancakes onto the griddle. Wait until the surface begins to bubble, then flip. Cook 1 more minute and serve.

"MY GRANDCHILDREN ALWAYS BEG FOR THIS ONE!"

> Sharon

APPETIZERS

BREADS

BREAKFAST & BRUNCH

ENTRÉES

VEGETABLES & SIDE DISHES

SALADS

SOUPS

DESSERTS

grandma p's oatmeal pancakes

Joe Piasecki > *Streator, Illinois*

Serves 4

INGREDIENTS

1 cup regular oatmeal, uncooked
1 1/2 cups buttermilk
1/8 cup brown sugar, packed
2 eggs
1/4 cup margarine, melted
1 cup sifted all-purpose flour
1 teaspoon baking soda

PREPARATION

Combine the oatmeal and buttermilk in a bowl, mix and let stand for 10 minutes. Stir in the brown sugar, eggs, and margarine. Add the flour and baking soda. Stir with a wooden spoon until combined (do not overmix). Spoon pancake batter onto a lightly greased hot griddle; cook until pancakes are set.

Good with chilled applesauce instead of syrup or jelly. Can be wrapped and frozen to be reheated.

mock cheese soufflé

Michelle Stoken > *Pittsburgh, Pennsylvania*

Yields 1 soufflé

INGREDIENTS

6 slices bread, cubed
1/2 pound sharp cheddar, grated
6 eggs
2 cups milk
1 teaspoon dry mustard
1/2 teaspoon salt
2 tablespoons salted butter, melted

PREPARATION

Preheat oven to 250ºF. Place the bread cubes on a cookie sheet and bake for 20 minutes. Grease a 2-quart casserole. Arrange the bread cubes and cheese in layers in the casserole. Beat the eggs, then add the milk, mustard, and salt. Pour the mixture over the bread and cheese. Drizzle the butter over the casserole. Refrigerate overnight.

To bake, preheat the oven to 400ºF and bake casserole for 30 to 40 minutes. Let stand for 5 minutes, then serve.

quiche lorraine

Rob Lowrie > *Greenville, South Carolina*

Serves 6

INGREDIENTS

1 piecrust, rolled out
6 strips bacon
2 medium onions, chopped
1 1/2 cups (6 ounces) Swiss cheese, shredded
4 teaspoons all-purpose flour
4 eggs
2 cups half-and-half
1 teaspoon salt

PREPARATION

Preheat oven to 350ºF. Place the piecrust into 10-inch quiche plate and crimp edges. Fry the bacon strips in a skillet until very crisp and then remove them to a paper towel to cool. Sauté the onions in the bacon drippings until they start to caramelize, about 5 minutes. Mix the Swiss cheese and flour until the cheese is well dusted.

Spread the cheese and flour mixture evenly over the piecrust. Crumble the bacon and spread evenly over the cheese. Spread the sautéed onions evenly over the cheese and bacon.

In a medium bowl, beat the eggs, half-and-half, and salt until smooth. Slowly pour the mixture evenly over the cheese, bacon, and onion filling. Bake in the preheated oven for 1 hour or until firm in the center and golden brown. Transfer onto cooling rack for about 15 minutes. Serve warm with fruit and champagne.

APPETIZERS

BREADS

BREAKFAST & BRUNCH

ENTRÉES

VEGETABLES & SIDE DISHES

SALADS

SOUPS

DESSERTS

risotto colaziano
(breakfast risotto)

Sone Monteverdi > *Austin, Texas*

Serves 4

INGREDIENTS

3 cups apple juice
2 sticks cinnamon, broken in half
Pinch of nutmeg
2 cups 1 percent low-fat milk
2 tablespoons unsalted butter
1 1/2 cups Arborio rice
1/2 teaspoon salt
1/2 cup raisins
1/4 cup dark brown sugar for topping
1/2 cup milk or cream for topping

PREPARATION

In a saucepan, combine the apple juice, cinnamon sticks, and nutmeg. Bring to a boil over medium-high heat; immediately reduce heat to low and keep warm. At the same time, in a separate saucepan, warm the milk over medium-low heat; turn off heat and keep warm.

In a large non-aluminum saucepan, melt the butter over medium-low heat. Add the rice and salt and stir with a wooden spoon until the rice begins to turn translucent, 2 to 3 minutes. Ladle in about 1/2 cup of the hot apple juice and stir rice until it absorbs the juice. Continue adding juice about 1/4 cup at a time until absorbed. When all the juice has been absorbed, ladle in about 1/2 cup of the warm milk along with the raisins. Stir until milk is absorbed. Add the remaining milk the same way, stirring after each addition until fully absorbed before adding more milk. All liquid will have been added and rice will be tender in about 30 minutes. Test a few kernels; they should be creamy on the outside but firm to the bite at the center.

Remove pan from heat, cover, and let stand for about 5 minutes. Ladle risotto into warmed individual bowls. Add the brown sugar and cream to taste.

APPETIZERS

BREADS

BREAKFAST & BRUNCH

ENTRÉES

VEGETABLES & SIDE DISHES

SALADS

SOUPS

DESSERTS

savory egg, ham and cheese bake

Jessica Martin > *Plymouth, Minnesota*

Serves 10

INGREDIENTS

1 loaf of French bread, cubed
1 pound ham, cubed
1/2 pound cheddar cheese, cubed
3 eggs
2 cups milk
1/2 teaspoon salt
1/2 teaspoon dry mustard
1/2 cup (4 ounces/1 stick) **salted butter**

PREPARATION

Grease a 9 by 13-inch baking pan. Combine the bread, ham, and cheese in the baking pan. In a mixing bowl, mix the eggs and milk together with the salt and mustard. Pour over the bread mixture, coating evenly. Melt the butter and pour over the entire mixture. Cover and refrigerate for 24 hours. To bake, preheat oven to 325°F, and bake covered for 45 minutes. Uncover and bake an additional 15 minutes or until the top is golden brown.

" AS A YOUNG CHILD, THE ANTICIPATION OF OPENING GIFTS ON CHRISTMAS MORNING WAS OVERWHELMING, ESPECIALLY SINCE THIS BRUNCH CASSEROLE WAS SERVED *BEFORE* WE EXCHANGED GIFTS. MY FAMILY LEISURELY ENJOYED EVERY LAST MORSEL, WHILE MY EAGERNESS TO OPEN THOSE BRIGHTLY COLORED PRESENTS STACKED EVER SO GENTLY UNDER THE TWINKLING TREE GREW WITH EVERY BITE I TOOK.

NOW AS THE AROMA FROM THIS COMFORTING BRUNCH CASSEROLE FILLS MY OWN KITCHEN, I THINK BACK TO THOSE WONDERFUL CHRISTMAS MORNINGS. I APPRECIATE THE MEMORIES, THE SMELL, AND THE TASTE THIS SAVORY BRUNCH CASSEROLE EVOKES, AND I HAVE COME TO REALIZE HOW SPECIAL THOSE MOMENTS REALLY WERE. IT WAS NOT ABOUT THE PRESENTS; IT WAS ABOUT THE JOY AND LOVE SHARED BY MY FAMILY ON THOSE CHRISTMAS MORNINGS. "

> Jessica

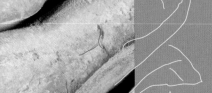

spinach omelet "muffins"

Linda Chirash > *Rosemont, Illinois*

Serves 3 to 4

INGREDIENTS

1 (16-ounce) bag frozen chopped spinach, thawed
1 small onion, chopped
1 clove garlic, chopped, or 1 teaspoon garlic powder or garlic salt
1 to 2 tablespoons olive oil or margarine
6 large eggs, beaten well
3/4 cup Swiss cheese, grated (or other cheese as desired)
1/4 cup fresh parsley, chopped, or 1 tablespoon dried parsley (optional)
Salt and black pepper

PREPARATION

Preheat oven to 350ºF. Thaw the spinach in a strainer and press out some of the liquid. (Another option is to cook the spinach and drain it; either method works.) Sauté the onion and garlic in the olive oil or margarine until golden brown. Mix with the spinach. Add the beaten eggs to the spinach mixture and mix well. Add the grated cheese and mix well. Add parsley and salt and pepper to taste.

Line a muffin tin with foil cupcake cups (not paper) and spray them on the bottom and sides with vegetable oil spray. Spoon the spinach mixture into each cup until almost full. Mixture can also be put directly into a well-greased muffin tin.

Bake for 25 to 30 minutes until edges start to get lightly golden. Remove from oven and serve or let cool.

Other options include adding small quantities of chopped peppers or tomatoes, substituting chopped broccoli for spinach, or adding basil. Muffins can be stored in a sealable bag and refrigerated for a few days, then reheated in the microwave (don't overcook) or served at room temperature.

entrées

beef stroganoff

Jim Jefferson > *Dunkirk, New York*

Serves 4

INGREDIENTS

2 pounds stew beef, cubed
1 package dry onion soup mix
1 (10.75-ounce) can cream of mushroom soup
1 (8-ounce) can mushrooms
1 can of milk (soup can size)
8 ounces sour cream
1 pound wide egg noodles, cooked and drained

PREPARATION

Preheat the oven to 325ºF. In a large mixing bowl, combine the beef, onion soup mix, mushroom soup, mushrooms, and milk, and mix well. Put these ingredients into a casserole dish, and cover. Bake for 3 hours. Remove from the oven, set aside for several minutes, and stir in the sour cream. Serve over noodles.

green bean & hamburger casserole

Debi Coonce > *Ypsilanti, Michigan*

Serves 4 to 6

INGREDIENTS

1 pound ground beef
1 small onion, peeled and chopped
1 (16-ounce) can green beans, drained
1 bag tater tots
1 (10.75-ounce) can cream of chicken soup
1 cup whole milk

PREPARATION

Preheat the oven to 350ºF. Brown the ground beef and chopped onion; season to taste. Pour into a 3-quart baking dish. On top, lay the green beans, and a layer of tater tots. In separate bowl, mix the cream of chicken soup and milk. Pour this over all the ingredients. Bake for 1 hour, or until the top is golden brown.

> "THIS IS A LONGTIME FAMILY RECIPE THAT IS EASY TO MAKE AND GOOD AS LEFTOVERS TOO."
>
> > Debi

APPETIZERS

BREADS

BREAKFAST & BRUNCH

ENTRÉES

VEGETABLES & SIDE DISHES

SALADS

SOUPS

DESSERTS

beefsteak pie
with potato crust

Sherrill Gladman > *Clearwater, Florida*

Serves 4 to 6

INGREDIENTS

1 pound round steak, cut into 1-inch cubes
6 tablespoons flour
3 tablespoons shortening, or more as needed
3 small onions, thinly sliced
1 1/2 teaspoons salt
1 teaspoon paprika
1/4 teaspoon black pepper
Pinch of thyme
Pinch of garlic salt
2 1/2 cups water
4 medium-sized potatoes, peeled and thinly sliced

PREPARATION

Preheat the oven to 350ºF. In a large mixing bowl, dredge the meat in 3 table-spoons of the flour. Heat the shortening in a skillet over medium heat, and cook the cubes, a few at a time, until very brown and crusty, for about 15 minutes. Repeat until all the meat is browned. Add the onions to the skillet, and cook until golden brown, about 15 minutes, adding more shortening as needed.

Put the meat and onions into a 2-quart baking dish. Sprinkle with the remaining 3 tablespoons flour and the salt, paprika, pepper, thyme, and garlic salt. Pour the water over the top.

Bake 45 minutes to 1 hour, or until the meat is tender. Remove from the oven, and increase the oven temperature to 450ºF. Place the potato slices on top of the meat, and sprinkle with additional salt and paprika if desired. Return to the oven, and bake 20 minutes or until the potatoes are browned and tender.

blazy's pepperoni-studded lasagna

Boneita Page > *Charlotte, North Carolina*

Serves 8 to 10

INGREDIENTS

2 pounds lasagna sheets
2 tablespoons olive oil
2 cups hand-cut 1/8-inch slices pepperoni
4 cups tomato sauce, recipe follows
2 pounds bulk Italian sausage, cooked
1 pound ricotta
1 pound shredded mozzarella
3/4 cup grated parmesan cheese

INGREDIENTS FOR TOMATO SAUCE

3 ounces extra-virgin olive oil
1 yellow onion, peeled and minced
5 medium-sized garlic cloves, crushed
6 cups skinned and diced Roma tomatoes
2 tablespoons thinly sliced fresh basil leaves
1 tablespoon minced fresh oregano leaves
Salt and freshly ground black pepper

PREPARATION

Preheat the oven to 375ºF. In a large stockpot, bring 6 quarts of water to a boil over medium-high heat, add a pinch of salt, and cook the lasagna sheets until almost done. Drain, and shock the sheets in an ice bath. In a medium saucepan, heat the olive oil over medium heat, and sauté the pepperoni until crispy. Remove from the heat, and drain on a paper towel. In a 10 by 14 by 3-inch baking pan or dish, pour 1 cup of the tomato sauce in the bottom and around the sides.

Layer the lasagna sheets on the bottom of the pan, overlapping by 1/2 inch. Add one-third the amount of the sausage, one-third the amount of the ricotta, and one-third the amount of the mozzarella, and sprinkle generously with the parmesan cheese. Add 1/2 cup tomato sauce and 1/4 cup of pepperoni. Repeat this 2 more times. Top the very top lasagna sheets with the remaining ricotta, tomato sauce, mozzarella, and pepperoni, and dust with the parmesan. Bake for about 45 minutes. Remove from the oven; let sit for 15 minutes. Cut, and serve immediately.

PREPARATION FOR TOMATO SAUCE

In a medium saucepan, heat the olive oil. Add the onion, and cook over medium to low heat until transparent. Add the garlic, and cook until almost brown. Add the tomatoes, and cook for 1/2 hour over low to medium heat. Add the basil and oregano, and continue to cook for another 1/2 hour. Season to taste with salt and pepper, cool, and store in the refrigerator until ready to use.

APPETIZERS

BREADS

BREAKFAST &
BRUNCH

ENTRÉES

VEGETABLES &
SIDE DISHES

SALADS

SOUPS

DESSERTS

chuck wagon chili

Kimberly Cook > *Mount Airy, Maryland*

Serves 8 to 10

INGREDIENTS

2 pounds ground beef
1 pound smoked sausage
2 onions, peeled and minced
6 garlic cloves, minced
1 (16-ounce) can cut green beans, drained
1 (15-ounce) can kidney beans, drained
2 (15-ounce) cans pinto beans, drained
1 (14-ounce) can sliced stewed tomatoes
1 (14-ounce) bottle ketchup
1 (7-ounce) can diced green chilies
3 tablespoons chili powder
1 jalapeño pepper, seeded and diced, or more as desired
1 teaspoon salt
1/2 teaspoon black pepper

PREPARATION

In a large skillet or pot, brown the ground beef, sausage, and onions over medium heat. Drain off excess fat. Add all the garlic, green beans, kidney beans, pinto beans, tomatoes, ketchup, chilies, chili powder, jalapeño pepper, salt, and pepper, and cook a minimum of 2 hours. Add more jalapeño peppers to make the dish hotter, if you wish. After browning the meat, you can cook this dish in a crockpot for 4 or more hours.

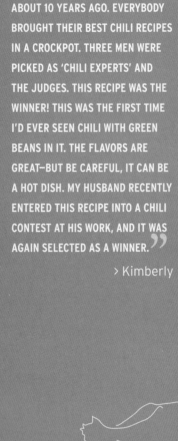

> "OUR NEIGHBORHOOD HAD A CHILI COOK-OFF CONTEST ONE FALL ABOUT 10 YEARS AGO. EVERYBODY BROUGHT THEIR BEST CHILI RECIPES IN A CROCKPOT. THREE MEN WERE PICKED AS 'CHILI EXPERTS' AND THE JUDGES. THIS RECIPE WAS THE WINNER! THIS WAS THE FIRST TIME I'D EVER SEEN CHILI WITH GREEN BEANS IN IT. THE FLAVORS ARE GREAT—BUT BE CAREFUL, IT CAN BE A HOT DISH. MY HUSBAND RECENTLY ENTERED THIS RECIPE INTO A CHILI CONTEST AT HIS WORK, AND IT WAS AGAIN SELECTED AS A WINNER."
>
> > Kimberly

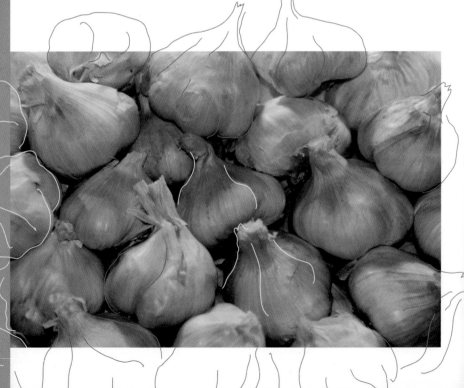

74

country-style steak and mushroom gravy

Suzanne McAlhaney > *Gilbert, South Carolina*

Serves 4 to 6

INGREDIENTS

3/4 cup all-purpose flour
1 teaspoon salt
1/4 teaspoon black pepper
6 cubed steaks
3/4 stick butter
1 (10 1/2-ounce) **can cream of mushroom soup**
1/2 (10 1/2-ounce) **can water**

PREPARATION

Preheat the oven to 325ºF. In a large mixing bowl, combine the flour, salt, and pepper, and dredge the steaks. Heat the butter in a large skillet over medium heat, and brown the steaks on both sides. Put the steaks into a roasting pan.

In the same skillet with the steak drippings, combine the soup and water, and heat over medium heat until boiling. Pour the mixture over the steaks, and cover the pan with aluminum foil. Bake for 45 minutes. Remove the foil, and bake 15 minutes more. The steak can be served over rice.

APPETIZERS

BREADS

BREAKFAST & BRUNCH

ENTRÉES

VEGETABLES & SIDE DISHES

SALADS

SOUPS

DESSERTS

gulumpkies (cabbage rolls)

Mary Adderhold > *Olive Branch, Mississippi*

Serves 6

> *MY GRANDMOTHER TAUGHT MY MOM HOW TO MAKE THESE WHEN SHE WAS A LITTLE GIRL. MY MOM TAUGHT ME TO MAKE THESE WHEN I WAS A LITTLE GIRL. THE BIG INSIDE JOKE WAS THAT MY GRANDMOTHER ALWAYS SAID HER CABBAGE ROLLS WERE MUCH BETTER THAN HER MOTHER-IN-LAW'S!*
>
> > Mary

INGREDIENTS FOR CABBAGE

12 cabbage leaves

INGREDIENTS FOR FILLING

1 pound ground beef
1/2 pound pork sausage, crumbled
3/4 cup regular rolled oats
1/2 cup finely chopped onion
1 egg
2 teaspoons salt
1 teaspoon pepper
1/2 cup whole milk

INGREDIENTS FOR SAUCE

2 (8-ounce) **cans tomato sauce** (may need 3)
1/2 cup water
3 tablespoons sugar
2 tablespoons vinegar
1/4 cup cold water
2 tablespoons cornstarch

PREPARATION

Preheat the oven to 350ºF. Spray a 9 by 12-inch baking pan with nonstick spray. To prepare the cabbage leaves, bring a large pot of salted water to a boil, and cook the leaves for 3 minutes, or until slightly limp. Drain, and set aside.

PREPARATION FOR FILLING

To make the filling, in a large mixing bowl combine all the ingredients, mixing well. Divide into 12 parts, and place a scoop in the center of a cabbage leaf. Roll the leaf around the filling, and fasten it shut with a toothpick. Place it in the pan, and repeat until the ingredients are used up.

PREPARATION FOR SAUCE

To make the sauce, in a small bowl, combine the tomato sauce, 1/2 cup water, sugar, and vinegar, and stir well. Pour over the rolls. Bake for 40 to 45 minutes. Remove the rolls from the pan and take out the toothpicks. In a separate small bowl, stir together the 1/4 cup water and cornstarch, and slowly stir it into the sauce. Bring the sauce to a boil, and cook until thickened. Pour over rolls.

dump stew

Kathy Berry > *Dallas, Texas*

Serves 4 to 6

INGREDIENTS

2 tablespoons vegetable oil
1 medium onion, peeled and chopped
1 pound ground beef
2 cans minestrone soup
1 (10-ounce) **can of Ro-Tel diced tomatoes and green chilies**
1 (14.5-ounce) **can diced tomatoes**
1 (10-ounce) **can Ro-Tel diced Mexican tomatoes**

PREPARATION

To make the stew, in a large saucepan heat the oil over medium heat, and sauté the onion. Stir in the ground beef and brown. Stir in the soup, Ro-Tel, tomatoes, and Mexican tomatoes, and reduce the heat to medium-low. Cook for 20 minutes. Quick, easy, and an inexpensive way to feed a group! As with most stews, it's better after it sits overnight.

easy sauerkraut with apple and kielbasa

Kathy Reyher > *Allentown, Pennsylvania*

Serves 4

INGREDIENTS

1 pound sauerkraut
1 pound kielbasa or other smoked sausage, halved
3 to 4 tart cooking apples, thickly sliced
1/2 cup firmly packed brown sugar
3/4 teaspoon salt
1/8 teaspoon pepper
1/2 teaspoon caraway seeds
3/4 cup apple juice

PREPARATION

To prepare the sauerkraut, rinse it and squeeze it dry. Place half the sauerkraut in a slow cooker. Place the sausage on top of the sauerkraut. Continue to layer in the apples, brown sugar, salt, pepper, and caraway seeds. Top with the remaining sauerkraut, and pour apple juice over all. Cover, and cook on low for 6 to 8 hours, or until the apples are tender. Stir before serving.

APPETIZERS

BREADS

BREAKFAST & BRUNCH

ENTRÉES

VEGETABLES & SIDE DISHES

SALADS

SOUPS

DESSERTS

english muffin pizzas

Melissa Hudson > *New Smyrna Beach, Florida*

Serves 3 to 6

INGREDIENTS FOR TOPPINGS

Pepperoni
Crumbled and browned Italian sausage and/or beef
Black olives, pitted
Chopped green peppers, mushrooms, and onions
Pineapple bits
Ham (any other ideas that come up!)

INGREDIENTS FOR MUFFINS

6 English muffins, halved
1 jar pizza or spaghetti sauce
1 to 2 cups shredded mozzarella

PREPARATION

Preheat the oven to 375ºF. Place the toppings in individual bowls. To make the pizzas, place the English muffin halves on a baking sheet. Spoon about 1 table-spoon sauce onto each half a muffin, or to taste. Add toppings to each half, depending on taste, and top with mozzarella.

Bake for about 15 minutes, or until the cheese is melted and lightly brown. Cool and enjoy! If you have little ones, let them make their own.

> "MY FAMILY ENJOYS THESE WHEN WE NEED THAT EXTRA TIME TO SPEND TOGETHER AND DURING SLEEPOVERS (ADD BANANA SPLITS AND IT IS A MAKE-IT-YOURSELF NIGHT!). THE KIDS LOVE MAKING THEIR OWN PIZZAS AND SEEING HOW DIFFERENT EACH ONE COMES OUT."
>
> > Melissa

more (ground beef casserole)

Alan Myers > *Los Angeles, California*

Serves 4 to 6

INGREDIENTS

1 1/2 pounds ground beef
1 quart whole milk
1 cup uncooked white rice
1 (14.5-ounce) can large tomatoes
1 (14.5-ounce) can cream-style corn
1 medium onion, chopped
Salt and freshly ground black pepper to taste

PREPARATION

Preheat the oven to 375ºF. Grease a 3-quart casserole dish. To prepare the dish, in a large mixing bowl, mix together all the ingredients, breaking up the meat. Put it into the casserole. Bake for 1 1/2 hours, stirring 2 to 3 times during cooking.

> "MY SON MADE THIS MEAT DISH A LOT WHEN HE WAS SINGLE. THIS IS A GREAT DISH FOR SINGLE PEOPLE. ENJOY!"
>
> > Alan

fall pumpkin casserole

Charlotte Anderson > *Oklahoma City, Oklahoma*

Serves 4 to 6

INGREDIENTS

1 **medium pumpkin** (make sure it will fit in your oven!)
2 to 4 cups long-grain or Spanish rice
2 tablespoons vegetable oil
1 pound lean ground beef
1 pound mild Italian sausage
1 medium onion, peeled and diced
1 (28-ounce) **can Ro-Tel mild tomatoes**
1 (16-ounce) **can cut green beans** (optional)
1 (16-ounce) **package shredded mozzarella**
1 (16-ounce) **package shredded cheddar**

PREPARATION

Preheat the oven to 350ºF. Cut the top off the pumpkin, and remove the seeds and fibers. To make the casserole, cook the rice according to package instructions. In the meantime, heat the oil in a large skillet over medium heat, and brown the ground beef and sausage; drain well. Set the meat aside, and sauté the onions in the same skillet. Stir the meat with the onions. To fill the pumpkin, layer the ingredients with rice, meat mixture, tomatoes, green beans, and the cheeses, repeating this procedure three times, ending with the cheeses. Place the lid back on top of the pumpkin, and put it on a baking sheet.

Bake for 2 1/2 to 3 hours. Once pumpkin is soft, it's ready to eat.

> "I LOVE THE FALL AND COOKING MOUTH-WATERING DISHES MADE WITH PUMPKIN! THE SEASON JUST WOULDN'T BE THE SAME WITHOUT OUR FALL RECIPES, WHICH ALL INCLUDE PUMPKIN: SOUP, CHILI, BREAD PUDDING, RISOTTO, LASAGNA, COOKIES, HUMMUS, FUDGE, AND ICE CREAM. BUT, OUR FRIENDS, FAMILY AND FELLOW EMPLOYEES LOOK FORWARD EACH YEAR TO CELEBRATING WITH THIS HARVEST CASSEROLE THAT IS BAKED RIGHT IN THE PUMPKIN. ABSOLUTELY DELICIOUS!
>
> P.S. PUMPKINS ARE FUN CONTAINERS FOR BAKING NUMEROUS RECIPES SUCH AS PUMPKIN BREAD PUDDING. A LARGE PUMPKIN CAN BE CLEANED AND A SPIGOT INSERTED IN THE LOWER PART OF THE PUMPKIN FOR SERVING A PUNCH OR WITCHES BREW TOO! SMALL PUMPKINS CAN BE USED FOR BAKING CRÈME BRÛLÉE OR HOLDING PUMPKIN CHILI OR SOUP."
>
> > Charlotte

APPETIZERS

BREADS

BREAKFAST & BRUNCH

ENTRÉES

VEGETABLES & SIDE DISHES

SALADS

SOUPS

DESSERTS

granny's cowboy stew

Karen Hood > *St. Louis, Missouri*

Serves 8

INGREDIENTS

6 slices bacon
1 cup diced onion
1/2 cup diced green pepper
1 clove garlic, crushed
1 1/2 pounds ground beef
2 (13-ounce) cans diced tomatoes
1 teaspoon salt
1/4 teaspoon black pepper
1 tablespoon chili powder
1 (12-ounce) can whole kernel corn, drained
1 (15.5-ounce) can red kidney beans, drained
2 cups diced potatoes

PREPARATION

To make the stew, in a large saucepan, cook the bacon over medium heat until crisp; drain on paper towels. Crumble, and set aside.

In the same skillet, sauté the onion, green pepper, and garlic in the bacon fat until tender. Add the ground beef; cook until it is well browned, breaking up with a fork as it cooks. Add the tomatoes, salt, pepper, and chili powder; cover; simmer 30 minutes. Add vegetables; cook 30 more minutes until potatoes are tender. Sprinkle with bacon. For a substitute, you can add a can of mixed vegetables if you want.

"MY MOM MADE THIS EVERY WINTER AS I WAS GROWING UP. SHE SAID SHE HELPED HER MOM MAKE IT FOR HER DAD AFTER A LONG DAY ON THE FARM. IT WOULD MAKE THE HOUSE SMELL SO GOOD. MY WHOLE FAMILY LOVES IT. UNFORTUNATELY, I LOST MY MOM IN SEPTEMBER, BUT HER COWBOY STEW WILL LIVE ON FOR YEARS TO COME. I MAKE THE STEW NOW AND PLAN TO PASS IT ON TO MY DAUGHTER AND GRANDDAUGHTER. I MADE IT FOR MY HUSBAND TO TAKE TO DEER CAMP THIS YEAR. HE SAID THE BOYS LOVED IT. NOW THEY WANT THE STEW AS A YEARLY TRADITION."

> Karen

ground beef and zucchini casserole

Cheryl Hill > *Las Vegas, Nevada*

Serves 4 to 6

INGREDIENTS FOR CASSEROLE

1 tablespoon cooking oil
1 pound ground beef chuck or round
1 medium onion, chopped
1 to 2 cloves chopped fresh garlic
4 to 5 fresh zucchini
1 tablespoon seasoning salt
Black pepper to taste

INGREDIENTS FOR CHEESE SAUCE

1 (12-ounce) **can evaporated milk**
1 pound (or more) **mild cheddar cheese**
1/4 cup (1/2 stick) **butter or margarine**
1 cup **shredded cheese** (for topping)

PREPARATION FOR CASSEROLE

Preheat the oven to 350ºF. In a large skillet, heat the oil over medium heat, and sauté meat, onions, and garlic. Add seasonings, cook until the meat is browned through and crumbly; drain well. In a large saucepan, bring 6 cups of lightly salted water to a boil over medium heat. Cut the zucchini into even round circles, and add to the water; cook until tender but don't overcook! Drain well.

PREPARATION FOR CHEESE SAUCE

To make the cheese sauce, in a medium saucepan, heat the milk over very low heat, and add the cheese and butter. Let the cheese melt, stirring constantly. The mixture should be smooth and not lumpy. Remove from the heat.

In a 3-quart baking dish, layer the meat, zucchini, and cheese sauce. After the final layer, sprinkle shredded cheese on top. Bake just until cheese melts on top. Enjoy!

APPETIZERS

BREADS

BREAKFAST & BRUNCH

ENTRÉES

VEGETABLES & SIDE DISHES

SALADS

SOUPS

DESSERTS

guinness stew & soda bread

Craig Mariutto > *Indianapolis, Indiana*

Serves 12

INGREDIENTS FOR STEW

2 1/2 pounds beef or lamb stew meat
2 tablespoons salt
1/4 tablespoon black pepper
2 tablespoons olive oil
1 quart stout beer or 2 (1-pint) cans
1/2 ounce Worcestershire sauce
1/4 cup dried thyme
2 tablespoons unsalted butter
1/2 pound pearl onions
1/2 pound celery, coarsely chopped
1/2 pound carrots, coarsely chopped
2 tablespoons chopped fresh garlic
8 ounces all-purpose flour
1 pound red potatoes, quartered
About 1 cup beef broth

INGREDIENTS FOR BREAD (YIELDS 1 LOAF)

1 3/4 cups buttermilk
2 eggs, well beaten
2 tablespoons butter, melted
3 cups all-purpose flour
2/3 cup sugar
4 tablespoons baking powder
4 teaspoons baking soda
4 teaspoons salt

PREPARATION FOR STEW

In a large bowl, toss the meat with the salt and pepper until well coated. Heat the oil in a heavy-bottomed pot over medium heat. Add the meat, and sauté until browned evenly. Add the beer, Worcestershire sauce, and thyme. Bring to a boil, and reduce the heat to low. Allow the meat to cook until tender, about 1 hour.

Strain the meat, reserving the liquid. Set the meat aside. Heat the butter in the pot over medium heat, and add the onions, celery, carrots, and garlic. Sauté until the vegetables are tender. Stir in the flour to make a roux, and cook for 3 to 5 minutes, stirring constantly. Slowly stir all the reserved liquid back into the pot to prevent lumping. Stir in the beef and potatoes, and use broth to adjust the consistency, if needed. Cook over low heat until the potatoes are tender.

Remove from the heat, and cool.

PREPARATION FOR SODA BREAD

Meanwhile, preheat the oven to 300ºF. Grease one 9-inch loaf pan. To prepare the soda bread, in a large mixing bowl, combine the buttermilk, eggs, and butter, beating well with a portable mixer. Fold in the flour, sugar, baking powder, baking soda, and salt. Spoon the mixture evenly into the prepared pan.

Bake for 35 to 45 minutes, until a fork comes out clean.

deb's meat loaf

Debbie Williams > *Paducah, Kentucky*

Serves up to 6

INGREDIENTS FOR SECRET SAUCE

1 (15-ounce) **can of tomato sauce**
2 tablespoons brown sugar
1 tablespoon vinegar
1 teaspoon Worcestershire sauce
1/2 teaspoon salt
1/4 teaspoon dry mustard
1/2 teaspoon chili powder

INGREDIENTS FOR MEAT LOAF

2 pounds lean ground beef
1/2 cup evaporated milk
1/3 cup regular rolled oats
1/4 cup chopped onions
1 teaspoon salt
1/2 teaspoon pepper

PREPARATION FOR SAUCE

Preheat the oven to 350ºF. To make the Secret Sauce, heat the tomato sauce, brown sugar, vinegar, Worcestershire sauce, salt, mustard, and chili powder in a small saucepan over medium heat. Cook, stirring, for 5 minutes.

PREPARATIONS FOR MEAT LOAF

To make the meat loaf, put the ground beef into a large mixing bowl, and crumble it. Pour one-half the sauce mixture over the crumbled meat, and mix well with the milk, oats, onions, salt, and pepper. Form the meat mixture into a loaf shape, and put it into a baking dish; cover it with the remaining sauce.

Bake for 50 minutes. If you're in a hurry, you can flatten the mixture into a 12-inch-square microwave-safe baking dish about 2 inches deep and cook in the microwave for 10 to 15 minutes or until done.

APPETIZERS

BREADS

BREAKFAST & BRUNCH

ENTRÉES

VEGETABLES & SIDE DISHES

SALADS

SOUPS

DESSERTS

hearty beef-and-macaroni casserole

Linda Crouch > *Greenville, South Carolina*

Serves 4 to 6

INGREDIENTS

1 1/2 pounds ground chuck
1 (6-ounce) **can tomato paste**
1 (14.5-ounce) **can beef and macaroni**
1 (15.5-ounce) **can kidney beans or hot beans (hot beans are better)**
Shredded cheese

PREPARATION

Preheat the oven to 350ºF. Heat a large skillet over medium heat, and sauté the meat, stirring to cook through and brown. Drain excess fat. Stir in the tomato paste, and mix well. In a baking dish, stir in the beef and macaroni, and beans, and mix well. Stir in the meat mixture.

Bake for 35 to 40 minutes. Top with shredded cheese, and bake until cheese is melted. Serve with salad and garlic bread.

> " MY MOTHER DEVELOPED THIS RECIPE AND IT IS ALWAYS A FAVORITE FOR NEWCOMERS TO THE NEIGHBORHOOD AS A WELCOME DINNER. "
>
> > Linda

hobo dinner

Mary Ann Steeg > *Allentown, Pennsylvania*

Serves 4

INGREDIENTS

1 pound ground beef
5 potatoes, peeled and sliced
4 large carrots, peeled and sliced
1 onion, peeled and sliced into rings
Salt and freshly ground black pepper
Garlic salt

PREPARATION

Preheat oven to 400ºF. Line a 9 by 13-inch baking pan with aluminum foil. To prepare the dinner, shape the ground beef into 4 patties, and place them in the prepared pan. Layer the vegetables on top of the patties, starting with the potatoes, then carrots, and finally the onion rings. Season with salt, pepper, and garlic salt to taste. Cover with foil, and seal the edges.

Bake for 1 hour, or to desired doneness. Instead of burgers, you may use boneless chicken breasts or thighs or thinly sliced steak. You may also make individual foil packages, and cook them on grill or over an open fire. Great for camping.

> " I USED TO MAKE INDIVIDUAL PACKAGES FOR MY KIDS WHEN THEY WERE YOUNGER EVEN IF WE WERE EATING AT HOME. THAT WAY YOU CAN PUT MORE OF SOME INGREDIENTS AND LESS OF OTHERS DEPENDING ON LIKES AND DISLIKES. (IF YOU HAVE A TEENAGE SON WITH A VORACIOUS APPETITE, YOU MAY WANT TO INCLUDE TWO BURGERS WITH A SLICE OF ONION BETWEEN THEM, AND THEN STACK THE VEGGIES ON TOP.) "
>
> > Mary Ann

italian beef roast

Rich Maaske > *Hastings, Minnesota*

Serves 6 to 8

INGREDIENTS

3 1/2 pounds boneless rump roast
1 teaspoon dried oregano
1 teaspoon chili powder
1 teaspoon onion salt
1 teaspoon garlic powder
2 cups water (reserved from cooking roast)
4 beef bouillon cubes
1/2 green pepper, thinly sliced
1 medium onion, thinly sliced

PREPARATION

Preheat the oven to 325ºF. Place the meat in a roasting pan, and cook for 2 1/2 hours. Cool, and refrigerate overnight. Slice thick when cold. To make the sauce, in a large saucepan, combine the oregano, chili powder, onion salt, garlic powder, water, beef cubes, green pepper, and onion. Heat the mixture over medium-low heat for 20 minutes. Preheat the oven to 325ºF. Put the roast into a 9 by 13-inch pan. Pour the sauce over the meat, and cook, covered, for 1 hour. Serve on Italian rolls. Reserve meat juices to pour over the sandwiches or for dipping. This recipe freezes well.

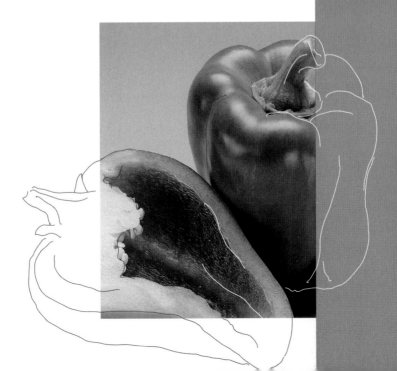

APPETIZERS

BREADS

BREAKFAST & BRUNCH

ENTRÉES

VEGETABLES & SIDE DISHES

SALADS

SOUPS

DESSERTS

" THIS WAS ADAPTED FROM A
RECIPE IN A COOKBOOK THAT
DID EVERYTHING FROM SCRATCH,
INCLUDING TOMATO SAUCE. THE
FAMILY ENJOYED IT, BUT THE
COOKING WAS TOO TIME-CONSUMING.
I MODIFIED THE RECIPE AND IT
TURNED OUT JUST ABOUT AS
GOOD. "

> Joe

marilyn's chili con carne pie

Joe Piasecki > *Streator, Illinois*

Serves 4 to 6

INGREDIENTS

2 tablespoon vegetable oil
1 1/2 pounds ground turkey, chicken, or beef
1 package Chili Man seasoning mix
1 (16-ounce) can kidney beans, drained and rinsed
1 (16-ounce) can tomato sauce
1/4 cup hot water
Additional seasonings to taste
1 package Jiffy Cornbread Mix
2 tablespoons whole milk

PREPARATION

Preheat the oven to 375°F. To prepare the chili, heat the oil in a large skillet over medium heat, and sauté the meat, stirring to cook through and brown. Drain excess fat. Stir in the Chili Man seasoning, the beans, tomato sauce, and hot water. Mix well, and let the meat cook for 10 minutes.

Meanwhile, make the cornbread following package instructions, but adding 2 tablespoons more milk to thin the batter. Spoon the meat mixture into a 3-quart baking dish, and pour the cornbread mixture over top, spreading it out to even it.

Bake uncovered for 20 minutes, or until the cornbread turns golden brown.

maw's hamburger noodle dish

Valerie Worthington > *Richmond, Virginia*

Serves 4 to 6

INGREDIENTS

8 ounces egg noodles
2 tablespoons vegetable oil
1 1/2 pounds ground beef
1 small yellow onion, peeled and diced
1 (10.5-ounce) can tomato soup, undiluted
8 ounces shredded cheddar cheese
Salt and freshly ground black pepper to taste

PREPARATION

Preheat the oven to 350ºF. To prepare the dish, bring a large pot of lightly salted water to a boil, and cook the noodles until tender; drain. In a large skillet, heat the oil over medium heat, and sauté the meat and onions until brown. Drain off excess fat. In a large mixing bowl, combine the tomato soup, cheese, the meat mixture, spices, and the noodles. Spoon the mixture into a 9 by 12-inch baking dish. Bake for 30 minutes.

> "THIS RECIPE IS FROM MY GRANDMOTHER, BETTY LOU ADAMS, OR AS I CALL HER 'MAW.' MY MOTHER USED TO MAKE THIS FOR ME GROWING UP, AND NOW I LOVE TO COOK IT FOR AN EASY SUNDAY NIGHT SUPPER. SOMETIMES I ADD SUN-DRIED TOMATOES AND WILD MUSHROOMS TO GIVE IT A LITTLE TWIST!"
>
> > Valerie

mexican stew

Leslie Needham > *Austin, Texas*

Serves 12

INGREDIENTS

2 tablespoons vegetable oil
2 pounds ground beef
1 pound hot breakfast sausage
1 medium onion, peeled and chopped
Salt and freshly ground black pepper to taste
3 (15-ounce) cans yellow hominy, undrained
4 (14.5-ounce) cans stewed tomatoes
2 (4-ounce) cans diced green chilies

PREPARATION

To make the stew, in a large saucepan, heat the oil over medium heat, and sauté the beef, sausage, and onions, stirring to cook through and brown. Drain excess fat. Add salt and pepper. Stir in the hominy, stewed tomatoes, and green chilies. Bring to a boil, and decrease the heat to low. Cook for 30 minutes to 1 hour.

> "THIS IS A RECIPE MY FAMILY GOT WHILE WE LIVED IN A TOWN ON THE BORDER OF TEXAS AND MEXICO. I PREFER IT A LITTLE SPICIER SO I WILL SOMETIMES USE RO-TEL BRAND TOMATOES INSTEAD OF PLAIN TOMATOES AND ADD ANOTHER CAN OF GREEN CHILIES. IT IS GREAT SERVED IN A BOWL AND EATEN WITH WARM TORTILLAS."
>
> > Leslie

mexican stuffed shells

Erin Silvia > *Columbia, Maryland*

Serves 4 to 6

INGREDIENTS

1 pound ground beef
1/2 cup chopped onion
1 garlic clove, minced
1 teaspoon chili powder
1/4 teaspoon ground cumin
1/4 teaspoon dried oregano
1/4 teaspoon salt
1/2 cup spicy or mild salsa
1/4 cup sour cream
3 ounces (about 12) jumbo pasta shells, cooked and drained
1 1/2 ounces coarsely shredded cheddar cheese
Shredded lettuce
Diced tomato

PREPARATION

Preheat oven to 350ºF. In a large skillet, sauté the beef, onion, and garlic over high heat, while stirring to cook through until brown. Add the chili powder, cumin, oregano, and salt. Toss to mix well. Cook 1 minute. Stir in the salsa, and cook 5 more minutes. Remove from the heat, and stir in the sour cream. Let cool slightly. Fill the shells with the mixture, and arrange them on a baking sheet. Cover the shells with aluminum foil.

Bake 15 minutes. Uncover, and sprinkle with the cheese. Bake uncovered until the cheese melts. To serve, top shells with the lettuce and tomato.

middle eastern beef kabobs

Al Sartain > *Montgomery, Alabama*

Serves 6

INGREDIENTS

3 tablespoons olive oil
3 tablespoons white vinegar
1 teaspoon salt
1 teaspoon coarsely ground black pepper
3 or 4 cloves garlic, minced
1/2 teaspoon ground cumin
3 pounds lean steak (top sirloin will do just fine)
Rice (optional)

PREPARATION

Begin preparation well in advance of the time you plan to serve. The steak should marinate for at least 2 hours before cooking. You will also need one skewer for each person you intend to serve. Be careful with the cumin! Don't overdo it or its flavor will be overpowering, but don't leave it out either. It is a key ingredient.

To prepare the marinade, in a large mixing bowl, stir together the olive oil, vinegar, salt, pepper, garlic, and cumin. Cut the steak into 1-inch cubes, and add the meat to the marinade, mixing well to ensure that each cube is coated. Cover the bowl with plastic wrap, and refrigerate for at least 2 hours.

When you're ready to cook, prepare a hot fire on the grill, setting the grill 4 to 6 inches from the coals. Oiling the grill is recommended. To cook, thread the meat, about 7 or 8 cubes, onto metal skewers, allowing one skewer per person. Grill for about 15 minutes for medium, turning at least once. Serve over a bed of rice (be as creative here as you wish) or with your choice of sides.

"THIS DISH DELIVERS A LOT OF 'BANG FOR THE BUCK.' FOR ONE THING, IT IS DESIGNED FOR ONE OF THE LESS EXPENSIVE CUTS OF MEAT. I USE THE TOP SIRLOIN, BUT I HAVE USED ROUND STEAK AS WELL. AND BECAUSE THE MEAT SERVES AS A GARNISH WHEN SERVED OVER RICE, IT ALLOWS YOU TO 'STRETCH' THE AMOUNT OF MEAT IN EACH SERVING. OF ALL THE THINGS I CONCOCT ON THE GRILL, THIS ONE GETS THE MOST REQUESTS FROM MY FAMILY. HOPE YOURS WILL ENJOY IT TOO!"

> Al

APPETIZERS

BREADS

BREAKFAST & BRUNCH

ENTRÉES

VEGETABLES & SIDE DISHES

SALADS

SOUPS

DESSERTS

prime rib with cabernet and port au jus

Mike Fairchild > *Durham, North Carolina*

Serves 10 to 12

INGREDIENTS FOR PRIME RIB

1 (8 to 10-pound) boneless prime rib
2 cups water
1 large yellow onion sliced in 1/4-inch slices
6 sprigs fresh rosemary, or 2 tablespoons dried
4 bay leaves
3 carrots cut into 2-inch pieces
4 stalks celery, cut into 2-inch pieces
1 tablespoon minced garlic
1 tablespoon olive oil
2 tablespoons kosher salt
1 tablespoon coarsely ground black pepper
1 teaspoon paprika
1 teaspoon ground ginger

INGREDIENTS FOR AU JUS

1 cup pan drippings
1 1/2 cups Cabernet Sauvignon
1 1/2 cups port
1 cup beef stock

PREPARATION FOR PRIME RIB

Remove meat from refrigerator at least 1 hour before roasting. Preheat the oven to 400ºF. Pour the water in the bottom of a large roasting pan fitted with a rack. Spread onion, rosemary, and bay leaves on rack or bones. Place the carrots and celery around the rack on the bottom of the pan. Mix garlic in olive oil, and rub the mixture into the meat. Mix salt, pepper, paprika, and ginger together, and rub over the surface of the roast.

Roast, uncovered, for 15 or 20 minutes, or until slightly browned. Cover with aluminum foil, decrease the heat to 325ºF, and roast about 2 hours more, or until the internal temperature is 115ºF in the center. Check temperature frequently with meat thermometer. Remove the roast from the pan, and place it on a serving platter. Tent with foil until the internal temperature reaches 120ºF. Slice, and serve with au jus.

" MY CHRISTMAS TRADITION STARTED SEVERAL YEARS AGO WHILE I WAS IN RESTAURANT OPERATIONS AND MY WIFE WAS WORKING IN RETAIL. DUE TO OUR HOLIDAY WORK SCHEDULES, IT WAS IMPOSSIBLE TO TRAVEL OUT OF STATE TO SEE EITHER OF OUR FAMILIES OVER THE HOLIDAYS. TO COMPENSATE FOR THIS, WE BEGAN HOLDING THANKSGIVING AND CHRISTMAS DINNERS FOR OUR FRIENDS WHO WERE ALSO 'ORPHANED' DURING THE HOLIDAYS DUE TO SIMILAR DEMANDING WORK SCHEDULES. THIS RECIPE EVOLVED INTO OUR 'SIGNATURE' ENTRÉE, OVER THE COURSE OF SEVERAL YEARS. IT WORKS WELL FOR A PARTY, SINCE THE PRIME RIB AND AU JUS MAY BE PREPARED AHEAD. SERVE WITH A HEARTY PINOT NOIR OR CABERNET. "

> Mike

PREPARATION FOR AU JUS

Remove the rack or bones from the roasting pan, and spoon off fat. Pour off pan drippings, reserving 1 cup. Place the roasting pan on top of stove, and over medium heat, brown the vegetables to caramelize them lightly. Add the Cabernet, port, and 1 cup pan drippings, and cook to reduce the liquid by one-half. Add the stock, and continue cooking to reduce the liquid until slightly thickened. Pour through a strainer, and serve with the roast.

For Buffet Style: Once meat reaches 120ºF internal temperature place roast in refrigerator uncovered to stop cooking process. Remove so the roast doesn't over-chill and cover with foil. Place 1 cup au jus and 1 cup water in sauté pan and heat until boiling. Dip each roast slice into au jus to reheat or cook longer for those well-done meat eaters. To serve buffet style, double the au jus recipe.

pumpkin stew

Diane Jennings > *Chicago, Illinois*

Serves 8 to 10

INGREDIENTS

1 pound beef stew meat, cubed
1 cup water
3 large potatoes, peeled and cut into 1-inch cubes
4 medium carrots sliced
1 large green pepper, cut into 1/2-inch pieces
4 garlic cloves minced
1 medium onion, chipped
2 teaspoons salt
1/2 teaspoon pepper
2 tablespoons instant beef bouillon granules
1 (14 1/2-ounce) can tomatoes, undrained, cut up
1 pumpkin (10 to 12 pounds)
2-3 tablespoons oil

PREPARATION

In a Dutch oven, brown the meat in 2 tablespoons oil. Add the water, potatoes, carrots, green pepper, garlic, onion, salt, and pepper. Cover and simmer for 2 hours. Stir in bouillon and tomatoes. Wash the pumpkin: cut a 6 to 8-inch circle around the top stem. Remove top and set aside: discard seeds and loose fibers from inside. Place pumpkin in a shallow sturdy baking pan. Spoon stew into pumpkin and replace the top. Brush outside of pumpkin with remaining oil. Bake at 325ºF for 2 hours or just until the pumpkin is tender (do not overbake). Serve stew from pumpkin, scooping out a little pumpkin with each serving.

speedy shepherd's pie

Katie Picciariello > *Bensenville, Illinois*

Serves 4 to 6

INGREDIENTS

1 pound ground beef
2 slices bread, torn into coarse crumbs
2/3 cup milk
1/4 cup diced onion
1 tablespoon Worcestershire sauce
1 egg, lightly beaten
1 teaspoon salt
3 cups hot mashed potatoes
1 cup finely diced American cheese

PREPARATION

In a large mixing bowl, mix together the beef, bread, milk, onion, Worcestershire sauce, egg, and salt. Spread the mixture into a 9-inch microwavable baking dish. Microwave on high for 7 minutes. Cover the meat with the potatoes, and sprinkle with the cheese. Microwave for 8 minutes, or until the cheese melts. Let stand 3 minutes before serving.

stew to warm the heart

Bonnie Harloff > *Rosemont, Illinois*

Serves 4 to 6

INGREDIENTS

1 can French onion soup
4 large red potatoes, peeled and diced
1 (10.5-ounce) can cream of tomato soup
4 sticks celery, diced
1 (10-ounce) bag small whole carrots
1 (10.5-ounce) can golden mushroom soup
2 pounds of stew meat, cubed and seasoned with steak seasoning
1 tablespoon of minced garlic (jar)
Mushrooms, small package, diced (optional)

PREPARATION

In a crockpot, begin by layering the ingredients in the following order. Pour onion soup over the potatoes. Pour tomato soup over the celery and carrots. Pour golden mushroom soup over the stew meat. Spread minced garlic and mushrooms over golden mushroom soup.

Cook on low for 8 hours. Stir and mix all ingredients after 4 hours. Serve with freshly made rolls and salad.

ENTRÉES

"THIS RECIPE IS A COMBINATION OF MY MOTHER-IN-LAW'S INGREDIENTS AND MY MOM'S, WHO ADDED GOLDEN MUSHROOM SOUP TO ALMOST EVERYTHING! NOT ONLY DO THE KIDS ENJOY IT, BUT THEIR FRIENDS WANT TO BE INVITED ON STEW NIGHT!"

> Bonnie

spendini

Bob Aiken > *Rosemont, Illinois*

Serves 8 to 10

INGREDIENTS

1 jar or more of bay leaves
2 to 3 cans Italian-seasoned breadcrumbs
1 cup chopped fresh parsley
1/2 cup grated parmesan cheese
1/2 teaspoon salt
1/4 teaspoon pepper
4 cups olive oil
3 large Spanish onions
4 pounds tenderloin or top round, sliced paper-thin in 3 by 5-inch strips
Lemon wedges to serve on each plate

PREPARATION FOR THE DISH

Preheat the oven to 350ºF. Bring a large pot of water to a boil, and cook the bay leaves for 10 minutes. Remove them, and set aside. In a large mixing bowl, combine 2 cans of breadcrumbs with the parsley, cheese, salt, and pepper. Slowly stir in olive oil, adding enough until the breadcrumbs are moist but not soggy. Pour the remaining olive oil into a separate bowl. Cut onions into wedges, and put in another bowl.

PREPARATION FOR THE MEAT

Dip each piece of meat into the olive oil, letting the excess drip off. Roll the meat in the breadcrumb mixture until well coated. Starting at the shorter end of the meat, roll it up, and set aside. Repeat until all the meat is coated.

PREPARATION FOR THE SKEWER

Thread a wedge of onion, a bay leaf, and a roll of meat onto a skewer. Repeat step, while leaving space at each end of the skewer. Repeat until all the ingredients are used up.

Bake for 15 minutes, and then broil for 2 minutes on each side. Serve with lemon wedges on the side. The trick to this dish is to ask the butcher to cut the meat into paper-thin slices. You will need wooden skewers, which should be soaked for 1/2 hour before using. You can use the 5 to 6-inch skewers to prepare individual servings. Fettuccini Alfredo and sautéed cherry tomatoes make great side dishes for this meal!

> "THIS RECIPE IS FOR A WONDERFUL ITALIAN ENTRÉE, AND HAS BEEN SERVED AT OUR FAMILY GATHERINGS FOR MANY YEARS. THIS IS MY FAVORITE DISH, AND MY FAMILY USUALLY SERVES IT ON MY BIRTHDAY. I HOPE YOU ENJOY IT AS MUCH AS I DO."
>
> > Bob

APPETIZERS

BREADS

BREAKFAST & BRUNCH

ENTRÉES

VEGETABLES & SIDE DISHES

SALADS

SOUPS

DESSERTS

steak and grits

Jeff Bland > *Roanoke, Virginia*

Serves 8

INGREDIENTS

2 pounds beef tenderloin, cubed
Blackened spice
1 cup (2 sticks) butter
1 cup diced andouille sausage
1/4 cup diced yellow onion
1/4 cup diced bell pepper, red and/or green
1/4 cup diced celery
1 tablespoon minced garlic
3 tablespoon all-purpose flour
2 cups beef stock
1 cup heavy cream
Salt and freshly ground black pepper
1 cup sliced green onions, sliced
Cooked grits

PREPARATION

Preheat a large skillet over medium-high heat. Season the beef cubes with the blackened spice to taste, and set aside. Add the butter to the skillet, and sear the beef. Remove from the pan and set aside.

Into the same skillet, stir in the sausage, onion, pepper, celery, and garlic, sautéing for 3 to 5 minutes. Add the flour, and stir until slightly golden, another 3 to 5 minutes. Add the beef stock, 1 cup at a time, stirring until it becomes sauce-like. Add the cream, blending well, and bring to a low boil. Cook until the sauce coats the back of a spoon. Just before you are ready to serve, add in the beef cubes, and cook 2 to 4 minutes.

Taste and adjust seasoning with salt and pepper. Just before plating, stir in the green onions. Serve the steak and sauce over grits. I like to use stone-ground coarse grits, but the instant will work just as well. Have the grits ready for when the meat is cooked.

sylvia's stuffed steak

Renee Foulis > *Newberry, South Carolina*

Serves 4 to 6

INGREDIENTS

1 double round steak
1/2 cup self-rising flour
1 1/2 cups chopped onion
1/2 cup finely chopped green peppers
1 (6-ounce) can sliced mushrooms
8 to 10 slices bacon
2 cups of water
Salt and pepper

PREPARATION

Tenderize the steak by pounding on both sides. Add the salt and pepper to taste. Lay the steak flat on the counter and spread the flour evenly over the steak (on face side only). Cover the steak with the onions, peppers, and mushrooms. Then lay bacon slices side by side until ingredients are covered. Roll as if making a "jelly roll" and secure with toothpicks or metal skewers.

Brown in a small amount of oil, turning to brown evenly. Add the 2 cups water, cover and simmer 45 minutes. Add more water as needed. Cool, remove from pan 15 minutes before slicing.

the duke's texas chili

Melinda Freeman > *Salem, Missouri*

Serves 12

INGREDIENTS

3 pounds ground beef
1 large onion, chopped
1/2 bell pepper, chopped
1 jalapeno, chopped
1/2 teaspoon cumin
1 1/2 teaspoons sugar
4 tablespoons chili powder
3 cloves garlic, minced
3 bay leaves
1 (13-ounce) can tomato sauce
2 (15.5-ounce) cans red kidney beans

PREPARATION

Brown the meat in a skillet. Drain the grease. Add to a crockpot. Add all the other ingredients. Cook on low 4 to 6 hours. Remove bay leaves before serving.

"I GUESS MOM THOUGHT THAT WE WERE TIRED OF FRIED STEAK, OR MAYBE SHE WAS AND SO SHE CREATED THIS RECIPE. THIS ALSO WAS THE FIRST MEAL I EVER MADE MY HUSBAND, WHO IS A CHEF. HE SEEMED IMPRESSED BY THE SIMPLICITY BUT DID TELL ME I NEEDED TO GO TO 'GREEN BEAN' SCHOOL."

> Renee

"MY GRANDMOTHER, DOROTHY DEMAINE, NAMED THIS DISH AFTER A NICKNAME MY GRANDFATHER, CHARLES, HAD AS A BOY. GRANDFATHER GREW UP IN PINE BLUFF, ARIZONA, DURING THE GREAT DEPRESSION. HE WAS VERY ATHLETIC AND SPENT MORE TIME PLAYING SPORTS THAN DOING CHORES. HIS FATHER WOULD GET IRRITATED WITH HIM BECAUSE GRANDFATHER ALWAYS SEEMED TO MANAGE TO GET HOME AFTER THE CHORES WERE ALREADY DONE FOR THE DAY. HIS FATHER WOULD SAY, 'WELL, THE GRAND DUKE IS FINALLY HOME!' THE NAME DUKE STUCK WITH HIM EVER SINCE."

> Melinda

APPETIZERS

BREADS

BREAKFAST & BRUNCH

ENTRÉES

VEGETABLES & SIDE DISHES

SALADS

SOUPS

DESSERTS

taco pie

Joan Miller > *Battleboro, North Carolina*

Serves 6 to 8

INGREDIENTS

1 taco dinner kit (includes shells, seasoning packet, and sauce)
1 pound ground beef
3/4 cup water
2 tablespoons butter
2 tablespoons all-purpose flour
1 cup whole milk
1/4 teaspoon salt
1 (8-ounce) container sour cream
2 cups grated cheddar or Mexican blend cheese

PREPARATION FOR PIE

Take the ingredients out of the dinner kit and set aside. Preheat the oven to 350ºF. Heat a large skillet over medium heat, and sauté the meat, stirring to cook through and brown. Drain excess fat. Stir the taco seasoning packet, 3/4 cup water, and 1/4 cup taco sauce into the ground beef. Bring to a boil. Reduce the heat to low and cook 10 minutes, stirring occasionally. Turn off the heat.

PREPARATION FOR WHITE SAUCE

In a heavy saucepan, melt the butter, and add the flour, stirring constantly until smooth. Keep stirring, and cook about 1 minute. Gradually add the milk, and cook over medium heat, stirring constantly, until thickened and bubbling. Remove from the heat and stir in salt and sour cream.

Break the taco shells into halves and put enough shells in the bottom of a glass pie pan to cover. Spoon the ground beef mixture over the shells. Cover the ground beef with another layer of shell halves. Spread the white sauce over the shell layer and top with the grated cheese.

Bake for 20 to 25 minutes, or until the cheese is melted and the sauce is bubbling. Remove from the oven, and let it sit for 5 or 10 minutes, then cut into wedges or squares, and serve with a drizzle of taco sauce and a small dollop of sour cream. Of course, you could also garnish with any of your favorite taco toppings. This dish is good served with Spanish rice and a salad.

ENTRÉES

upper peninsula pasties

MaryKay Skrypec > *Rosemont, Illinois*

Serves 6

INGREDIENTS FOR THE CRUST

4 cups flour
2 cups shortening
1 tablespoon white vinegar
1 egg (or equivalent egg substitute), **lightly beaten**
Whole milk to 1 cup

INGREDIENTS FOR FILLING

1 to 1 1/2 pounds boneless round steak (or more tender cut), **cut into 1/4 to 1/2-inch cubes**
4 to 5 potatoes, peeled and sliced 1/2-inch long by 1/4-inch thick
4 carrots, sliced 1/4-inch thick
1 large yellow or Vidalia onion, diced
1/2 cup (1 stick) **butter**

PREPARATION FOR CRUST

To prepare the pie crust, in a large mixing bowl, combine the flour and shortening. In a separate measuring cup, put the vinegar and egg, and fill the cup to the top with the milk. Stir the milk into the flour until the mixture forms dough. Roll it into a ball, and chill briefly for easier rolling.

PREPARATION FOR FILLING

In a large mixing bowl, combine the meat, potatoes, carrots, and onions, and set aside. Preheat the oven to 425°F. On a lightly floured surface, roll out the dough to the thickness of a piecrust. Cut out rounds the size of a dinner plate. Put about 1 cup filling mixture on one half of the round, and dot it with 1 tablespoon butter. Fold the other half over the filling, and crimp the edges closed. Using a fork or knife, poke several holes in the top to allow steam to escape. Repeat until all the ingredients are used up. Put the pies on a baking sheet. Bake 10 minutes. Decrease the oven temperature to 350°F, and bake about 45 minutes more. Remove from the oven. Place a clean towel lightly over the pasties for 10 minutes to let them steam.

> "THIS IS A HERITAGE RECIPE FROM MY MOM'S UPPER PENINSULA OF MICHIGAN UPBRINGING WHERE THIS TYPE OF FOOD IS A CLASSIC FOR LUMBERJACKS AND MINERS. WE ATE THESE OFTEN ON FAMILY TRIPS OR AT HOME. THEY ARE GREAT WITH ADDED BUTTER OR LOTS OF KETCHUP (MONARCH KETCHUP, OF COURSE!)."
>
> > MaryKay

APPETIZERS

BREADS

BREAKFAST & BRUNCH

ENTRÉES

VEGETABLES & SIDE DISHES

SALADS

SOUPS

DESSERTS

new york maple lamb brochettes

Robert J. More > *Albany, New York*

Serves 4 to 6

INGREDIENTS FOR MARINADE

1 1/2 cups vegetable oil (not olive oil)
1/2 cup julienned shallots or sweet onion
1 teaspoon whole peppercorns
3 to 4 sprigs fresh thyme, or 1 teaspoon dried
3 tablespoons New York maple syrup
1 tablespoon sea or kosher salt
8 each Mission figs, fresh or dried, quartered
2 each (8-bone racks) lamb racks (or other cut), cut into individual chops

INGREDIENTS FOR DRESSING
(YIELDS 1 PINT)

2/3 cup balsamic vinegar
1 1/2 cups extra-virgin olive oil
1 tablespoon sea or kosher salt
1 teaspoon black pepper
1 teaspoon dried basil
1/2 teaspoon dried thyme
1 teaspoon dried parsley
1/2 teaspoon cracked or ground fennel

INGREDIENTS FOR SALAD

1 pound bag mesclun mix, or other favorite greens
1 (8-ounce) jar or can roasted red peppers, cut into strips
4 ounces bleu cheese crumbles

PREPARATION FOR MARINADE

In a small saucepan, combine the vegetable oil, shallots or onion, peppercorns, thyme, maple syrup, and salt. Heat over medium heat. Once the mixture starts to bubble, turn off the heat, stir, and let it sit for 2 minutes. Arrange the lamb and the figs in a large baking dish, and pour the marinade over them. Set aside in a cool place, or refrigerate for up to 48 hours.

PREPARATION FOR DRESSING

In a small bowl, combine all the ingredients and mix thoroughly. (Substitute your favorite store-bought Balsamic if desired.)

To serve, in a large mixing bowl, toss the greens with enough dressing to coat, and mound the mixture on individual plates. Garnish each serving with red pepper strips. Grill or sauté the meat, about 2 minutes per side, and arrange the chops fanned out on one side of the greens. Place the figs around the side of the plate, and top with the blue cheese.

Note: You may substitute your favorite cut of lamb. Also, be careful grilling the marinated product. Wipe off excess oil to avoid dangerous flare-ups on an open-fire grill.

barbecue ham

Robert Campbell > *Altoona, Pennsylvania*

Serves 8

INGREDIENTS

2 pounds chipped ham, shredded
1 large can of Manwich Barbecue Sauce (Sloppy Joe)
1 (6-ounce) small can tomato paste
1/2 cup firmly packed brown sugar
1 teaspoon Worcestershire sauce
Salt and freshly ground black pepper
Garlic salt

PREPARATION

Rinse the ham in hot water, drain, and set aside. Combine the remaining ingredients in a crockpot and cook on low. Add ham about 2 hours before serving, and continue cooking. Serve with rolls.

APPETIZERS

BREADS

BREAKFAST & BRUNCH

ENTRÉES

VEGETABLES & SIDE DISHES

SALADS

SOUPS

DESSERTS

glazed pork roast

Christina Brown > *Greensburg, Pennsylvania*

Serves 8

INGREDIENTS

1 (5-pound) **boneless pork loin**
2 cloves **garlic, sliced**
Salt and freshly ground black pepper
1/2 cup **sugar**
1 tablespoon **cornstarch**
1/4 cup **apple cider vinegar**
1/4 cup **water**
2 tablespoons **soy sauce**

PREPARATION

Preheat the oven to 325°F. Make 8 to 10 1/2-inch slits on the surface of the roast, and stuff a garlic slice into each slit. Season the meat with salt and pepper to taste. Place the pork in a roasting pan on the middle oven rack. Bake, uncovered, until internal temperature reaches at least 150°F, depending on your desired doneness.

Meanwhile, put the sugar, cornstarch, vinegar, water, and soy sauce in a small saucepan. Heat, stirring occasionally, until the mixture begins to bubble and thickens slightly. Brush the roast with the glaze 3 or 4 times during the last 30 minutes of cooking. When the roast is done, let it sit for 15 to 20 minutes. Slice, and pour remaining glaze over slices. Serve.

stuffed pork tenderloin

Wes Daniel > *Prattville, Alabama*

Serves 8

INGREDIENTS

1 (2-pound) **pork tenderloin**
3 cups **blue cheese crumbles**
4 finely sliced **green onions**
Salt and freshly ground black pepper to taste

PREPARATION

Preheat the oven to 300°F. Using a sharp paring knife, cut lengthwise slits into tenderloin. In a small bowl, blend the blue cheese crumbles and onions into a paste. Stuff the paste into the slits. Turn the roast over, and tie it with butcher's twine. Roast for 1 hour.

hutspot (old-fashioned dutch dish)

Samantha Jameson > *Houston, Texas*

Serves 8

INGREDIENTS

5 pounds potatoes, peeled and cubed
5 pounds yellow onions, quartered
5 pounds carrots, peeled and cut into chunks
2 eggs
1/2 cup (1 stick) **butter**
2 pounds smoked rope sausage (pork or beef), **cut into 3-inch pieces**
Gravy (optional)

PREPARATION

In a large pot filled with lightly salted water, cook the potatoes, onions, and carrots over medium heat until all the vegetables are soft. Drain, and put the vegetables into a large mixing bowl. Add the eggs and butter, and using a potato masher, mash until most of the lumps are gone.

In a large skillet, cook the sausage pieces, and when heated through, place on top of the Hutspot. Serve with gravy, if desired.

italian sausage and potatoes

Darlene Brown > *Berwyn, Illinois*

Serves 4

INGREDIENTS

1 pound Italian sausages cut in 4-inch pieces
2 potatoes, unpeeled and quartered
1 green pepper, cut into strips
1 onion, thinly sliced
1 tablespoon dried oregano
Garlic powder
1 can stew tomatoes (optional)

PREPARATION

Preheat the oven to 425°F. In a baking dish, layer the sausage, potatoes, green peppers, and tomatoes, repeating the layers until the ingredients are used up. Place onion slices on top. Sprinkle with the oregano and garlic powder to taste. Fill the baking dish halfway with water, and cover it with aluminum foil. Bake for 45 minutes.

"MY MOTHER GREW UP IN HOLLAND WHERE THIS WAS A GREAT DISH ON COLD DAYS AND VERY INEXPENSIVE TO FEED A FAMILY. DUTCH FARMERS WOULD MAKE THIS OFTEN. MY MOTHER RAISED MY SISTER AND ME ALONE ON $600 A MONTH; WE ATE THIS OFTEN. IT SOUNDS STRANGE I KNOW, BUT I PROMISE IT IS YUMMY!"

> Samantha

APPETIZERS

BREADS

BREAKFAST & BRUNCH

ENTRÉES

VEGETABLES & SIDE DISHES

SALADS

SOUPS

DESSERTS

grilled pork tenderloin with peanut sauce

Cindy Gordon > *Sarasota, Florida*

Serves 10 to 12

"AFTER ENJOYING PORK SATAY AS A FIRST COURSE AT AN INDONESIAN RESTAURANT, I RE-CREATED THIS AT HOME, USING FAIRLY COMMON INGREDIENTS. WHEN I TAKE THIS TO A POTLUCK, IT GOES VERY QUICKLY AND I GET MANY REQUESTS FOR THE RECIPE."

> Cindy

INGREDIENTS FOR PORK

1 pork tenderloin (about 2 pounds)
1 tablespoon minced garlic

INGREDIENTS FOR MARINADE

1/2 cup teriyaki sauce
1 tablespoon minced fresh ginger
1 tablespoon brown sugar
2 teaspoons chili oil

INGREDIENTS FOR PEANUT SAUCE

1 (13.5-ounce) can coconut milk
1/2 cup peanut butter (for best results do not use a natural peanut butter)
Juice of 1/2 lime
1/4 teaspoon lime zest
1 tablespoon brown sugar
2 tablespoons teriyaki sauce
1 teaspoon minced fresh ginger
Dash chili oil

INGREDIENTS FOR GARNISH

Chopped peanuts
Minced cilantro
Minced scallions
Lime wedges

PREPARATION FOR PORK

Using a sharp paring knife, slice off the silver skin (membrane) and any excess fat. Rub with the minced garlic, and set aside in a large roasting pan.

To prepare marinade, in a large baking dish, combine all the marinade ingredients. Put the pork in the marinade, and let it marinate for at least 1/2 hour, turning once or twice.

PREPARATION FOR PEANUT SAUCE

Meanwhile, in a large saucepan, combine all the ingredients and bring the mixture to a boil over medium heat. Decrease the heat to low, and cook until the mixture thickens slightly. Keep warm.

Preheat the grill. Remove the pork from the marinade and grill to desired doneness, minimum 160°F. Let the pork rest for 10 minutes, and slice into 1/2-inch pieces. Arrange the pieces on a platter. Nap the pork slices with a small portion of the peanut sauce; put the remaining sauce in a serving dish. Garnish the pork with the peanuts, cilantro, scallions, and lime wedges.

jamie's secret marinated tenderloin of pork

Jamie Collier > *Mobile, Alabama*

Serves 8

INGREDIENTS

4 cups liquid steak seasoning/marinade
2 cups water
1 cup red wine
3 tablespoons chopped garlic
2 tablespoons Creole seasoning
1 to 2 pork tenderloins, 1.5 to 2 pounds each

PREPARATION

To prepare the marinade, in a large bowl, combine the steak seasoning, water, wine, garlic, and Creole seasoning, mixing well. Transfer the mixture to a square baking pan. This will help the tenderloin lay flat. The container should be slightly longer than the tenderloins. Rinse the tenderloins in cold water, and place them into the marinade to marinate for about 2 hours.

Preheat the grill. Grill the tenderloins, cooking them to an internal temperature of 165°F. Remove them and place them into an air-tight plastic container. This is the most important step as this is what makes them moist. Let the tenderloins stay in the container for 10 to 15 minutes. Slice and serve. Serve the sliced pork with a soft yeast roll and red pepper jelly.

APPETIZERS

BREADS

BREAKFAST & BRUNCH

ENTRÉES

VEGETABLES & SIDE DISHES

SALADS

SOUPS

DESSERTS

old-fashioned-way meat sauce

Pat Mulhern > *Rosemont, Illinois*

Serves 4

INGREDIENTS

1 pound or more of pork, pork ribs, pork butt, or pork shoulder with bone
2 tablespoons oil
1 large onion, chopped
1 clove garlic, chopped
1/4 cup white or red wine
3 (28-ounce) cans of whole peeled tomatoes, or 1 basket of fresh tomatoes
1 tablespoon salt

INGREDIENTS FOR TOMATO SAUCE

1/2 cup fresh basil, chopped fine
1 cup parsley, chopped fine
3 (28-ounce) cans of water from the tomato cans, or equal amount of water if using fresh tomatoes
Pinch salt

PREPARATION FOR MEAT

Brown the meat (cut fat off, if any) in oil. Add the onion and garlic and simmer while stirring. Stir in about 1/4 cup of the wine. Let it evaporate. Add the canned tomatoes (or the freshly made tomato sauce, recipe below), salt, basil, and parsley. Then fill each of the 3 cans from the tomatoes with water to "rinse" your cans and add that water to the pot. Cook uncovered or partially covered, never cover your sauce completely, always leave a vent.

PREPARATION FOR TOMATO SAUCE

Wash, core, and seed a basket of fresh tomatoes, and put in strainer. Salt tomatoes in layers as you go along, a little salt, not much. Let sit for 2 hours or so. Process in a blender or processor. Use right away as tomato sauce or freeze for later use. You will have a nice fresh sauce. There is a big difference between fresh and canned.

upside down pizza

Betsy Taylor > *Raleigh, North Carolina*

Serves 8

INGREDIENTS FOR FILLING

1 pound ground beef or sausage
1 cup chopped onions
1 cup chopped green peppers
2 cups pizza or spaghetti sauce
2 tablespoons Italian seasoning
1 (6-ounce) jar sliced mushrooms, drained
1 (8-ounce) package sliced pepperoni
2 cups grated mozzarella cheese

INGREDIENTS FOR CRUST

2 eggs
1 cup whole milk
1 1/2 tablespoons vegetable oil
1 cup flour
1/2 cup grated parmesan cheese

PREPARATION FOR FILLING

Preheat the oven to 400°F. Grease a 9 by 13-inch baking pan. In a large skillet, sauté the beef or sausage, onions, and peppers over medium heat until the beef or sausage is thoroughly cooked. Add the sauce and seasoning, stirring well. Pour the mixture into the prepared pan. Arrange the mushrooms and pepperoni slices over the top, and cover with the grated mozzarella cheese.

PREPARATION FOR CRUST

In a separate bowl, beat the eggs well with a whisk. Add the milk and oil; beat with a portable mixer on low until blended. Add the flour, and beat until mixed well. Pour the mixture over the top of the meat, and sprinkle with the parmesan cheese. Bake, uncovered, for 20 minutes. Let stand a few minutes before cutting. This recipe freezes well.

APPETIZERS

BREADS

BREAKFAST &
BRUNCH

ENTRÉES

VEGETABLES &
SIDE DISHES

SALADS

SOUPS

DESSERTS

pasta in a pot

Kathy Gwynn > *Las Vegas, Nevada*

Serves 6 to 8

INGREDIENTS

1 to 1 1/2 pounds sausage, hot or mild
1 small green bell pepper, seeded and diced
1 small onion, cubed
8 ounces shredded fresh mushrooms
1 pound box pasta, preferably mostaccioli
32 ounces tomato sauce
8 ounces shredded mozzarella
10 slices provolone (not thinly sliced)
8 ounces sour cream

PREPARATION FOR DISH

Preheat the oven to 350°F. In a large skillet over medium heat, sauté the sausage, peppers, onions, and mushrooms, stirring often.

PREPARATION FOR PASTA

Bring a large pot of salted water to a boil, and cook the pasta until al dente. Drain, and return the pasta to the pot. Spoon a little of the plain tomato sauce into the bottom of a lasagna pan. Mix the sausage, peppers, onions, and mushrooms into the remaining tomato sauce. Put half the pasta into the pan. Spoon one-third of the sauce mixture over pasta. Spoon on half the sour cream and spread around evenly. Layer on 5 pieces of provolone. Sprinkle on a third of the mozzarella. Repeat the layers, and top with the remaining sauce mixture and the remaining mozzarella. Bake for 1 to 1 1/2 hours, or until hot.

penne with sausage, onions, and peppers

Fabian Sriwardene > *Annandale, Virginia*

Serves 4 to 6

INGREDIENTS

1 (16-ounce) **box penne pasta**
2 pounds hot or sweet Italian sausage links
2 white onions, diced
1 green bell pepper, seeded and diced
1 red bell pepper, seeded and diced
1 yellow bell pepper, seeded and diced
1 clove garlic, diced
4 ounces grated parmesan cheese
4 tablespoons extra-virgin olive oil
Sea salt to taste
Parsley sprigs for garnish

PREPARATION

Bring a large pot of salted water to a boil, and cook the pasta until just tender. Drain, and put it into a large bowl. In a saucepan, bring water to the boil, and cook the sausage until firm. Drain, and cut each link into 6 or 7 pieces. Heat a skillet over medium heat, and sauté the sausages until brown. Add 1 tablespoon of the olive oil to the skillet, and sauté the vegetables for 7 to 10 minutes, or until soft. To the pasta, add 3 tablespoons of the olive oil and the parmesan cheese, and toss gently. Add the sausages, vegetables, and salt, and toss again. Garnish with the parsley, and serve. Serve this with a side salad with a creamy dressing.

APPETIZERS

BREADS

BREAKFAST & BRUNCH

ENTRÉES

VEGETABLES & SIDE DISHES

SALADS

SOUPS

DESSERTS

pesto penne florentine

Lynn Zehnder > *Rosemont, Illinois*

Serves 8

INGREDIENTS

1 pound Italian pork or turkey sausage
1 onion, diced
3 garlic cloves, minced
2 (24-ounce) jars pasta sauce
1 (6-ounce) jar sliced mushrooms
6 tablespoons basil pesto
Salt and freshly ground black pepper
1 pound penne pasta
1/2 pound smoked Gouda or mozzarella cheese, finely diced
1 cup grated parmesan cheese
1 (6-ounce) bag fresh baby spinach

PREPARATION FOR DISH

Preheat the oven to 375°F. Spray a 9 by 13-inch baking dish with olive oil cooking spray. Heat a large Dutch oven over medium heat, and cook the sausage, breaking up the meat and cooking it until no pink remains. Add the onion, and sauté for 10 minutes, or until soft, stirring frequently. Add the garlic, and cook for 3 minutes. Add the pasta sauce and mushrooms, and continue cooking for 10 to 15 minutes. Stir in the pesto, and add salt and pepper to taste, stirring well. Set aside.

PREPARATION FOR PASTA

Bring a large pot of salted water to a boil, and cook the pasta until just tender. Drain. Spread a thin layer of the sauce over the bottom of the pan. In a large bowl, combine the pasta with the remaining sauce, the smoked Gouda or mozzarella cheese, 1/3 cup of the parmesan cheese, and the spinach leaves. Mix well to combine. Spoon the mixture into the prepared pan, and sprinkle the remaining 2/3 cup parmesan cheese on top.

Bake for about 30 minutes, or until the pasta begins to bubble and the cheese starts to brown. Add a salad and warm crusty bread and it's a great meal that will easily serve 8 people. This pasta freezes well and can be reheated in the microwave.

ribs and kraut

Karen Hood > *St. Louis, Missouri*

Serves 8

INGREDIENTS

2 slabs ribs, cut into 8 pieces
3 quarts sauerkraut
Salt and freshly ground black pepper

PREPARATION

Preheat the oven to 350°F. To prepare the ribs, rinse the meat, and quarter the slabs. To prepare the sauerkraut, rinse it, and drain. In a 9 by 13-inch roasting pan, layer 1 quart sauerkraut, and sprinkle with salt and pepper to taste. Put the 4 pieces of ribs on top, and season with salt and pepper. Layer another quart of sauerkraut on the ribs, and season with salt and pepper. Put the last 4 ribs on top of the sauerkraut, and season with salt and pepper. Top with the remaining quart of sauerkraut, and season with salt and pepper. Cover the pan with aluminum foil. Bake for 1 1/2 hours or until the ribs are done. These ribs will be very tender.

simply delicious pork

Michael Beck > *Fairburn, Georgia*

Serves 6 to 8

INGREDIENTS

Olive oil for rubbing
5 pounds bone-in pork loin roast
Kosher salt and freshly ground black pepper
2 (16-ounce) **cans cannelloni beans, drained**
2 (16-ounce) **cans sauerkraut, drained**

PREPARATION

Preheat the oven to 500°F. To prepare the roast, rub olive oil over the whole roast, and sprinkle it with salt and pepper. Roast for 20 minutes, or until crisp. Decrease the temperature to 300°F and bake for 1 1/2 hours. Add the beans and sauerkraut, arranging them around the pork. Continue baking for another 30 to 40 minutes. Remove from the oven, and ladle the juices from the bottom of the pan on the beans and sauerkraut before serving. Serve with applesauce on the side. Tastes even better reheated the next day.

> "MY FAMILY HAS BEEN IN THE RESTAURANT BUSINESS FOR MORE THAN 50 YEARS. MY DAD STARTED AS A COOK ON A NAVY SHIP. HE WENT ON TO RUN MANY OF HIS OWN DOWN-HOME COUNTRY DINERS. I WORKED WITH MY DAD IN THE RESTAURANTS SINCE I WAS 12. I BOUGHT MY OWN RESTAURANT IN 1995, BUT I SOLD IT IN 2001 BECAUSE MY DAD WAS SICK WITH CANCER. HE IS GONE NOW, BUT I HAVE FOND MEMORIES OF HIM SHOWING ME HOW TO COOK. THIS RECIPE WAS A FAVORITE OF HIS CUSTOMERS."
>
> > Karen

APPETIZERS

BREADS

BREAKFAST & BRUNCH

ENTRÉES

VEGETABLES & SIDE DISHES

SALADS

SOUPS

DESSERTS

bahama chicken

Nicole Shipley > *Greensburg, Pennsylvania*

Serves 6 to 8

INGREDIENTS

8 (6-ounce) **boneless chicken breast halves**
Juice of 2 lemons
Juice of 2 limes
1 cup firmly packed brown sugar
1 tablespoon coarse-grain or Dijon mustard
1/2 cup red wine vinegar
1 tablespoon minced garlic
1 cup vegetable oil
Sprigs fresh mint, chopped

PREPARATION

Pound the chicken breasts to a uniform thickness. In a large mixing bowl, combine the lemon juice, lime juice, brown sugar, mustard, vinegar, and garlic. Whisk until the sugar is completely dissolved. Slowly whisk in the oil to form an emulsion. Put in the chicken breasts, making sure the breasts are covered. Cover and refrigerate for at least 30 minutes or up to 8 hours.

At least 1 hour before cooking, bring the chicken to room temperature. Grill or broil the breasts, as desired. Place them on a serving platter, and sprinkle with the mint. This chicken goes great over rice pilaf and grilled vegetables.

barbara's barbecue chicken

Rod McKenrick > *Kinston, North Carolina*

Serves 4

INGREDIENTS

1 (2 1/2 to 3-pound) fryer or 4 whole chicken breasts, halved
Salt and freshly ground black pepper
1/4 (1/2 stick) cup margarine
1/4 cup lemon juice
1/4 cup Worcestershire sauce
1/4 cup ketchup
1/4 cup cider vinegar

PREPARATION

Preheat the oven broiler. Line a large baking dish with aluminum foil.

To prepare this dish, sprinkle each piece of chicken with salt and pepper, and place them in the prepared baking dish skin side up. Broil the chicken until it starts to darken; remove it from the broiler. Decrease the temperature to 350°F.

Meanwhile, in a small saucepan heat the margarine, lemon juice, Worcestershire sauce, ketchup, and vinegar, and bring to a boil. Pour the sauce over the chicken, and place it in the oven. Bake for 45 minutes or until done. Baste the chicken with the sauce several times during baking.

> "MY WIFE, JAN'S, MOTHER (BARBARA SMITH) MADE THIS BARBECUE CHICKEN FOR HER WHEN SHE WAS A CHILD. IT WAS HER FAVORITE DISH. NOW OUR CHILDREN (TARYN, ERYN, AND RYLEE) ARE GROWING UP LOVING THIS DISH, TOO. IT HAS BECOME OUR FAMILY FAVORITE; WE CALL IT BARBARA'S BARBEQUE CHICKEN. BARBARA FOUND THIS RECIPE IN *MCCALL'S* MAGAZINE IN THE MID-1960S AS PART OF AN ARTICLE ABOUT PRESIDENT LYNDON B. JOHNSON (IT WAS ONE OF HIS FAVORITES), AND SINCE ADAPTED IT. THE SAUCE IS DELICIOUS SERVED OVER CREAMED POTATOES. THE RECIPE CAN ALSO BE USED FOR CHICKEN COOKED ON THE GRILL."
>
> > Rod

APPETIZERS

BREADS

BREAKFAST & BRUNCH

ENTRÉES

VEGETABLES & SIDE DISHES

SALADS

SOUPS

DESSERTS

bowtie chicken pasta

Jennifer Adams-Delph > *Greensboro, North Carolina*

Serves 6

INGREDIENTS

2 tablespoons olive oil
1 medium onion, chopped
1 cup shredded carrots
4 cloves garlic, minced
2 cups frozen broccoli florets
1 1/2 cups fresh or canned diced tomatoes
1 teaspoon salt
1/4 teaspoon black pepper
2 cups cooked cut-up chicken
1 cup chicken broth
4 cups hot cooked bowtie pasta
1 (8-ounce) bag grated parmesan cheese
2 tablespoons chopped fresh parsley

PREPARATION

In a large skillet or Dutch oven, heat the oil over medium heat. Sauté the onion, carrots, and garlic for about 3 minutes. Add the broccoli, and cook, stirring occasionally, until the broccoli is crisp but tender. Add the tomatoes, salt, and pepper. Cook another 3 minutes. Add the chicken and broth, and cook another 3 to 4 minutes. Toss the mixture with the pasta, cheese, and parsley. Serve hot.

chicken and cheese

Mitch Hughes > *San Francisco, California*

Serves 4

INGREDIENTS

1 1/2 pounds boneless skinless chicken
8 ounces sliced Swiss cheese
1 (12-ounce) can cream of celery soup, undiluted
1 tablespoon sherry wine or white wine
Breadcrumbs

PREPARATION

Preheat the oven to 375°F. To prepare the dish, put the chicken into a baking dish. Place the cheese slices on top of the chicken. Combine the soup with the wine and spoon over the cheese. Bake for 15 to 25 minutes, or until the chicken reaches 165°F. Sprinkle the breadcrumbs over the soup, and bake until golden brown. Remove from the oven, and let it cool for 10 minutes before serving. This dish goes great with wild rice.

" THIS RECIPE CAME FROM MY MOTHER-IN-LAW WHO LIVES OUTSIDE OF CHICAGO. MY WIFE AND I MOVED TO SAN FRANCISCO FIVE YEARS AGO AND THIS ALWAYS REMINDS US OF HOME. "

> Mitch

brunswick stew

Susan Clark > *Lexington, South Carolina*

Serves 12 to 15

INGREDIENTS

8 ounces lean boneless pork, diced
8 ounces boneless skinless chicken breast, diced
1 (10-ounce) package frozen baby lima beans, thawed
1 (10-ounce) package frozen corn kernels, thawed
1 (16-ounce) package frozen creamed corn, thawed
1 (28-ounce) can diced tomatoes
1 (14-ounce) bottle ketchup
1 (16-ounce) container chicken broth
1 large onion, diced
1 large potato, peeled and diced
Worcestershire sauce to taste
Hot sauce
Salt and freshly ground black pepper

PREPARATION

Place all the ingredients in a large crockpot, stirring well; the mixture will be thick. Cook on high for 8 hours. Taste and adjust seasoning. This stew is great for a crowd when served with corn bread or rice. It also freezes well.

chicken and rice casserole

Chad Steinert > *Indianapolis, Indiana*

Serves 6

INGREDIENTS

2 cups chicken, cooked and diced
6 cups cooked rice
1 (10.75-ounce) can cream of celery soup
1 (10.75-ounce) can cream of chicken soup
3/4 cup sour cream
3/4 cup mayonnaise
1/2 cup chopped celery
1/2 cup water chestnuts (optional)
8 ounces of shredded cheddar cheese

PREPARATION

Grease a 9 by 13-inch pan. In a large bowl, mix together the chicken, rice, soups, sour cream, mayonnaise, celery, and water chestnuts. Place in the prepared pan. Sprinkle the cheese on top. Bake at 375°F for about 30 minutes, or until the cheese is hot and bubbly.

APPETIZERS

BREADS

BREAKFAST & BRUNCH

ENTRÉES

VEGETABLES & SIDE DISHES

SALADS

SOUPS

DESSERTS

cheesy italian chicken

Debbie Williams > *Paducah, Kentucky*

Serves 4

INGREDIENTS

1 cup seasoned breadcrumbs
3 whole boneless chicken breasts
2 eggs, lightly beaten
3 tablespoons vegetable oil
6 slices mozzarella cheese
1 pint heavy cream
1 cup freshly grated parmesan cheese
2 tablespoons chopped fresh parsley
Salt and freshly ground black pepper

PREPARATION

Preheat the oven to 350°F. To prepare the dish, put the breadcrumbs into a shallow bowl. Dip the chicken breasts into the eggs, and coat each in breadcrumbs. Set aside. In a large skillet, heat the oil over medium heat. Put the chicken into the skillet, and cook lightly on both sides until brown. Remove from the pan, and place the chicken in a baking dish. Top each breast with a slice of mozzarella.

In a saucepan, mix together the cream, parmesan cheese, parsley, and salt and pepper to taste. Cook over medium heat until the mixture is hot and has thickened. Pour it over the chicken.

Bake for 25 minutes, or until the cheese is melted and light golden brown.

Note: This is great served over your favorite pasta!

chicken and never-fail dumplings

Melinda Freeman > *Salem, Missouri*

Serves 4

INGREDIENTS FOR CHICKEN

4 boneless chicken breasts
6 cups water
2 stalks celery, chopped
1 onion, chopped
4 chicken bouillon cubes
1 (10-ounce) can cream of chicken soup
Salt and pepper

INGREDIENTS FOR DUMPLINGS

1 1/2 cups flour
3 tablespoons shortening
1/2 teaspoon salt
1 egg
5 tablespoons cold water

PREPARATION FOR CHICKEN

Wash and remove skin from the chicken breasts; pat dry. Place in a crockpot. Add the water, celery, onion, bouillon, soup, and salt and pepper to taste; stir. Set the crockpot on low and cook at least 8 hours.

PREPARATION FOR DUMPLINGS

Mix all the dumpling ingredients into a soft dough. Divide into 3 parts. Roll out in thin sheets and allow to dry for 30 minutes. Cut into strips and drop into crockpot. Cook until tender.

"MY GRANDMOTHER, DOROTHY DEMAINE, TOLD ME THIS RECIPE HAS BEEN IN OUR FAMILY FOR OVER 100 YEARS. SHE WAS A TERRIFIC COOK AND A GENTEEL SOUTHERN BELLE. SHE PASSED AWAY A FEW MONTHS AGO LEAVING MANY LOVING, WONDERFUL MEMORIES AND MANY, MANY RECIPES. EVERY TIME I USE HER RECIPES, THE SMELLS REMIND ME OF MY GRANDMOTHER DOROTHY."

> Melinda

APPETIZERS

BREADS

BREAKFAST & BRUNCH

ENTRÉES

VEGETABLES & SIDE DISHES

SALADS

SOUPS

DESSERTS

chicken paprikás with hungarian dumplings

Jill Wayland > *Sykesville, Maryland*

Serves 6

INGREDIENTS FOR PAPRIKÁS

1 tablespoon olive oil or more as needed
2 medium onions, chopped
1 large clove garlic, chopped
Flour for dredging
1 (3-pound) **chicken, cut into serving pieces**
1 teaspoon salt
1 teaspoon freshly ground black pepper
3 tablespoons Hungarian paprika (all sweet or half sweet and half hot)
1 (4-ounce) **can tomato sauce**
Up to 1 cup water or chicken stock
1 cup sour cream (optional)

INGREDIENTS FOR DUMPLINGS

3 cups sifted all-purpose flour
1 teaspoon salt
3 eggs
Cold water
2 tablespoons butter or oil

PREPARATION FOR PAPRIKÁS

In a stockpot, heat the olive oil over medium-low heat, and add the onions and garlic, stirring often, until softened. Put the flour into a mixing bowl. Rub the chicken with the salt and pepper, and dredge each piece in flour. Push the onions and garlic aside in the pot. Add the chicken to the pot. Lightly brown the chicken on all sides. Gently stir the paprika into the chicken mixture. Cover the pot, and decrease the heat to low. (The low heat will begin to draw the juices out of the chicken. This should take about 15 minutes but check the pot occasionally.) When about 1 inch of juice appears, stir in the tomato sauce and up to 1 cup of the water or stock. Continue cooking until the chicken is tender. Before serving, you may stir 1 cup sour cream into the gravy, if desired.

PREPARATION FOR DUMPLINGS

In a large mixing bowl, stir together the flour and salt. Make a well in the center of the flour, and add the eggs. Beat with a sturdy wooden spoon, adding enough cold water to make the dough come together. Keep beating until the dough comes away from the sides of the bowl and starts to blister. Let the dough rest for 45 minutes. Put the dough on a wet cutting board, and using a sharp knife, cut off irregular pieces about the width of a pencil and about 1 inch long. Drop into boiling salted water. Dumplings are done a few seconds after they rise to the water's surface. Skim them off the surface, and drain in a colander. Put them in a bowl, and add the butter or oil and serve with the chicken and gravy.

Chicken Paprikás is traditionally served with small dumplings or wide noodles.

creamed chicken casserole

Beth Zubalik > *Greensburg, Pennsylvania*

Serves 6

INGREDIENTS FOR CHICKEN

4 chicken breasts (skin on)
4 chicken thighs (skin on)
4 cups corn flakes, crushed

INGREDIENTS FOR CREAM SAUCE

1/4 (1/2 stick) **cup butter**
3 tablespoons all-purpose flour
1 cup whole milk
3/4 cup grated sharp cheese
1 cup chicken broth
3 to 4 strips crisp bacon

PREPARATION FOR CHICKEN

Preheat the oven to 350°F. Grease a 9 by 13-inch baking pan. In a large steamer, steam the chicken, and when it is cool enough to handle, remove the skin and bones, and cut the chicken into bite-sized pieces. Put 2 cups of the crushed corn flakes into the bottom of the prepared pan.

PREPARATION FOR CREAM SAUCE

In a large saucepan, heat the butter over medium heat until melted, and stir in the flour, cooking for 1 minute. Stir in the milk, cheese, and chicken broth, and continue cooking and stirring until the sauce has thickened.

Stir in the chicken until it is completely mixed. Pour the chicken into the casserole over the corn flakes. Top with the remaining 2 cups of corn flakes, and crumble the bacon on top. Bake for 30 minutes.

APPETIZERS

BREADS

BREAKFAST & BRUNCH

ENTRÉES

VEGETABLES & SIDE DISHES

SALADS

SOUPS

DESSERTS

crockpot dressing

Twyla McCree > *Huntingdon, Tennessee*

Serves 16

> "OUR CHURCH YOUTH GROUP PREPARES A THANKSGIVING MEAL EVERY YEAR FOR OUR ELDERLY AND SHUT-IN MEMBERS. THIS IS THE MAIN DISH; EVERYONE LOVES IT!"
>
> > Twyla

INGREDIENTS

1 (5 to 7-pound) **chicken**
1 large pan cooked cornbread
1 box chicken-flavored stuffing
4 eggs, well beaten
1 medium onion, finely chopped
1/4 cup chopped celery
1 teaspoon salt
1/4 teaspoon black pepper
1 (10.75-ounce) **can cream of chicken soup**
1 (10.75-ounce) **can cream of celery soup**
1 (29-ounce) **can chicken broth**
2 tablespoons margarine

PREPARATION

Put the chicken, with enough water to cover, into a large stockpot, and bring to a boil over medium heat. Decrease the heat to low, and cook until the chicken is cooked through. Remove from the heat, strain, and reserve the cooking liquid.

When the chicken is cool enough to handle, remove the skin and bones, and discard. In a large mixing bowl, crumble the cornbread and mix with the stuffing until well combined. Add the eggs, onion, celery, salt, pepper, cream of chicken soup, cream of celery soup, and the chicken broth. Stir in the chicken pieces. Spoon the mixture into a large crockpot, and dot the top with the margarine. (I recommend using a crockpot liner for easy cleanup.) Cover, and cook on low for 4 hours or on high for 2 hours. Stir well after the first hour of cooking.

five-bean chili

Boston Chisum > *Atlanta, Georgia*

Serves 8 to 12

INGREDIENTS

3 pounds ground chuck (or turkey)
1 large onion, chopped
1 small bell pepper, chopped
1 cup cooked red beans
1 cup cooked black beans
1 cup cooked pinto beans
1 cup cooked lima beans
1 cup cooked dark red beans
2 cloves fresh garlic, chopped
4 cups pureed tomatoes
1 tablespoon cayenne pepper
Chili powder (as desired)
1 tablespoon brown sugar
Salt and pepper

PREPARATION

Brown the ground meat with the onions and peppers. Add the rest of the ingredients and cook for 1 1/2 to 2 hours. Enjoy with friends and family.

> "WHEN I WAS 10 YEARS OLD, MY MOTHER BECAME ILL AND WAS IN THE HOSPITAL FOR MORE THAN SIX MONTHS. MY FATHER, MY OLDER BROTHER, MY 5-YEAR-OLD BROTHER, AND I WERE LEFT AT HOME. MY DAD WAS A PLUMBER USUALLY ON 24-HOUR CALL BECAUSE OF THE COLD TEMPERATURES IN CHICAGO, SO HE MADE THIS CHILI FOR US, AND WE LOVED IT. WELL, AS CHRISTMAS ROLLED AROUND AND MY MOM WAS STILL SICK, WE HAD THE TASK OF COOKING THE HOLIDAY DINNER. MY BROTHER AND I MADE A HUGE POT OF THIS FIVE-BEAN CHILI. WE ALSO HAD NACHO CHIPS, SHREDDED CHEESE, BAKED POTATOES, AND SOUR CREAM. MY DAD CAME IN LATE ON CHRISTMAS EVE. WHEN HE WOKE UP CHRISTMAS AFTERNOON, HE TOOK ONE LOOK AT THE TABLE ALL SET UP AND SMILED. WE PIGGED OUT AND THEN WENT TO THE HOSPITAL TO SEE MY MOM."
>
> > Boston

"THIS IS MY MAW MAW MEDLIN'S RECIPE. EVERY SUNDAY WE WERE GREETED AT THE DOOR WITH HER HUG AND THEN WALKED INTO THE KITCHEN TO THE SMELL OF CHICKEN FRYING ON THE STOVE. THESE ARE HER 'REQUIREMENTS' FOR GOOD FRIED CHICKEN."

> Jessie

jessie medlin's southern fried chicken

Jane Medlin-Smith > *Fort Mill, South Carolina*

Serves 9

INGREDIENTS

1 (3 to 5-pound) **frying chicken, cut into serving pieces**
4 cups (1 quart) **buttermilk**
1 1/2 cups all-purpose flour for dredging
Shortening for frying
1/2 cup margarine
Salt and freshly ground black pepper to taste

PREPARATION

Rinse the chicken and remove all skin. Add salt and pepper to taste. Pour the buttermilk into a bowl and dip the chicken into buttermilk until coated. Place the flour in brown paper bag. Piece by piece, remove chicken pieces from buttermilk and place them into the paper bag. Shake the bag to coat the chicken with the flour.

In a cast-iron frying pan over medium to high heat, place one large scoop of shortening. Add the margarine to the shortening and allow it to melt. Once the shortening and margarine are melted, carefully place chicken into the hot oil. Fry 3 to 4 pieces at a time, taking care not to crowd the chicken in the pan. Fry the chicken until golden brown and thoroughly cooked (internal temperature of 165°F). Transfer chicken from frying pan and place on aluminum foil lined with paper towels.

jim's greek chicken

Jim Carlson > *Milwaukee, Wisconsin*

Serves 4 to 6

INGREDIENTS

4 to 6 boneless chicken breasts
6 ounces crumbled feta cheese, or enough to cover the chicken breasts
1 lemon
1 (10-ounce) can diced tomatoes
1 jar kalamata olives, sliced or halved
Salt and freshly ground black pepper

PREPARATION

Preheat the oven to 350°F. Place the chicken breasts flat in a baking dish; season with salt and pepper. Cover each breast with crumbled feta cheese. Squeeze fresh lemon juice over each breast. Bake for 20 minutes. Meanwhile, in a large skillet over medium heat, sauté the diced tomatoes (include the juice) and kalamata olives (with or without olive juice as desired). Cook for 20 minutes while the chicken is cooking. Stir occasionally, as some of the liquid will reduce in the skillet.

After 20 minutes, spoon the tomato/olive mixture on top of each chicken breast in the baking dish. Return the chicken to the oven, and cook an additional 30 minutes, or longer as needed until chicken is thoroughly cooked (internal temperature of 165°F).

APPETIZERS

BREADS

BREAKFAST & BRUNCH

ENTRÉES

VEGETABLES & SIDE DISHES

SALADS

SOUPS

DESSERTS

king ranch chicken

Neely Baker > *Hopkinsville, Kentucky*

Serves 6 to 8

INGREDIENTS

1 whole chicken
1 tablespoon poultry seasoning
1 tablespoon salt
1 tablespoon black pepper
1 teaspoon garlic powder
2 (10.75-ounce) **cans cream of chicken soup**
2 (10.75-ounce) **cans cream of mushroom soup**
2 whole jalapeños, seeded and chopped
1 large onion, chopped
10 corn tortillas cut into bite-sized pieces
8 ounces cheddar cheese, shredded
8 ounces mozzarella cheese, shredded

PREPARATION

To prepare the chicken, in a large stockpot, put the chicken in water to cover, and add 1/2 tablespoon poultry seasoning, 1/2 tablespoon salt, 1/2 tablespoon black pepper, and 1/2 teaspoon garlic powder. Bring water to a boil, and decrease the heat to medium-low, cooking until the chicken is cooked through (internal temperature of 165°F). Strain the liquid and set the chicken aside to cool. When the chicken is cool enough to handle, remove the cooked meat from the skin and bones.

Preheat the oven to 350°F. Blend the remaining 1/2 tablespoon poultry seasoning, 1/2 tablespoon salt, 1/2 tablespoon black pepper, and 1/2 teaspoon garlic powder, along with the onion, jalapeños, cream of mushroom soup, and cream of chicken soup in a food processor until pureed. In a large ovenproof casserole, combine the cooked chicken and the liquid mixture. Sprinkle the shredded cheese and tortillas over the casserole. Bake for about 1 hour.

krause funeral casserole

Michael Hutchison > *Pittsford, New York*

Serves 6

INGREDIENTS

2 tablespoons vegetable oil
1 medium onion, sliced
1 pound ground beef or turkey
1 (16-ounce) package wide egg noodles
3 medium stalks celery, sliced
1 (10.75-ounce) can cream of mushroom soup
1 (10.75-ounce) can chicken and rice soup

PREPARATION

Preheat the oven to 350°F. To prepare the casserole, in a large skillet, heat the oil over low heat, and sweat the onion to soften. When the onion starts to caramelize, add the meat, increase the heat to medium, and cook the meat until browned. To prepare the pasta, bring a large pot of salted water to a boil, and cook the pasta until just tender. Drain, and rinse in cold water.

Place the meat, onion, celery, noodles, cream of mushroom soup, and chicken and rice soup in an ovenproof casserole. Pour I soup can full of water into the mixture, and stir well. Bake for 30 minutes, or until thoroughly heated. Serve with a loaf of warm crusty bread.

> "I CAN REMEMBER TAKING THIS DISH TO THE HOME OF EVERY RELATIVE AND FRIEND WHO EXPERIENCED A LOSS WHEN I WAS A CHILD. MOM ALWAYS DOUBLED THE RECIPE SO WE HAD SOME FOR DINNER, TOO. AFTER SOME TIME HAD PASSED AND NO FUNERALS HAD TAKEN PLACE ... WELL, WE KIND OF MISSED THE DISH. WE MAKE IT SOMEWHAT REGULARLY NOW AS IT'S SIMPLE ENOUGH FOR THE KIDS TO HELP, AND WE CAN HELP THE KIDS WITH THEIR HOMEWORK AS IT BAKES."
>
> > Michael

APPETIZERS

BREADS

BREAKFAST & BRUNCH

ENTRÉES

VEGETABLES & SIDE DISHES

SALADS

SOUPS

DESSERTS

lemon chicken

Keith Lampkin > *Greensburg, Pennsylvania*

Serves 6 to 8

INGREDIENTS

8 to 10 (5-ounce) boneless chicken breasts
1 1/2 cups all-purpose flour
Salt and freshly ground black pepper to taste plus 1 teaspoon black pepper
2 cups instant mashed potato flakes
1 cup grated parmesan cheese
1 tablespoon garlic powder
2 large eggs
1/4 cup water
3 tablespoons vegetable oil
3 lemons

PREPARATION

Preheat the oven to 350°F. Line a baking sheet with aluminum foil sprayed with nonstick cooking spray. Using a meat mallet, pound all the breasts to a uniform thickness. On a plate, mix 1 cup flour, and season with salt and pepper. On a second plate, combine potato flakes, cheese, and remaining 1/2 cup flour with the garlic powder and 1 teaspoon pepper. Mix well.

In a small bowl, beat the eggs with 1/4 cup water, and whisk together.

In a large skillet, heat the oil over medium-high heat. Coat the chicken in the flour mixture, shaking off excess, dunk the pieces in the eggs, and then dip into the potato mixture until well covered. Transfer the chicken to the skillet, and cook until browned on each side, about 2 minutes per side. After all the chicken is browned, transfer to the prepared baking sheet. Bake for 25 minutes. When done, take chicken out and squeeze juice from 2 lemons over the chicken, and serve with parsley and thinly sliced lemons from the last lemon, as garnish. This goes great with mashed potatoes and green beans.

mom's chicken and dumplings

Karen Hood > *St. Louis, Missouri*

Serves 4 to 6

INGREDIENTS

4 to 6 quarts water
1 whole chicken, cut up
1 large jar chicken base
2 cans jumbo butter-flavored biscuits (8 biscuits each)

PREPARATION

In a 6 to 8-quart pot, put in the chicken pieces, and cover with water, about 4 to 6 quarts. Bring the water to a boil over medium heat, and cook the chicken for 45 minutes to 1 hour, or until done. Remove the chicken from the pot, and set aside to cool.

Use the leftover cooking water and add enough water to reach 3 to 3 1/2 quarts. Add 1/2 jar of the chicken base to water, and bring to a boil over medium-high heat. Cut each biscuit in half and each half into thirds for a total of 96 pieces. When the water boils, drop the biscuits into the water, one at a time; they will float to the surface while cooking. (Stay by the stove to keep the pot from boiling over.) After they have cooked for about 20 minutes, turn the heat down to medium heat, and cook for about another 30 minutes. Stir often to keep biscuits from sticking to the bottom. The juice will thicken as the biscuits cook. This is a rich, filling dish that is easy to make.

> "WINTER TIME IS A GREAT TIME FOR THE HOMEMADE ONE-POT DISHES. I HAVE BEEN MAKING THIS DISH FOR MY FAMILY FOR MANY YEARS. I HAVE ENJOYED ALL THE FAMILY GATHERINGS AROUND THE TABLE ON A COLD WINTER NIGHT AND THE CONVERSATIONS WE HAD ABOUT OUR DAY. EVERYONE ALWAYS LOOKED FORWARD TO MOM'S CHICKEN-AND-DUMPLINGS NIGHT. YOUR FAMILY WILL LOVE THIS DISH TOO. HOPE YOU MAKE MANY MEMORIES OF YOUR OWN. THIS IS A GREAT WAY TO BRING THE FAMILY TOGETHER."
>
> > Karen

APPETIZERS

BREADS

BREAKFAST & BRUNCH

ENTRÉES

VEGETABLES & SIDE DISHES

SALADS

SOUPS

DESSERTS

paul's chicken and broccoli ziti

Paul Willis > *Woburn, Massachusetts*

Serves 4

INGREDIENTS

1 pound ziti
1 tablespoon olive oil
4 skinless, boneless chicken breast halves (2 pounds), trimmed of fat and sliced into bite-sized pieces
2 cloves garlic, crushed (or 2 teaspoons minced garlic)
1/2 cup dry white wine
1 cup chicken stock (if using canned, College Inn brand preferred)
2 tablespoons butter
2 tablespoons all-purpose flour
4 tablespoons grated Romano cheese
2 cups broccoli florets
2 sprigs parsley, finely chopped (optional)
2 sprigs basil, finely chopped (optional)
Salt and pepper to taste

PREPARATION

In a large pot, prepare ziti according to the package directions; drain and set aside. Meanwhile, in a large sauté pan, heat the olive oil over medium to high heat. Add the chicken and sauté until brown on both sides. Add the garlic and sauté lightly for 2 minutes. Add the white wine and chicken stock, and bring to a simmer. In a separate sauté pan, melt the butter and add the flour, mixing to a sandy consistency. Add the flour mixture to the chicken, stirring well to avoid lumps. Add the grated cheese and broccoli to the chicken. Let it cook until the broccoli is tender but not mushy. Sprinkle with parsley and basil if desired, season to taste with salt and pepper. Combine the ziti with the chicken and broccoli.

saltine chicken

Cindy B. Rutt > *Slatington, Pennsylvania*

Serves 4 to 6

INGREDIENTS

2 pounds boneless chicken thighs or breasts
1/4 cup olive oil
1/2 cup powdered ranch dressing mix
1 to 1 1/2 sleeves of salted saltine crackers, crushed

PREPARATION

Preheat the oven to 400°F. In a large re-sealable bag, combine the oil, ranch dressing mix, and crushed crackers. Add the chicken pieces to the bag; shake to coat the chicken. Transfer the coated chicken into a 9 by 13-inch pan. Bake for 20 to 30 minutes, or until the chicken is cooked to the proper temperature (160°F).

my own chicken piccata

Cheryl Mulvihill > *Atlanta, Georgia*

Serves 4 to 6

INGREDIENTS

4 to 6 boneless, skinless chicken breasts
1 cup all-purpose flour
1 tablespoon dried basil
1/2 cup olive oil
Lemon juice from 2 lemons or 1/3 cup freshly squeezed lemon juice
1/2 cup white wine
1/4 cup capers
Salt and freshly ground black pepper to taste

PREPARATION

To prepare this dish, using a meat mallet, tenderize the chicken breasts by pounding them flat. In a separate bowl, combine the flour with the basil, salt, and pepper, and dredge each piece of chicken.

In a large skillet, heat the olive oil over medium heat, and pan-fry the breasts for about 5 minutes on each side. Sprinkle on more dried basil as desired. Add the lemon juice, wine, and capers. Decrease the heat to medium-low, and cook for a further 15 to 20 minutes. Place chicken on a warm platter, and pour the gravy from the pan over it. Garnish with lemon slices.

APPETIZERS

BREADS

BREAKFAST & BRUNCH

ENTRÉES

VEGETABLES & SIDE DISHES

SALADS

SOUPS

DESSERTS

"THIS IS MY FAVORITE CHICKEN DISH BECAUSE EACH TIME I PREPARE IT, I RECALL THE DAY IT CAME TO BE. I HAVE THREE DAUGHTERS. AS THEY GET OLDER, THEY ENJOY WORKING WITH ME IN THE KITCHEN. ONE SATURDAY, WE WERE TRYING TO COME UP WITH A NEW CHICKEN DISH. THEY WERE GETTING SILLY THROWING THE CHICKEN IN A BAG WITH INGREDIENTS THEY WERE GRABBING OUT OF THE KITCHEN CABINETS. WHAT I REMEMBER MOST IS ALL OF US LAUGHING SO HARD. SINCE THEN WE HAVE COME UP WITH SEVERAL MORE TASTY CREATIONS. THE FOOD, SURPRISINGLY, ALWAYS ENDS UP TASTING VERY GOOD, BUT THE TIME WE SPEND TOGETHER IS WHAT I ENJOY THE MOST."

> Cindy

"I TYPICALLY MEASURE NOTHING WHEN I COOK, SO I TOOK A STAB AT THE QUANTITIES OF THE INGREDI-ENTS. THIS RECIPE MAY REQUIRE A FEW TRIES TO GET IT JUST RIGHT OR TO YOUR OWN TASTE, BUT WHEN YOU DO, IT'S SURE TO BECOME A FAVORITE. MY FAMILY AND GUESTS LOVE THIS DISH. IT'S SIMPLE TO MAKE, AND IS GREAT WITH RICE AND A SALAD."

> Cheryl

stuffed mexican peppers

Cindy Gordon > *Sarasota, Florida*

Serves 4

> "I ENJOY SHOPPING AT PRODUCE MARKETS AND ALTHOUGH THESE COLORFUL PEPPERS ARE FRESH AND ATTRACTIVE, IT IS HARD TO IMAGINE WHAT TO DO WITH THEM. THIS RECIPE IS A CROSS BETWEEN A TRADITIONAL STUFFED PEPPER AND A CHILE RELLEÑO. THE CHICKEN AND CORN BALANCE NICELY WITH THE ZESTY SAUCE AND THE CHEESE. WHEN I SERVED THIS TO MY HUSBAND, HE ASKED WHY IT TOOK 22 YEARS OF MARRIAGE FOR ME TO COME UP WITH THIS TASTY RECIPE."
>
> > Cindy

INGREDIENTS

4 long Mexican green or red chilies (6 to 8 inches long, mild to medium; or a poblano pepper may be used)
3 ears corn
4 chicken breasts, preferably free range, trimmed of fat
2 tablespoons vegetable oil
1 medium onion, thinly sliced
1 jalapeño pepper, seeded and minced
2 fresh tomatoes, chopped
2 cups prepared pasta sauce, any vegetable variety
1 cup prepared salsa
6 to 8 ounces shredded cheese, preferably mixed Mexican variety
Seasoned salt and freshly ground black pepper to taste

PREPARATION

Prepare the fire in a charcoal grill, or heat the gas grill. Seed the peppers, and split them lengthwise to lay flat. Do not cut through. Sweat the peppers on a hot grill until they just start to blister. On the same grill, roast the corn and cook the chicken until lightly browned. Wrap the corn in foil if the ears are browning too quickly. Remove the corn and chicken, and cool slightly.

Preheat the oven to 350°F. In a small skillet, heat the oil over low heat, and sauté the onion until caramelized. Add the jalapeño, and cook for 2 to 3 minutes more. Cut the corn from the cob. Shred the chicken, using your fingers. Combine the corn, chicken, tomatoes, and onion-jalapeño mixture. Set aside.

In a large mixing bowl, mix the pasta sauce and the salsa together. Pour into the bottom of a rectangular baking dish. Lay the Mexican peppers over the sauce. Top each pepper with one-quarter of the chicken mixture. Top with the cheese.

Cover with aluminum foil and bake for 15 minutes. Remove the foil, and bake for 5 minutes more. To serve, season with salt and pepper. Spoon the sauce over the peppers when serving.

sweet and sour chicken

Bea Foster > *Tampa, Florida*

Serves 4 to 6

INGREDIENTS

1 whole chicken, cut up into serving pieces
1 egg
1 cup whole milk
All-purpose flour for dredging (about 1 1/2 cups)
Shortening for frying
1 (6-ounce) can frozen lemonade, thawed (do not add water)
3 tablespoons ketchup
3 tablespoons brown sugar
1 tablespoon vinegar
1 teaspoon soy sauce
Salt and freshly ground pepper to taste

PREPARATION

In a mixing bowl, combine the egg and milk. Dip the chicken pieces into the liquid, then roll in flour and add salt and pepper to taste. In a frying pan, melt shortening, and add chicken. Cook until brown on both sides. After nicely browned on both sides, remove from heat and remove chicken, pouring off excess shortening.

Into the same frying pan, add the lemonade, ketchup, brown sugar, vinegar, and soy sauce. Stir well, and transfer the chicken back to the pan. Cover and cook for about 15 minutes on each side until chicken is thoroughly cooked (165°F). Serve on a bed of cooked rice, using the remaining sauce as a gravy for the rice.

"MY FAMILY LIKES THIS SO WELL I SOMETIMES DOUBLE THE RECIPE SO WE HAVE ENOUGH TO GO AROUND. GREAT FOR COMPANY."

> Bea

APPETIZERS

BREADS

BREAKFAST & BRUNCH

ENTRÉES

VEGETABLES & SIDE DISHES

SALADS

SOUPS

DESSERTS

teriyaki chicken drumettes

Sandee Chaffino > *Tracy, California*

Serves 6

INGREDIENTS

3 tablespoons vegetable oil
1 cup chopped yellow onion
2 tablespoons freshly grated garlic
1 tablespoon freshly grated ginger
1 1/2 cups soy sauce
1 cup sugar
1 to 2 jalapeño peppers, slit open but whole
3 pounds chicken drumettes

PREPARATION

To prepare the sauce, heat the oil over medium heat in a large skillet or wok, and sauté the onion, garlic, and ginger; do not brown. Add the soy sauce, sugar, and jalapeño peppers. Cook until the sugar dissolves, and let stand for 20 minutes. Taste it and strain out the peppers if the sauce is too spicy.

Pour the sauce into a large bowl, and marinate chicken for a minimum of 6 hours. To serve, deep-fry the chicken until dark brown and cooked through.

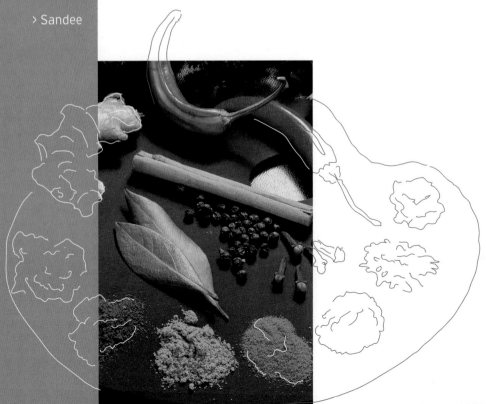

virginia chikahominy chicken

Lori Goodbody > *Salisbury, Maryland*

Serves 4 to 6

INGREDIENTS

1 cup seasoned bread crumbs
2 pounds chicken breast fillets
8 slices applewood smoked bacon
8 slices Havarti cheese
2 tablespoons chicken base
2 tablespoons butter
2 cups water for grits
2 cups uncooked enriched grits
1 teaspoon chicken seasoning
20 spears fresh asparagus
1/2 cup water for asparagus
Salt and freshly ground pepper to taste

PREPARATION FOR CHICKEN

Preheat the oven to 350°F. Spray a baking pan with nonstick cooking spray.

Lightly bread each chicken breast in the seasoned bread crumbs, and wrap each fillet with a slice of bacon in a "spiral" from top to bottom. Place the chicken in the oven for 15 to 20 minutes, or until golden brown and the bacon is cooked. Turn the oven off, place one slice of cheese on top of each piece of bacon-wrapped chicken, and return to the oven until cheese is melted.

PREPARATION FOR GRITS

In a saucepan, combine the chicken base, butter, chicken seasoning, and water. Bring to a boil, add the grits, and cook until desired consistency. For moister grits, gradually add more water (one tablespoon at a time); for drier grits use less water. Add salt and pepper to taste.

PREPARATION FOR ASPARAGUS

Wash fresh asparagus spears; trim approximately 1/2 inch off bottom where the green part begins. Bring a shallow saucepan with 1/2 cup water to a boil, and cook asparagus for about 5 minutes, or until bright green and tender yet still firm.

To serve, place a spoonful of grits in the center of plate and place 2 chicken fillets on top of the grits. Place 5 asparagus spears around the edge of the bowl with the ends stuck slightly into grits, tips pointing out. You can easily substitute rice for the grits or other seasonal fresh vegetables for the asparagus.

> " I CREATED THIS RECIPE IN 2006 WHILE LIVING IN WILLIAMSBURG, VIRGINIA. WE WERE PREPARING FOR THE 400TH ANNIVERSARY CELEBRATION OF OUR COUNTRY'S FIRST SETTLERS AT JAMESTOWN. THE NEW SETTLERS, ALONG WITH THE LOCAL INDIAN TRIBES, INCLUDING THE CHIKAHOMINY INDIANS, COLLABORATED AND COMBINED THEIR KNOWLEDGE, RESOURCES, AND CULTURES TO HELP CREATE WHAT OUR COUNTRY IS TODAY. I WANTED TO COMBINE SOME OF THE SAME INGREDIENTS AND FLAVORS OF THE REGION WHILE KEEPING THE RECIPE EASY, AND THE PRESENTATION IS BEAUTIFUL. "
>
> > Lori

APPETIZERS
BREADS
BREAKFAST & BRUNCH
ENTRÉES
VEGETABLES & SIDE DISHES
SALADS
SOUPS
DESSERTS

yellow rice stuffed cornish hens

Linda Kull > *Cabot, Arizona*

Serves 2 to 4

INGREDIENTS

2 (1-pound) **Cornish hens**
1 package yellow rice mix
1/2 cup (1 stick) **salted butter or margarine**
1 yellow onion, chopped
1 tablespoon chopped garlic
1/2 pound fresh mushrooms, chopped
Chicken stock (optional)
1 cup white or Marsala wine
Salt and freshly ground black pepper to taste

PREPARATION

Preheat the oven to 350°F. Rinse the Cornish hens, and pat dry, making sure no giblets are inside. Set aside.

Cook yellow rice according to package directions. (Chicken stock may be substituted for water.) Meanwhile, in a small skillet, melt 1 tablespoon butter (or margarine); when melted, add the onion and garlic, cook until soft, and add the chopped mushrooms. When rice is cooked, remove from heat and stir the onion, garlic, and mushrooms into the cooked rice mixture; let cool to the touch, about 15 minutes.

Stuff hens with the rice mixture, and tie the legs together to keep the stuffing in. Place them in a glass baking dish. Add the remaining butter.

Put the dish into the oven. When the butter has melted, add the wine to the melted butter, and baste the hens. Baste several times during roasting of hens. Roast 1 to 1 1/2 hours, or until the hens' juices run clear. Serve with fresh vegetables, such as broccoli or green beans.

grilled tilapia filets in a puttanesca/tomatillo cream

Marten Cabrera > *Chicago, Illinois*

Serves 5

INGREDIENTS

1/2 cup fresh lime juice
6 garlic cloves, crushed
1 jalapeño chili, seeded and de-veined
5 (6-ounce) **tilapia fillets**
Salt and freshly ground black pepper
3/4 pound tomatillos, husked, rinsed, and coarsely chopped
1 cup coarsely chopped cilantro with stems
1/2 cup coarsely chopped flat-leaf parsley
1/2 teaspoon ground cumin
1/4 teaspoon ground cinnamon
2 tablespoons coarsely ground black pepper
1/2 cup water
3 tablespoons olive oil
1 cup chopped cippolini onions
1 (28-ounce) **can of roasted crushed tomatoes**
3 tablespoons chipotle peppers
1/4 cup fresh basil, roughly chopped
1 tablespoon of fresh rosemary
1/2 teaspoon ground aniseed
1/2 teaspoon ground coriander
1/2 cup sour cream

PREPARATION

Prepare oven to broil. In a bowl, prepare a marinade for the tilapia by mixing 2 tablespoons of lime juice, 3 crushed garlic cloves, and half of a jalapeño pepper, diced. Sprinkle the fillets with salt and pepper, and add them to the marinade. Refrigerate for 30 minutes.

In a food processor, add the tomatillos, cilantro, the remaining half of the jalapeño, 3 tablespoons of lime juice, parsley, ground cumin, 1 garlic clove, cinnamon, 1/2 tablespoon of black pepper, and a pinch of salt. Add water until the mixture becomes smooth. In a sauté pan over medium heat, add 1/2 tablespoon olive oil. Add the remaining 2 garlic cloves and the chopped onions and cook until they become translucent. Add the roasted tomatoes, chipotle peppers, basil, rosemary, anise seed, and coriander, and let it simmer for about 15 minutes. Then add the tomatillo mixture and let it cook for about 8 minutes. Add the sour cream and let it cook for another 5 minutes.

Broil the tilapia filets for about 4 minutes on each side. Serve on a platter and add the puttanesca/tomatillo sauce over the fish.

> "GROWING UP IN MEXICO CITY WITH AN ITALIAN HERITAGE HELPED ME DEVELOP AN ACQUIRED TASTE FOR BOTH WORLDS. SINCE AN EARLY AGE, I WAS EXPERIMENTING WITH TRADITIONAL MEXICAN STAPLE DISHES WITH A SOUTHERN ITALIAN FLAIR. THIS IS ONE EXAMPLE."
>
> > Marten

APPETIZERS

BREADS

BREAKFAST & BRUNCH

ENTRÉES

VEGETABLES & SIDE DISHES

SALADS

SOUPS

DESSERTS

baked stuffed shrimp

Shawn O'Rourke > *Phoenix, Arizona*

Serves 6 to 8

INGREDIENTS

1 cup chopped mushrooms
1/3 cup chopped onion
1 clove garlic, finely chopped
1 teaspoon chicken bouillon
1/4 cup (1/2 stick) **butter or margarine**
1 1/2 cups soft breadcrumbs (3 slices bread)
1 tablespoon chopped pimento
1 pound jumbo raw shrimp with tail on, peeled and de-veined
Melted margarine or butter
Chopped parsley (optional)

PREPARATION

Preheat oven to 400°F. Grease a shallow baking dish. In a large skillet over medium heat, combine and cook the mushrooms, onions, garlic, and bouillon in butter until tender. Remove from the heat. Stir in crumbs and pimento. Cut a slit along the underside of each shrimp; do not cut through. Brush the entire shrimp with butter. Mound the stuffing mixture in the hollow of each shrimp. Place the stuffed shrimp in the prepared baking dish. Bake shrimp for 10 to 12 minutes, or until shrimp are cooked through. Garnish with parsley, if desired. Shrimp should look like a scorpion.

chesapeake bay
crab cakes

Bruce Shumaker > *Richmond, Virginia*

Serves 4

INGREDIENTS

1 egg
2 tablespoons mayonnaise
1/2 teaspoon pepper
1 table Worcestershire sauce
1/2 cup chopped parsley
1 teaspoon Dijon mustard
1 tablespoon baking powder
1 tablespoon fresh lemon juice
1/4 cup breadcrumbs
1 tablespoon Old Bay seasoning
1 pound backfin or lump crabmeat
2 tablespoons vegetable oil

PREPARATION

In a large bowl, combine the egg, mayonnaise, pepper, Worcestershire sauce, parsley, mustard, baking powder, lemon juice, breadcrumbs, and Old Bay seasoning. Carefully fold in the crab, trying not to break up the lumps. Form into 4 patties, cover, and refrigerate for at least 30 minutes. In a large skillet, heat the oil over medium heat, and fry the crab cakes for 4 to 5 minutes on each side or until they are golden brown. Serve with rice and a lemon wedge.

" WE USED TO 'CHICKEN NECK' FOR CRABS OFF A PIER AT OUR FRIEND'S HOUSE ON THE CHESAPEAKE BAY, AND WHAT WE DIDN'T EAT RIGHT AWAY, WE WOULD EAT THE NEXT DAY ON A PICNIC TABLE IN FRONT OF THE HOUSE. "

> Bruce

APPETIZERS

BREADS

BREAKFAST & BRUNCH

ENTRÉES

VEGETABLES & SIDE DISHES

SALADS

SOUPS

DESSERTS

crab cakes

Ginger Catoe > *Lugoff, South Carolina*

Serves 2 to 4 depending on size of crab cake

INGREDIENTS

1/4 cup (1/2 stick) margarine, at room temperature
1 tablespoon minced onion
1/2 teaspoon salt
1/2 teaspoon pepper
1/2 teaspoon Worcestershire sauce
1 tablespoon minced parsley
1 tablespoon cold water
1 tablespoon lemon juice
1 cup soft bread crumbs
2 2/3 cups crabmeat
Crushed saltine crackers, about 1/4 to 1/2 sleeve

PREPARATION

Preheat the oven to 450°F. Line a baking sheet with brown paper. In a mixing bowl, combine the margarine, onion, salt, pepper, Worcestershire sauce, parsley, water, lemon juice, bread crumbs, and crab meat; let sit for 5 minutes. Shape crab mixture into patties and dredge in the saltine cracker crumbs. Bake crab cakes for 15 to 20 minutes.

creole shrimp

Vicki Sears > *Houston, Texas*

Serves 6

INGREDIENTS

2 pounds large to jumbo shrimp, peeled, de-veined, and butterflied
3 tablespoons champagne vinegar
2 teaspoon Creole seasoning
1/2 teaspoon ground cumin
1/2 teaspoon crushed red pepper
2 cloves pressed garlic
1 tablespoon olive oil
Remoulade sauce or tortillas for serving

PREPARATION

Prepare the fire in a charcoal grill. In a large mixing bowl, combine the vinegar, Creole seasoning, cumin, red pepper, garlic, and olive oil. Add the shrimp and marinate in the refrigerator for at least 30 minutes. Grill the shrimp over medium-hot coals for 5 to 7 minutes, turning once. Serve with a remoulade sauce or in tortillas as shrimp tacos.

linguini with vegetables and shrimp

Jennifer Shea > *Mesa, Arizona*

Serves 4 to 6

INGREDIENTS

2 tablespoons extra-virgin olive oil
4 cloves garlic, chopped
1 cup diced onion
1 cup thinly sliced carrots
1 cup sliced zucchini
1 cup sliced yellow squash
1 cup broccoli florets
1 cup chicken stock
1/2 teaspoon crushed red pepper
1/2 teaspoon salt
1/2 teaspoon black pepper
1 pound large shrimp, cleaned and de-veined
1 pound linguini
1/4 cup grated parmesan or Romano cheese

PREPARATION

In a large deep skillet, heat the olive oil over medium heat and sauté the garlic without burning it. Add the onions and carrots, and sauté 3 to 4 minutes. Add the zucchini, squash, and broccoli, and sauté 3 to 4 minutes. Add the chicken stock, crushed red pepper, salt, and pepper, and cook for about 5 minutes. Add the shrimp, and cook until the shrimp turn pink (about 3 to 5 minutes), being careful not to overcook the shrimp.

Meanwhile, cook the linguini according to package directions. Drain the pasta, reserving 1 cup pasta cooking water. Add the linguini directly to the skillet with the vegetables and shrimp, adding some pasta water if the mixture is too dry. Adjust the seasonings, toss to combine, and serve immediately with grated parmesan or Romano cheese. This recipe can easily be halved for just two people or doubled for a large group.

APPETIZERS

BREADS

BREAKFAST & BRUNCH

ENTRÉES

VEGETABLES & SIDE DISHES

SALADS

SOUPS

DESSERTS

"WITH MY ITALIAN HERITAGE (MY GRANDPARENTS WERE BORN IN NAPLES, ITALY), THERE IS NO GREATER COMFORT FOOD FOR MY FAMILY THAN PASTA. AND NO GREATER AROMA THAN SAUTÉED GARLIC! WHEN MY CHILDREN WERE YOUNG AND OUR BUDGET WAS STRETCHED, I OFTEN PREPARED THIS DISH WITHOUT THE SHRIMP AND USED ANY VEGETABLES I HAD IN THE REFRIGERATOR."

> Jennifer

quick fish bake

Ginny Birkett > *Ormond, Florida*

Serves 4

INGREDIENTS

1 pound flounder fillets (can be frozen but separated)
1 (10.75-ounce) can cream of shrimp soup
1 cup seasoned breadcrumbs
2 or 3 teaspoons melted butter

PREPARATION

Preheat the oven to 350°F. To prepare the fish, lay the fillets out flat on the bottom of a baking dish. Pour the undiluted soup over the fish, and spread evenly. Stir the breadcrumbs together with the butter to moisten, and sprinkle them over the fish. Bake, uncovered, for about 30 minutes, or until bubbly and the fish is tender.

Suggestion: Serve over prepared white rice. It's amazing how nicely this recipe works with thin fish fillets that are frozen!

salmon arlene

Kevin L. Hagan > *Gaithersburg, Maryland*

Serves 4 to 6

INGREDIENTS

2 tablespoons olive or canola oil
1 medium onion, chopped
4 to 6 cloves chopped fresh garlic
3/4 cup chopped cilantro
3/4 cup chopped flat leaf parsley
1 1/2 to 2 pounds salmon fillets
Equal parts white wine and chicken broth to cover fillets
Salt and freshly ground black pepper to taste

PREPARATION

In a large skillet, heat the oil over medium heat, and sauté the onion and garlic until partially cooked. Add the cilantro and parsley to the onion and garlic mixture. Season the salmon fillets with salt and pepper, and place them on the onion mixture, skin side up. Pour the white wine and chicken broth into the skillet until the salmon is almost covered. Heat until boiling, cover with lid, and decrease the heat to low. Add more liquid (equal parts chicken broth and white wine) as necessary to cover salmon during cooking, about 20 minutes.

Remove the skin, and turn fillet over onto a plate. For a more flavorful, slightly thicker sauce, continue to cook the sauce mixture down a bit, then cover the salmon with the sauce and serve.

This recipe pairs nicely with white rice and a mild Chardonnay or Zinfandel wine.

"MY BEST FRIEND'S MOM FROM CLEVELAND, OHIO, CREATED THIS SALMON DISH. MY FRIEND AND I WERE ROOMMATES IN GRADUATE SCHOOL IN WASHINGTON, D.C., AND HIS FAMILY QUICKLY EMBRACED ME AS A MEMBER OF THEIR FAMILY. WHENEVER HIS MOM CAME FOR A VISIT, SHE MADE THIS DISH FOR US. IT WAS ABSOLUTELY ONE OF OUR FAVORITES. IN HONOR OF HER, EVERYONE STARTED REFERRING TO IT AS SALMON ARLENE. WHEN I MENTIONED U.S. FOODSERVICE WAS PUBLISHING THIS COOKBOOK FOR CHARITY, SHE GENEROUSLY OFFERED TO SHARE HER RECIPE."

> Kevin

shrimp scampi

Patricia Scranton > *Bridgeport, New Jersey*

Serves 4

INGREDIENTS

8 ounces spaghetti
1 pound asparagus, cleaned and trimmed
3/4 cup (1 1/2 sticks) butter
1/4 cup Old Bay seasoning
2 heaping tablespoons minced garlic
Peppercorns and cracked black pepper to taste
2 1/2 pounds (26 to 30) shrimp, cleaned and peeled

PREPARATION

Prepare the pasta according to the package directions. Drain and set aside. In a separate large saucepan, cook the asparagus until just tender, drain, and set aside.

In another large saucepan, melt the butter, and add the Old Bay seasoning, garlic, and pepper, stirring to combine. Add the shrimp to the saucepan, and cook, stirring, for 5 to 6 minutes. Decrease the heat to low. Add the asparagus and spaghetti, and toss to combine. Serve hot.

stuffed baked lobster

Dana Flynn > *New Sy, Florida*

Serves 4

INGREDIENTS

4 female lobsters
1 box Ritz crackers, crushed
1 pound backfin crabmeat
2 tablespoons Old Bay seasoning
1 cup (2 sticks) butter, melted

PREPARATION

Preheat the oven to broil. To prepare the dish, use a lobster pot with a steamer insert to steam the lobsters for 10 minutes. When the lobsters are cooked and cool enough to handle, split them down the center of the underbelly with sharp knife. In a large bowl, combine the crackers, crabmeat, Old Bay seasoning, and 1/2 cup butter, blending into a firm stuffing. Do not remove anything from lobster belly; fill the chest cavity with the stuffing, and glaze the top with the remaining melted butter. Bake or broil on high until the stuffing is crisp on the outside. The lobsters may need more melted butter brushed over them while baking.

> "THIS IS MY NEW HUSBAND'S RECIPE. WE HAVE BEEN MARRIED SEVEN WEEKS. COOKING THIS RECIPE WAS ONE OF THE WAYS HE WON MY HEART. HE USED TO EAT THIS DISH AT HIS UNCLE'S RESTAURANT WHEN HE WAS A CHILD. WHEN HE GREW UP, HE BEGGED HIS GRANDMOTHER FOR THE RECIPE; SHE FINALLY GAVE IT TO HIM SINCE HE LOVED IT SO MUCH. WHENEVER HE IS BACK HOME WITH HIS FAMILY, THEY ALWAYS ASK HIM TO COOK THIS MEAL."
>
> > Dana

enchilada casserole

Mark Wenzel > *Plymouth, Minnesota*

Serves 6

INGREDIENTS

2 (16-ounce) **cans enchilada sauce**
1 (10.75-ounce or 14.7-ounce) **can condensed tomato soup**
1 (19-ounce) **bag restaurant-style corn tortilla chips**
2 (16-ounce) **cans black beans, drained**
16 ounces shredded cheddar cheese
1 large onion, diced

PREPARATION

Preheat oven to 350°F. In a bowl, combine the enchilada sauce with the tomato soup. Layer 1/3 of the tortilla chips in the bottom of a casserole dish, using just enough to cover the bottom. Layer the beans, cheese, and onion over the tortilla chips. Pour 1/3 of the tomato and sauce mixture over the chips. Continue to layer until all chips are used, making sure to reserve some sauce for the top. Cover the casserole dish with aluminum foil and bake for 30 to 45 minutes.

hungarian fried cabbage

Laurie Kennedy > *Denver, Colorado*

Serves 4 to 6

INGREDIENTS

1 large head cabbage, cored and halved
3 tablespoons butter or margarine
1 large onion, or as many as desired, halved
1 pound egg noodles (or other kinds of pasta as desired)
1/4 tablespoon caraway seeds
Salt and freshly ground black pepper to taste

PREPARATION

Shred the cabbage by placing the cabbage half flat side down and using a sharp knife, slice into desired thickness. Slice the onion to desired thickness.

In a large skillet or Dutch oven, melt butter over medium heat. Place the cabbage and onion in the skillet. Season with the caraway seeds, salt, and pepper. Cover the skillet, and decrease the heat to medium-low. The cabbage will cook in its own juices. Check on cabbage mixture, and turn in skillet every 5 minutes or so. Meanwhile, prepare the pasta according to the package directions. When cooked, drain the pasta and add it to the skillet to combine with the cabbage mixture. Cook until heated through. Serve as a main dish or as a side.

ENTRÉES

"THIS IS THE BASIC RECIPE. YOU CAN SERVE THIS AS A SIDE DISH WITH PORK CHOPS, OR YOU CAN BE CREATIVE. SOME SUGGESTIONS INCLUDE MIXING IT WITH ONE POUND OF FRIED BULK SAUSAGE. (I HAVE SLICED TWO TO THREE APPLES WITH THIS AND ADDED THE APPLES TO THE CABBAGE MIXTURE TO COOK TOGETHER.) OR TRY POLISH SAUSAGE SLICED IN ONE-INCH BITE SIZES. (ADD THIS TO YOUR CABBAGE AND ONION, AND LET THEM SIMMER AT THE SAME TIME. THE FLAVOR OF THE POLISH SAUSAGE SEASONS THE CABBAGE WONDERFULLY.) MY HUSBAND'S FAVE IS WITH ONE POUND OF COTTAGE CHEESE…DON'T KNOCK IT UNTIL YOU TRY IT. HIS MOM WOULD MAKE HOMEMADE NOODLES AND ONION GRAVY (ONIONS, FLOATING IN BUTTER, LITERALLY). THEN SHE WOULD MIX THE NOODLES, ONION GRAVY, AND ONE POUND OF COTTAGE CHEESE. CABBAGE AND NOODLES, CHEAP AND EASY."

> Laurie

grandma striney's pyrohy
(ukrainian pierogi)

Ashley Lyerly > *Lenexa, Kansas*

Yields 50 pyrohy

INGREDIENTS

5 pounds potatoes, peeled and quartered
1 to 1 1/2 pounds Velveeta cheese
1 to 2 cups (2 to 4 sticks) **butter**
10 cups (2 1/2 pounds) **all-purpose flour**
3 eggs
2 to 2 1/2 cups water (retained from boiling the potatoes)

PREPARATION

In a large stockpot with salted water, cook the potatoes until tender. Drain, reserving 2 to 2 1/2 cups of the cooking liquid. In a large mixing bowl, mash (do not whip) the potatoes with 1/2 pound of the butter and 1 pound of the Velveeta (or to taste), and set aside. In a second large mixing bowl, combine the flour and eggs, slowly beating in the warm potato water with a sturdy wooden spoon. Mix and knead until a soft dough is formed. Turn out the dough onto a lightly floured surface. Roll out the dough to about 1/4-inch thick, and cut into 4 to 5-inch squares. Spread the potato mixture onto the dough squares. Fold the dough over the potato mixture to form triangle-shaped dumplings.

In a large stockpot, bring water to a boil. Drop a few dumplings into the boiling water without crowding the pot. When they float to the surface, cook for about 5 minutes. Remove with a slotted spoon, and put them into a baking dish. Repeat until all the dumplings are cooked. Layer the dumplings with the remaining melted butter and cheese. These can be refrigerated or frozen, then reheated, covered, in a moderate oven. Some like to serve these with sour cream or even salsa as an additional topping.

> "ANNA JENNY COOPER WAS BORN IN 1864 IN VIENNA, AUSTRIA, TO UKRAINIAN PARENTS. WITH HER FOUR CHILDREN SHE TRAVELED ALONE TO MEET UP WITH HER HUSBAND, ANDREW STRINEY, IN AMERICA. TRAGICALLY, HER BABY DIED ABOARD SHIP. A KIND GENTLEMAN GAVE HIS COAT TO WRAP THE BABY FOR BURIAL AT SEA. MY MOTHER, EVELYN, WAS GRANDMA'S ELEVENTH OF TWELVE CHILDREN. MY SISTERS AND I WERE VERY FORTUNATE TO HAVE THE BETTER OF TWO WORLDS, LIVING IN NEW YORK CITY THEN BECOMING PENNSYLVANIA COUNTRY GIRLS IN THE SUMMER WITH OUR 'BABA' AND OUR RELATIVES. I KNEW ONLY A FEW SENTENCES IN UKRAINIAN BUT WE COMMUNICATED WITH LOVE. BABA'S COURAGE WAS ALWAYS AN INSPIRATION TO ME. WE CALLED THE PYROHY 'THREE CORNERS' BECAUSE SHE MADE THEM INTO TRIANGLES. MY COUSINS AND I WOULD EAT 'THREE CORNERS' ALL DAY, COUNTING WHO ATE THE MOST. AFTER BABA DIED, MY MOTHER AND AUNTS TAUGHT ME AND MY CHILDREN HOW TO MAKE OUR VERY FAVORITE FOOD. NOT FOR DIETERS – IT'S A SPECIAL TREAT."

> Ashley

ENTRÉES

VEGETABLES &
SIDE DISHES

SALADS

SOUPS

DESSERTS

141

macaroni and cheese with bechamel sauce

Joe Zindle > *Crest Hill, Illinois*

Serves 4

INGREDIENTS

4 cups elbow macaroni
1/4 cup (1/2 stick) **butter**
1/2 cup all-purpose flour
4 cups whole milk (variation: substitute milk for spaghetti sauce or red sauce)
1 pound grated sharp cheddar cheese (grated/divided 2/3 and 1/3)
Salt and freshly ground black pepper to taste

PREPARATION

Preheat oven to 400°F. Prepare the pasta according to package directions; drain and set aside. Meanwhile, in a large skillet, melt the butter, whisk in the flour, and stir (do not brown). Add the milk, and stir until slightly thickened. Add two-thirds of the cheese, a little bit at a time. Stir until smooth and thickened. If the sauce is too thick, add a little more milk. Season with salt and pepper. Place the cooked macaroni in a 9 by 13-inch baking dish. Add the sauce and stir until all the noodles are coated. Sprinkle the remaining cheese on top. Bake in the lower third of the oven for 20 minutes, or until the cheese is lightly browned. Serve hot.

Variation: You can make this recipe with leftover spaghetti sauce, red sauce from a jar, or tomato sauce from a can. Just substitute spaghetti sauce for the milk. See above directions. This version is a good and different variation of an old favorite recipe.

vegetables & side dishes

arroz con gandules

Sammi Maldonado > *Lexington, South Carolina*

Serves 3 to 4

INGREDIENTS

1 1/2 cups salt pork, sliced in bite-sized pieces
4 ounces tomato sauce
2 tablespoons green olives
2 tablespoons sofrito
1 packet Goya Sazón with achiote
1 (16-ounce) can gandules (pigeon peas)
2 cups long or short-grain rice, rinsed
3 1/2 cups boiling water
2 tablespoons oil
Salt

PREPARATION

In a Dutch oven, fry salt pork in oil. Add the tomato sauce, olives, sofrito, and Sazón, and stir together. Cook at medium heat for 4 minutes. Add gandules and rice. Pour the boiling water into the pot so the rice is submerged 1 inch below the water. Do not cover. Let the rice absorb the water. When the water has been absorbed, stir gently from the bottom to the top, cover, and turn the heat to low. Cook for 25 to 30 minutes, until the rice is tender, stirring once. Salt to taste.

> "MY MOTHER-IN-LAW WAS FAMOUS FOR HER PUERTO RICAN DISHES, AND THIS WAS EVERYONE'S FAVORITE. WHEN SHE MOVED OUT OF STATE, I BECAME MY HUSBAND'S ONLY SOURCE FOR THIS AUTHENTIC PUERTO RICAN DISH."
>
> > Sammi

au gratin potatoes

Julie Heim > *Eagan, Minnesota*

Serves 12

INGREDIENTS

1 (16-ounce) container sour cream
1 (10.75-ounce) can cream of chicken soup
1 (8-ounce) bag shredded cheddar cheese
1 teaspoon salt
1 (2-pound) box frozen hash brown potatoes (not shredded)
1/2 cup melted butter or margarine

INGREDIENTS FOR TOPPING

2 cups crushed cornflakes
1/4 cup melted butter or margarine

PREPARATION

Preheat oven to 350°F. In a large mixing bowl, stir together sour cream and soup. Add cheese, salt, and hash browns. Pour in the melted butter and mix well. Transfer the mixture to a 9 by 13-inch baking pan, patting it into the pan. Combine the topping ingredients and spread over the potato mixture. Bake uncovered for 1 1/2 hours.

aunt shirley's potato bake

Edward Zakszeski > *Port Orange, Florida*

Serves 8 to 10

INGREDIENTS

6 medium or large potatoes
1 pint sour cream
10 ounces grated sharp cheese
3 tablespoons milk
Pinch of salt
Black pepper (optional)
1/4 cup (2 ounces/1/2 stick) butter
1/4 cup breadcrumbs

PREPARATION

Boil the potatoes (skins on) and refrigerate overnight. The next day, combine the sour cream, cheese, milk, salt, and pepper. Peel the potatoes and grate them into the cheese mixture. Combine well and spread into a buttered 9 by 13-inch baking dish. Combine the butter and breadcrumbs. Top the potato mixture with the crumb mixture. Bake at 350°F for 30 to 35 minutes, until bubbly at the edges. Note: Casserole can be made ahead of time and refrigerated until it's time to bake it.

avocado peach salsa

Doug Ricketts > *Cleveland, Ohio*

Serves 6 to 8

INGREDIENTS

2 cups diced fresh peaches
1 large tomato, diced
1/2 cup diced avocado
1 tablespoon minced red onion
1 tablespoon lime juice
1 teaspoon olive oil
1/4 teaspoon salt
1/4 teaspoon ground red pepper
1/4 teaspoon diced jicama
2 tablespoons diced green onions
2 tablespoons cilantro, chopped fine
Tortilla chips

PREPARATION

Combine first nine ingredients in a large bowl. Cover and chill. Before serving top with cilantro and green onions. Serve with tortilla chips.

baked artichokes

Janice Simonian > *Newnan, Georgia*

Serves 4

INGREDIENTS

2 (6.5-ounce) jars marinated artichoke hearts, chopped
1 medium onion, diced
2 cloves garlic, chopped
4 eggs
1/2 teaspoon salt
1/2 teaspoon pepper
1/2 teaspoon oregano
1/2 teaspoon tabasco sauce
1/2 tablespoon parsley
1/2 cup breadcrumbs
1/2 pound cheddar cheese, grated

PREPARATION

Preheat oven to 325ºF. Sauté onion and garlic in the juice of one jar of artichokes (discard the juice from the second jar of artichokes). In a bowl, combine artichoke hearts, eggs, spices, breadcrumbs, and cheese. Add onion and garlic, and mix well. Transfer to a 9 by 9-inch baking dish. Bake for 30 to 40 minutes.

baked creamed corn

Dianne Phillips > *Omaha, Nebraska*

Serves 6 to 8

INGREDIENTS

1 (14.75-ounce) can creamed corn
1 (14.75-ounce) can whole kernel corn
1 egg, beaten
1 cup sour cream
1 small box Jiffy corn muffin mix
1/2 cup (4 ounces/1 stick) margarine, melted

PREPARATION

Preheat oven to 350ºF. Mix all ingredients in a bowl. Transfer to a greased medium sized casserole dish. Bake for 35 to 45 minutes, or until browned. Recipe may be doubled.

APPETIZERS
BREADS
BREAKFAST & BRUNCH
ENTRÉES
VEGETABLES & SIDE DISHES
SALADS
SOUPS
DESSERTS

belfast "champ" potatoes

Trevon Pulsifer > *Rosemont, Illinois*

Serves 6

INGREDIENTS

5 pounds baking potatoes
1 bunch green onions, chopped
3/4 cup (6 ounces / 1 1/2 sticks) **unsalted butter**
8 ounces heavy cream
Salt and fresh ground pepper

PREPARATION

Peel potatoes, boil in salted water for 20 to 30 minutes, drain, and set aside. In a saucepan, melt a single pat of butter and sauté green onions until soft (3 minutes). Over low heat, add cream to the onions, then add the remaining butter and heat until melted. Pour the contents of the pan over the potatoes and mash or whip.

broccoli casserole

Mary Lynn Crosby > *Greensburg, Pennsylvania*

Serves 15 to 20

INGREDIENTS

1 bag (20 to 32 ounces) **frozen broccoli**
2 (10.75-ounce) **cans cream of mushroom soup**
2 cups shredded cheddar cheese
1 medium onion, diced
2 eggs, beaten
1 1/2 cups mayonnaise
1 sleeve Ritz crackers
1/2 cup (4 ounces/1 stick) **butter**

PREPARATION

Preheat oven to 350°F. Mix together soup, cheese, onion, egg, and mayonnaise. Steam broccoli, then add it to the mixture. Spray a 9 by 13-inch casserole dish with Pam; transfer the mixture to the dish. Smash the Ritz crackers and sprinkle them over the top of the casserole. Slice the butter into pats and lay them over the top of the casserole. Bake for 45 minutes.

carrot soufflé supreme

Christine Kakolewski > *Winter Haven, Florida*

Serves 10

INGREDIENTS

1 pound cooked carrots
3 large eggs
1/2 cup sugar
3 tablespoons all-purpose flour
1 teaspoon baking powder
1 teaspoon vanilla
1/2 cup butter, melted
Pinch of nutmeg

INGREDIENTS FOR TOPPING

1/3 cup crushed cornflakes
3 tablespoons brown sugar
1/4 cup chopped walnuts
Pinch of cinnamon
Pinch of nutmeg
1 tablespoon butter, melted

PREPARATION

Preheat oven to 350°F. Spray a 1 1/2-quart casserole dish with cooking spray. In a blender or food processor, place cooked carrots, eggs, sugar, flour, baking powder, vanilla, butter, and nutmeg. Blend well. Transfer to the casserole dish.

PREPARATION FOR TOPPING

Combine cornflakes, brown sugar, walnuts, cinnamon, nutmeg, and melted butter. Sprinkle on top of casserole. Bake for 45 minutes.

> " THIS SOUFFLÉ IS ON THE TABLE AT EVERY HOLIDAY MEAL AND SHOWS UP AT CHURCH FUNCTIONS AS WELL. IT'S ALWAYS A GREAT SUCCESS, AND THE RECIPE HAS BEEN GIVEN OUT MANY, MANY TIMES. "
>
> > Christine

consommé rice

Lissa Sullivan > *Greenville, South Carolina*

Serves 6

INGREDIENTS

1 cup uncooked white rice
1 (18-ounce) can French onion soup
1 (10.5-ounce) can beef consommé
4 teaspoons butter

PREPARATION

Preheat oven to 350°F. Spray an 8 by 8-inch casserole dish with Pam. Mix rice and soups in the dish. Place a teaspoon of butter in each corner. Bake uncovered for 50 minutes.

APPETIZERS

BREADS

BREAKFAST & BRUNCH

ENTRÉES

VEGETABLES & SIDE DISHES

SALADS

SOUPS

DESSERTS

cheesy hash brown casserole

Kevin Richards > *Irmo, South Carolina*

Serves 6 to 8

INGREDIENTS

1 (27-ounce) **package shredded hash brown potatoes**
16 ounces **shredded cheddar cheese**
1 (10.75-ounce) **can cream of chicken soup**
1 (16-ounce) **container sour cream**

PREPARATION

Mix all ingredients in a large bowl. Transfer the mixture to a 13 by 9-inch casserole dish. Bake for 30 to 45 minutes at 350°F, until cheese is melted and top is golden brown.

copper carrots

Marsha Giomariso > *Ormond Beach, Florida*

Serves 6 to 8

INGREDIENTS

2 pounds carrots
1 large onion
1 green pepper
1 cup granulated sugar
1 (10.75-ounce) **can tomato soup**
3/4 cup apple cider vinegar
1/2 cup canola oil
1 teaspoon Worcestershire sauce
1 teaspoon mustard
Pinch of salt and pepper

PREPARATION

Clean carrots and slice in small round pieces. Cook in a steamer until tender. Cool. Slice onion and green pepper. Mix in bowl with carrots.

In a saucepan, bring to a boil sugar, soup, vinegar, oil, Worcestershire sauce, mustard, and a pinch each of salt and pepper. Stir until sugar dissolves. Remove from heat and cool. Pour over vegetable mixture and mix well. Refrigerate and serve cold.

"MY MOTHER MADE THIS DISH EVERY YEAR FOR CHRISTMAS DINNER. SHE WOULD NOT MAKE IT AT ANY OTHER TIME OF YEAR. I'VE CARRIED ON THE TRADITION, EVEN THOUGH MY HUSBAND BEGS ME TO MAKE IT MORE OFTEN."

> Marsha

corn bread soufflé

Laura Anastasia > *Plymouth, Minnesota*

Serves 8 to 10

INGREDIENTS

1/2 cup (4 ounces/1 stick) **butter**
2 **eggs**
1 (8-ounce) **container sour cream**
1 (8.5-ounce) **box Jiffy corn muffin mix**
1 (14.7-ounce) **can corn, drained**
1 (14.7-ounce) **can creamed corn**
Salt and fresh ground pepper

PREPARATION

Preheat oven to 350°F. Microwave butter until softened (not melted). Add eggs and blend. Add sour cream and corn muffin mix. Add both cans of corn. Mix well and add salt and pepper to taste. Transfer to a greased 9 by 13-inch pan. Bake for 40 minutes, or until top is golden. Do not overcook. Let stand 10 minutes before serving.

cowboy beans

Mark Eggerding > *Rosemont, Illinois*

Serves 6 to 8

INGREDIENTS

1 pound **pork sausage**
1 cup **chopped onion**
1 cup **chopped celery**
1 (6-ounce) **can tomato paste**
1 (10.75-ounce) **can tomato soup**
1 cup **brown sugar**
2 teaspoons **powdered mustard**
1 (14-ounce) **can lima beans, drained**
1 (14-ounce) **can wax beans, drained**
1 (14-ounce) **can green beans, drained**
1 (14-ounce) **can kidney beans, drained**
1 (14-ounce) **can chili beans, drained**
2 (14-ounce) **cans pork and beans**

PREPARATION

Fry sausage, onion, and celery in a skillet. Transfer mixture to a large crockpot and add remaining ingredients. Cook approximately 4 hours on low.

APPETIZERS
BREADS
BREAKFAST & BRUNCH
ENTRÉES
VEGETABLES & SIDE DISHES
SALADS
SOUPS
DESSERTS

creamed corn

Lorie Golden > *Salem, Missouri*

Serves 4

INGREDIENTS

1/4 cup (2 ounces 1/2 stick) **butter**
1 (16-ounce) **package frozen corn**
2 tablespoons cornmeal
2 to 4 tablespoons granulated sugar

PREPARATION

Melt butter in a pan on the stove. Add all other ingredients. Cover and cook on low heat for 30 minutes.

> "THIS IS ONE OF MY KIDS' FAVORITE RECIPES. THEY LOVE THE SWEET SAUCE THAT COATS THE CORN – IT GETS THEM TO EAT THEIR VEGGIES!"
>
> > Lorie

crockpot chunky applesauce

Barbara Norton > *Bridgeport, New Jersey*

Yields 2 quarts

INGREDIENTS

8 cooking apples (such as Macintosh, Granny Smith)
1/2 cup water
2 teaspoons cinnamon
1 cup granulated sugar

PREPARATION

Peel, core, and slice apples. Combine with remaining ingredients in crockpot. Cover and cook on low for 8 to 10 hours. Stir occasionally while cooking. Freezes well.

> "I USUALLY DOUBLE THIS RECIPE. IT'S SO GOOD THAT MY FAMILY THINKS I SPEND A LOT OF TIME PREPARING IT. IT GIVES MY KITCHEN A WONDERFUL HOMEY AROMA."
>
> > Barbara

delicious potatoes

Judy Rende > *Plymouth, Minnesota*

Serves 8 to 10

INGREDIENTS

1 (32-ounce) **bag frozen hash brown potatoes (southern style)**
1 (10.75-ounce) **can cream of potato soup**
1 (10.75-ounce) **can cream of chicken soup**
1 (10.75-ounce) **can creamy onion soup**
1 (8-ounce) **container sour cream**
2 cups shredded cheddar cheese
1 cup shredded Swiss cheese

PREPARATION

Mix together hash browns, soups, sour cream, and 1 cup of shredded cheddar cheese. Spray a 9 by 13-inch pan with spray oil and transfer the mixture to the pan. Sprinkle the remaining cheddar and Swiss cheese on top. Bake at 325°F for 1 1/2 hours, or until cheese melts.

easy potato casserole

Walt Clark > *San Francisco, California*

Serves 12

INGREDIENTS

1 (32-ounce) **bag frozen Tater Tots**
4 cups grated sharp cheddar cheese
1 tablespoon soft butter
1 (16-ounce) **container sour cream**
1 (10.75-ounce) **can cream of mushroom soup**

PREPARATION

Preheat oven to 350°F. In a large bowl, mix all the ingredients and fold together. Spray an 11 by 13-inch glass baking pan with cooking spray. Transfer the potato mixture and spread it in the pan. Bake for 1 hour. Serve warm.

APPETIZERS

BREADS

BREAKFAST & BRUNCH

ENTRÉES

VEGETABLES & SIDE DISHES

SALADS

SOUPS

DESSERTS

> "EVERY TIME I MAKE THESE POTATOES, SOMEONE ASKS FOR THE RECIPE."
>
> > Judy

farmdale mac and cheese

Kevin L. Hagan > *Gaithersburg, Maryland*

Serves 10 to 12

INGREDIENTS

2 (8-ounce) **boxes macaroni or other pasta**
1/2 cup chopped onion
1/2 cup chopped pimiento
32 ounces grated cheddar cheese
1 1/2 cups whole milk
2 (10.75-ounce) **cans cream of mushroom soup**
Salt and fresh ground pepper
1 cup crushed goldfish crackers or breadcrumbs

PREPARATION

Preheat oven to 350°F. Cook and drain macaroni. In a 9 by 13-inch casserole dish, combine macaroni, onion, pimiento, and cheese (reserve 1/2 cup of cheese for topping). In a separate bowl, combine milk, soup, salt, and pepper. Whisk mixture to take out most of the lumps. Pour soup mixture into casserole dish and stir into macaroni mixture. Top with reserved cheese and crackers or breadcrumbs. Bake for 40 minutes.

green beans reggiano

Mark Moreno > *Williamsburg, Virginia*

Serves 12

INGREDIENTS

1/2 pound country ham pieces
2 cloves garlic, chopped
1/2 pound portobello mushrooms, sliced
2 to 3 pounds green beans, tipped
1 tablespoon sea salt
1 tablespoon ground black pepper
2 cups Parmigiano Reggiano cheese, shredded

PREPARATION

In a deep, heavy-bottomed coverable pan, sauté country ham and garlic in olive oil on medium heat until slightly browned. Add mushrooms, green beans, and salt and pepper. Cover and simmer for 1 hour, or until desired doneness, tossing occasionally. Serve on a large oval platter and top with Parmigiano Reggiano.

> " THESE GREEN BEANS ARE SERVED AT ALL FAMILY GATHERINGS. THEY ARE SO POPULAR THAT THEY'VE REPLACED SOME OF THE OTHER COVERED DISHES THAT PEOPLE USED TO BRING. "
>
> > Mark

good conversation starter tomato pie

Jane Medlin-Smith > *Fort Mill, South Carolina*

Serves 8

INGREDIENTS

1 unbaked deep-dish pie shell
3 medium tomatoes, sliced
1/2 teaspoon basil
1 bunch green onions
Salt and pepper
2 cups shredded sharp cheddar cheese
1 cup mayonnaise
2 eggs, beaten

PREPARATION

Preheat oven to 350°F. Bake unbaked pie shell for about 5 minutes. Remove pie shell from the oven and layer the tomatoes, basil, and green tips of the onions. Add salt and pepper to taste. In a bowl, mix the cheese, mayonnaise, and eggs. Pour the egg mixture over the tomato mixture. Cook for 45 minutes to an hour, or until golden brown.

Note: To serve this dish as an entrée, add cooked ground beef (about 1/2 pound) and use two tomatoes instead of three.

> "THE FIRST TIME I PREPARED THIS PIE WAS TO TAKE IT TO MY FIANCÉ'S FAMILY REUNION. IT GOT RAVE REVIEWS AND WAS A GOOD CONVERSATION STARTER AND HELPED ME MEET MANY PEOPLE I DIDN'T KNOW. I MET A DEAR LADY THAT DAY, AND WE FORMED A GREAT FRIENDSHIP. SHE PASSED AWAY A FEW YEARS LATER. I NEVER BAKE THIS PIE WITHOUT THINKING OF HER."
>
> > Jane

herb buttered peas

Maggie Goldsborough > *Columbia, Maryland*

Serves 4

INGREDIENTS

1 (10-ounce) **package frozen peas**
1/3 cup butter
1 to 3 tablespoons minced onion
1/4 teaspoon salt
1/4 teaspoon garlic powder
1/4 teaspoon crushed oregano leaves
1/8 teaspoon ground pepper
2 tablespoons sliced pimiento stuffed green olives

PREPARATION

In a 2-quart pan, cook peas according to package directions. Drain. Add remaining ingredients except olives. Heat through. Toss in olives just before serving. Note: 2 cups fresh peas can be substituted. Cook in boiling salted water 5 to 8 minutes or until tender.

hoppin' juan's black beans and rice

Ron Logan > *Raleigh, North Carolina*

Serves 4 to 6

INGREDIENTS

1 cup parboiled rice
24 ounces chicken broth
1 pound smoked beef sausage or polish sausage
1 cup diced onion
1 (15-ounce) **can black beans**
1 teaspoon ham base
1 cup tomato-based barbecue sauce

PREPARATION

Mix rice and broth in a 2.2-quart ceramic (microwave-safe) dish. Cover and cook in microwave for 22 minutes. Slice sausage in rounds and then in slivers and sauté with onion; drain off fat. In a small pot, heat beans, ham base, and barbeque sauce for 15 minutes. Take half the beans out of the pot, mash them, and return them to the pot (makes a thicker consistency). Add the onions and sausage to the beans and cook another 10 minutes. In a serving dish, pour the beans over the rice. Stir to blend well and serve.

" THIS IS AN EASY DISH TO BRING TO THE KITCHEN TABLE OR TO TAKE AS A COVERED DISH TO A PARTY. EVEN MY PERSNICKETY THREE-YEAR-OLD LIKES IT. "

> Ron

janet's spinach kugel

Rick Maltz > *Columbia, Maryland*

Serves 8 to 12

INGREDIENTS

1 pound wide noodles
2 (10-ounce) **boxes frozen chopped spinach**
8 large eggs
1 pint sour cream
6 ounces melted margarine
1 package onion soup mix
1 can French fried onions

PREPARATION

Preheat oven to 350°F. Cook noodles according to package instructions and drain them. Cook spinach according to package instructions and drain it. In a blender, mix eggs, sour cream, margarine, and onion soup mix until well blended.

Add blended mixture and chopped spinach to cooked noodles. Transfer the mixture to a 13 by 9-inch baking dish. Sprinkle the French fried onions on top of the noodles and bake for 1 1/2 to 2 hours. Check during baking and lightly cover with aluminum foil if necessary to keep the onions from getting too well done.

kiz linda's potatoes

Merrie Eads > *Peoria, Arizona*

Serves 6 to 8

INGREDIENTS

1 (8-ounce) **box instant mashed potatoes**
1 (16-ounce) **package cream cheese, softened**
1 bunch green onions, finely chopped
1 bunch fresh parsley, stemmed and finely chopped (not dried)
2 tablespoons melted butter

PREPARATION

Preheat oven to 400°F. Make potatoes according to the directions on the box. Mix in cream cheese. Stir in green onions and parsley. Transfer to a buttered baking dish. Brush with melted butter. Bake 25 to 30 minutes, until heated through and golden brown on top.

> "JANET WAS MY MOTHER'S BEST FRIEND. WHEN I WAS A KID, MY MOTHER WOULD MAKE THIS KUGEL FOR ME AS A SPECIAL TREAT. MY MOTHER HAS PASSED AWAY, BUT WE STILL MAKE THE DISH ON HOLIDAYS AND FOR SPECIAL MEALS."
>
> > Rick

> "MY GREAT AUNT, LINDA COOPER, BROUGHT THESE POTATOES TO A FAMILY DINNER 30 YEARS AGO. THEY ARE STILL A FAVORITE IN THE FAMILY COOKBOOK. WE USUALLY SERVE THEM WITH PRIME RIB, BUT RECENTLY THEY ACCOMPANIED CHICKEN WINGS FOR MY NIECE'S 13TH BIRTHDAY DINNER. THEY MAKE ANY MEAL OR POTLUCK SPECIAL."
>
> > Merrie

APPETIZERS

BREADS

BREAKFAST & BRUNCH

ENTRÉES

VEGETABLES & SIDE DISHES

SALADS

SOUPS

DESSERTS

loaded garlic smashed potatoes

Jim Weaver > *Virginia Beach, Virginia*

Serves 6 to 8

INGREDIENTS

6 slices bacon
1 bunch green onions, chopped
4 pounds red potatoes
2 medium garlic bulbs, roasted
1 (16-ounce) container sour cream
1 1/2 cups (6 ounces) shredded cheddar cheese
1/3 cup butter, softened
1/4 cup milk
1/2 teaspoon salt
1 tablespoon olive oil

PREPARATION

Cook the bacon in a large skillet until crisp. Drain on paper towels, reserving 2 tablespoons of drippings in the skillet. Crumble the bacon and return it to the skillet. Add green onions. Cook 1 minute or until green onions are tender. Set aside. Peel half the potatoes and cut the other half into 1/4-inch pieces. Cook peeled and unpeeled potatoes in boiling salted water 20 to 25 minutes. Drain and place in a large bowl.

Add roasted garlic pulp, bacon mixture, sour cream, 1 cup cheddar cheese, butter, milk, and salt. Mash with potato masher until blended. Spoon into a lightly oiled 9 by 13-inch baking dish and top with remaining cheese. Bake at 350°F for 10 minutes, or until cheese melts.

> " MY MOTHER-IN-LAW INTRODUCED ME TO THIS DISH. EVERY TIME I PREPARE IT, SOMEONE ASKS FOR THE RECIPE. "
>
> > Mike

macaroni casserole

Mike Pillion > *Manassas, Virginia*

Serves 8

INGREDIENTS

1 (14-ounce) can whole kernel corn
1 (14-ounce) can creamed corn
1/2 cup (4 ounces/1 stick) butter or margarine, cut into small pieces
1 cup uncooked elbow macaroni
2 cups Velveeta cheese, cubed

PREPARATION

Preheat oven to 350°F. Put all ingredients into greased casserole dish and stir together. Bake covered for 45 minutes. Remove from oven and stir. Continue cooking for additional 15 to 20 minutes, until top bubbles and browns.

mom's au gratin potatoes

Lisa Powers > *Streator, Illinois*

Serves 10 to 12

INGREDIENTS

6 to 8 large potatoes
1/2 cup chopped onion
1 cup Miracle Whip
3/4 (16-ounce) **brick Velveeta cheese, cubed**
6 slices cooked bacon, crumbled or cut

PREPARATION

Peel potatoes and boil them until tender (about 20 to 30 minutes). Cut potatoes into bite-sized chunks. Mix in a large bowl with onion, Miracle Whip, and cheese (reserve 1/4 cup of cheese). Transfer the mixture to a greased 13 by 9-inch baking pan. Top with the rest of the cheese and the bacon. Bake at 350°F for 30 minutes, or until the cheese starts to brown. Remove from the oven and let cool slightly before serving.

potato casserole

Sharon K. Parker > *Ormond Beach, Florida*

Serves 4 to 6

INGREDIENTS

1/4 cup (2 ounces/1/2 stick) **butter**
2 1/2 cups milk
1 cup half-and-half
6 ounces Idaho instant mashed potatoes (3 2-ounce packets)
4 ounces cream cheese
1 1/2 tablespoons sour cream
Pinch of salt, white pepper, and garlic salt
4 ounces shredded cheddar cheese

PREPARATION

Melt butter in a bowl in the microwave with milk and half-and-half (should be hot but not boiling). Use a whisk to mix in instant potatoes. Gradually add cream cheese and then sour cream, salt, pepper, and garlic salt to taste. If potatoes are stiff, add hot water (they should be very moist). Transfer to casserole dish and sprinkle the cheddar cheese over the top. Bake at 350°F for 20 to 30 minutes. Note: For a richer dish, add more butter and cream cheese.

APPETIZERS

BREADS

BREAKFAST & BRUNCH

ENTRÉES

VEGETABLES & SIDE DISHES

SALADS

SOUPS

DESSERTS

nonnie's pizza giena

Charles J. Murphy > *Sudbury, Massachusetts*

Serves 12 to 15

INGREDIENTS

2 pounds Parma prosciutto
1 pound sopressata (Italian dry-cured salami)
1/2 pound Genoa salami
1/2 pound sweet cappicola
3/4 pound grated Romano cheese
3 pounds ricotta cheese
8 eggs, beaten
2 pounds fresh farmer's cheese, drained and cubed
2 tablespoons crushed black pepper
2 (1-pound) balls pre-prepared pizza dough
1 egg beaten with 1 tablespoon water for egg wash

PREPARATION

In a large bowl, combine the prosciutto, sopressata, salami, cappicola, and dice to 1/2 inch with Romano cheese to aid adhering. In a separate bowl, mix the ricotta with the eggs until smooth. Add the farmer's cheese. Fold the meat and cheese mixture into the egg and cheese mixture. Once both are combined, add black pepper. Try not to crush the delicate cheese when mixing.

To bake, preheat the oven to 400°F. Brush a half-sheet pan with olive oil. Roll out one pizza crust so the crust overlaps the pan by 1 inch or so. Place the ingredients evenly within the pan. Roll out the top crust, and cover the filling. Seal the crusts by pressing the top and bottom edges together and rolling the dough inward. Brush all over the top with the egg wash. Make a small slit in the center, and place a small tube of aluminum foil in the hole to vent.

Bake for 30 minutes, then decrease the heat to 350°F, and cook for 30 to 40 minutes, or until golden brown. Let cool at least 3 hours before slicing (overnight is best). Serve with your favorite glass of wine. Refrigerate after serving.

quick and easy corn casserole

Dianna Rex > *Greenville, South Carolina*

Serves 6

INGREDIENTS

1/4 cup Egg Beaters
1/4 cup melted butter
1 (8.5-ounce) can whole kernel corn, drained
1 (15-ounce) can creamed corn
1 (8.5-ounce) package Jiffy corn muffin mix
1 (8-ounce) container plain low fat yogurt

PREPARATION

Preheat oven to 350°F. Spray a baking dish with Pam. Mix all ingredients in a bowl and transfer mixture to the baking dish. Bake for 45 to 60 minutes until firm.

super mushroom dish

Jack Collins > *Grass Valley, California*

Serves 6 to 8

INGREDIENTS

1 pound fresh mushrooms, sliced thin
1 tablespoon butter
1/3 cup sour cream
Salt and pepper
1 tablespoon all-purpose flour
1/2 cup grated Swiss cheese
1/4 cup chopped parsley

PREPARATION

Preheat oven to 425°F. Sauté mushrooms in butter for 2 minutes in a covered sauce pan. Blend in sour cream and flour. Add salt and pepper to taste and stir until the mixture boils. Transfer to an 8 by 10-inch casserole dish and sprinkle with Swiss cheese and parsley. Bake for 10 minutes.

MY MOTHER-IN-LAW WON FIRST PRIZE WITH THIS DISH IN A NEWSPAPER RECIPE CONTEST IN 1976 IN LAFAYETTE, CALIFORNIA. WE STILL LOVE THE DISH AND PREPARE IT AS A FAMILY TRADITION IN HER HONOR.

> Jack

APPETIZERS

BREADS

BREAKFAST & BRUNCH

ENTRÉES

VEGETABLES & SIDE DISHES

SALADS

SOUPS

DESSERTS

rosinski family baked beans

Cindy Rosinski > *Buffalo, New York*

Serves 12

INGREDIENTS

1 pound lean ground beef
1 pound bacon, diced
1 onion, chopped
1/2 cup ketchup
1/2 cup barbecue sauce
1 teaspoon salt
4 tablespoons mustard
4 tablespoons molasses
1 teaspoon chili powder
3/4 teaspoon black pepper
2 (16-ounce) cans red kidney beans
2 (16-ounce) cans pork and beans
2 (16-ounce) cans butter beans

PREPARATION

Preheat oven to 350°F. Grease a 9 by 13-inch casserole dish. In a large skillet, brown ground beef, bacon, and onion. Transfer to a large bowl, using a slotted spoon. In a small bowl, combine ketchup, barbecue sauce, salt, mustard, molasses, chili powder, and pepper. Add all the beans to the ground beef mixture. Stir, then add the ketchup/barbecue sauce mixture. Combine all ingredients thoroughly, then transfer to casserole dish. Bake for 1 hour.

scalloped pineapple

Kevin Edmonds > *Ridgeland, Mississippi*

Serves 6 to 8

INGREDIENTS

4 cups fresh breadcrumbs (8 slices of bread)
1 (20-ounce) can pineapple chunks, drained
3 eggs, beaten
2 cups granulated sugar
1 cup melted butter

PREPARATION

Preheat oven to 350°F. Combine all ingredients in a large mixing bowl. Transfer to a 2-quart greased baking dish and bake for 30 minutes. Serve warm as a side dish or with ice cream for a delightful dessert.

sweet onion and butternut squash quiche

Craig Mariutto > *Indianapolis, Indiana*

Serves 6 to 10

INGREDIENTS

1 (9-inch) deep-dish frozen pie shell
2 cups butternut squash, peeled and diced small
1 tablespoon vegetable oil
1 tablespoon salt
1 teaspoon white pepper
2 tablespoons sage
3 Vidalia onions, sliced thin
4 tablespoons butter
3 eggs
1 cup whole milk
2 tablespoons Worcestershire sauce
1/2 cup Asiago cheese, shredded

PREPARATION

Toss diced squash with oil, salt, pepper, and sage. Roast in a 350°F oven until soft. Heat a pan until smoking hot, then add sliced onions and butter. Cook the onions until they are golden to deep brown, stirring constantly to keep the butter from burning. Transfer onions to pie shell. Puree the squash with eggs, milk, and Worcestershire sauce, then pour the mixture over the onions; be sure all the onions are covered. Sprinkle cheese on top. Bake at 325°F for about 45 minutes, until the top of the pie is uniformly golden brown.

> REAL NEW ENGLANDERS EAT QUICHE, AND YOU CAN'T GROW UP IN NEW ENGLAND WITHOUT LEARNING HOW TO COOK FALL SQUASH. THIS QUICHE IS GREAT WITH A SALAD OR SOUP, OR ALL BY ITSELF.
>
> > Craig

APPETIZERS

BREADS

BREAKFAST & BRUNCH

ENTRÉES

VEGETABLES & SIDE DISHES

SALADS

SOUPS

DESSERTS

sweet potato "soufflé"

Glen Dusina > *Lexington, North Carolina*

Serves 8 to 10

INGREDIENTS

3 cups cooked sweet potatoes; peeled if baked, drained if boiled
3 eggs
1 stick melted butter or margarine
1/2 cup whole milk
1/4 cup light brown sugar
1/2 cup granulated sugar
1/4 teaspoon cinnamon
1 teaspoon vanilla extract
Pinch of nutmeg

INGREDIENTS FOR TOPPING

1 cup cornflakes
1/2 cup light brown sugar
1/3 cup melted butter
3/4 cup chopped pecans

PREPARATION

Preheat the oven to 350°F. In a large bowl, mash the sweet potatoes with a whisk or potato masher. Combine them with eggs, butter, milk, brown and white sugars, cinnamon, vanilla, and nutmeg. Transfer to a 9 by 12-inch casserole dish. Top with pecan topping and bake for 25 to 30 minutes.

PREPARATION FOR TOPPING

Crush the cornflakes into small pieces. In a mixing bowl, combine them with the sugar, butter, and pecans, and mix well. Top the soufflé with this mixture before baking.

salads

aegean greek shrimp salad

Doug Ricketts > *Cleveland, Ohio*

Serves 8

INGREDIENTS

2 1/2 cups romaine/iceberg lettuce blend
8 cooked large shrimp
1/4 cup diced tomato
3/8 cup (3 ounces) diced cucumber
1/4 cup Kalamata olives
1/8 cup (1 ounce) diced red onion
1/4 cup (2 ounces) sliced red bell pepper
1/8 cup (1 ounce) sliced green bell pepper
1/3 cup seasoned croutons
3/8 cup (3 ounces) Aegean Greek dressing

PREPARATION

In a serving bowl, combine the lettuce, shrimp, tomato, cucumber, olive, onion, and bell peppers. Top with croutons and dressing as desired.

aunt arnetta's apricot salad

Kate Clemmons > *Tecumseh, Kansas*

Serves 4 to 6

INGREDIENTS

2 large boxes apricot gelatin
1 (15 to 20-ounce) can crushed pineapple
2 cups buttermilk
12 ounces Cool Whip, slightly softened

PREPARATION

In a saucepan, combine the gelatin and pineapple on a stove over medium heat. Mix until the gelatin dissolves, remove from heat, and let cool. In a separate bowl, combine the buttermilk with the Cool Whip. Pour the gelatin mixture into the buttermilk and Cool Whip mixture, stir to combine. Pour mixture into mold. Chill overnight or until firm.

> "MY GREAT-AUNT ARNETTA USED TO BRING THIS TO FAMILY REUNIONS. IT IS EASY TO MAKE AND VERY FESTIVE. YOU CAN USE DIFFERENT FLAVORS OF GELATIN FOR SPECIAL OCCASIONS. I LIKE TO USE STRAWBERRY FOR VALENTINE'S DAY."
>
> > Kate

APPETIZERS

BREADS

BREAKFAST & BRUNCH

ENTRÉES

VEGETABLES & SIDE DISHES

SALADS

SOUPS

DESSERTS

avocado and grapefruit salad

Doug Ricketts > *Cleveland, Ohio*

Serves 4

INGREDIENTS

2 ounces baby greens
4 tablespoons poppy seed dressing
2 ounces red onion, thinly sliced
4 sections medium-sized pink grapefruit
4 slices medium-sized avocado

PREPARATION

Arrange the greens on a serving plate. In a separate mixing bowl, lightly toss the dressing with the onion, grapefruit, and avocado. Arrange on top of greens and serve.

belgium salad

Edward Zakszeski > *Port Orange, Florida*

Serves 12 to 16

INGREDIENTS

1/2 cup corn or canola oil
1/2 cup red wine vinegar
1 cup granulated sugar
1 teaspoon salt
1/2 teaspoon freshly ground black pepper
1 (15-ounce) can French-style green beans, drained
1 (15-ounce) can small peas, drained
1 (15-ounce) can white shoepeg corn, drained
1 cup celery, finely chopped
1 cup red pepper, finely chopped
1 medium onion, finely chopped
1 carrot, grated

PREPARATION

Heat the oil, vinegar, sugar, salt, and pepper until the sugar is dissolved. Set aside to cool. Drain the canned green beans, peas, and corn. In a large bowl, combine the green beans, peas, corn, celery, pepper, onion, and carrot. Pour the oil-and-vinegar mixture over the vegetables and stir. Chill before serving. This salad will keep for about one week in the fridge.

blt salad

Melinda Freeman > *Salem, Missouri*

Serves 6

INGREDIENTS

1 pound bacon
3/4 cup mayonnaise
1/4 cup milk
1 teaspoon garlic powder
1/8 teaspoon freshly ground black pepper
1 head of lettuce, washed and shredded
1/2 pound grape tomatoes
1 cup sharp cheddar cheese, shredded
2 cups seasoned croutons

PREPARATION

Remove the bacon from the package. Slice vertically through each slice. Separate the pieces and cook until evenly browned. Drain and set aside. In a small bowl, whisk together mayonnaise, milk, garlic powder, and pepper. Add salt to taste. In a large salad bowl, combine lettuce, tomatoes, bacon, and croutons. Toss with dressing and serve.

bountiful veggie salad

Maggie Goldsborough > *Columbia, Maryland*

Serves 6 to 8

INGREDIENTS

1 cup cauliflower, chopped
1 cup broccoli, chopped
1 cup celery, chopped
1 cup carrots, chopped
1 cup green peppers, chopped
1 cup cucumbers, peeled and seeded, chopped
1/2 cup mayonnaise
1/2 cup sour cream
1/4 cup French dressing
2 tablespoons granulated sugar
1/4 cup green onion, sliced
1 tablespoon tarragon vinegar
1 teaspoon salt

PREPARATION

In large bowl, toss all ingredients together. Cover and refrigerate 6 hours or overnight.

APPETIZERS

BREADS

BREAKFAST & BRUNCH

ENTRÉES

VEGETABLES & SIDE DISHES

SALADS

SOUPS

DESSERTS

broccoli salad

Karen Rogers > *Mooresville, North Carolina*

Serves 8 to 10

INGREDIENTS FOR SALAD

1 head broccoli, cut into small pieces
6 slices of bacon (or prepared bacon pieces)
1 cup shredded cheddar cheese
1 small onion, diced

INGREDIENTS FOR DRESSING

1 cup mayonnaise
1/2 cup granulated sugar
1/4 cup cider vinegar

PREPARATION

Fry the bacon until crisp and cut into pieces, or use prepared bacon pieces. Combine the broccoli, bacon, cheese, and onion. In a separate bowl, whisk together the mayonnaise, sugar, and cider vinegar. Add dressing to vegetables, stir to combine. Refrigerate until ready to serve.

chicken pineapple salad

Robert Campbell > *Altoona, Pennsylvania*

Serves 4

INGREDIENTS

2 cups cooked chicken, diced
1 (8 1/4-ounce) can pineapple chunks, drained
1 cup celery, diced fine
1/4 cup onions, diced fine
1/4 cup salted peanuts, chopped
Mayonnaise

PREPARATION

In a bowl, combine the chicken, pineapple, celery, onions, and peanuts. Add enough mayonnaise to bind the ingredients, and mix well. Chill for 2 1/2 hours before serving. Serve on a bed of salad greens or in a sandwich.

chrissie's potluck and party salad

Christine A. Dunn > *Columbia, Maryland*

Serves 10

INGREDIENTS

1 head iceberg lettuce, chopped
2 to 3 bags prepared salad greens (Mediterranean or mixed greens)
2 medium-sized cucumbers, chopped
2 medium-sized tomatoes, chopped
1 bag prepared baby carrots
1 red pepper, chopped
1 orange pepper, chopped
1 jar Kalamata olives (do not rinse)
1 jar chopped or whole mild banana peppers (do not rinse)
1 (12-ounce) jar of marinated mild cherry peppers, green and red (do not rinse)
Oil and vinegar, or any light balsamic vinaigrette dressing.

PREPARATION

In a bowl, combine the iceberg lettuce and prepared salad greens and set aside. In a separate bowl, combine the cucumbers, tomatoes, and peppers and set aside. In a large salad bowl, begin layering the salad. First add a layer of lettuce and greens, then the chopped vegetables, baby carrots, banana peppers, olives, and 3 or 4 cherry peppers, then add another layer of salad, and so on. Fill to the rim of the bowl, with a final top layer of chopped vegetables, carrots, peppers, and olives. Cover and chill for 1 hour. Serve with light balsamic vinaigrette dressing on the side.

> "YEARS AGO, I WORKED WITH FOUR SISTERS INNS, A PROMINENT BED-AND-BREAKFAST COMPANY IN CALIFORNIA. INNKEEPERS FROM THE INNS UP AND DOWN THE WEST COAST WOULD GATHER AT THE HEADQUARTERS IN MONTEREY FOR THEIR YEARLY MEETING. ALL OF THE FOOD WAS PROVIDED BY THE THREE LOCAL FSI INNS IN THE AREA. ONE OF THE INNKEEPERS WOULD ALWAYS MAKE THIS SALAD. AND AFTER EACH MEETING, I WOULD FORGET TO ASK FOR THE RECIPE, SO I HAD TO DEVELOP MY OWN VERSION. A LOT OF THE FLAVOR IN THIS SALAD COMES FROM THE INGREDIENTS, SO THERE IS LITTLE NEED FOR A LOT OF DRESSING. PLUS, EVERYONE GETS TO ENJOY ALL OF THE FLAVORS, NO MATTER IF THEY TAKE THE FIRST SERVING OR THE LAST. TO THIS DAY, I MAKE THIS SALAD FOR EVERY POTLUCK AND PARTY. IT IS ALWAYS A HIT. I HOPE THAT YOU ENJOY IT TOO."
>
> > Christine

APPETIZERS

BREADS

BREAKFAST & BRUNCH

ENTRÉES

VEGETABLES & SIDE DISHES

SALADS

SOUPS

DESSERTS

cindy's delight

Mike Spallato > *Pittsburgh, Pennsylvania*

Serves 12 to 18

INGREDIENTS

4 ounces fresh chopped garlic
2 cups (16 ounces) **balsamic vinegar**
3 cups (32 ounces) **red wine vinegar**
8 cups (64 ounces) **olive oil**
Salt and freshly ground pepper
4 cups Romano cheese
8 heads romaine lettuce, chopped
3 red onions, sliced
Sliced mushrooms

PREPARATION

In a large mixing bowl, mix the garlic, balsamic vinegar, red wine vinegar, oil, and salt and pepper to taste. In a separate bowl, combine the cheese, lettuce, onion, and mushrooms to taste. Pour enough dressing over the vegetables to coat the lettuce, toss and serve.

confetti coleslaw

Charla Peterson > *Thompson, North Dakota*

Serves 4 to 6

INGREDIENTS FOR SALAD

1 (7-ounce) **package ring macaroni** (cooked, drained, cooled)
1 (16-ounce) **bag coleslaw mix**
1 cucumber, sliced
1 green pepper, diced
1/2 red onion, diced
4 stalks celery, diced

INGREDIENTS FOR DRESSING

1 1/2 cup Miracle Whip
1/2 cup granulated sugar
1 teaspoon vinegar
Salt and freshly ground black pepper

PREPARATION

Cook the macaroni to desired firmness; drain and set aside to cool. In a bowl, mix the Miracle Whip, sugar, vinegar, and salt and pepper to taste. When the macaroni is cool, combine it with the coleslaw, cucumber, pepper, onion, and celery. Add the dressing, and chill before serving.

cookie salad

Annette Cassity > *Afton, Wyoming*

Serves 4 to 6

INGREDIENTS

2 cans mandarin oranges, drained
1 (20-ounce) can pineapple chunks, drained
3 bananas cut in small pieces
1 small package instant vanilla pudding mix
1 tub Cool Whip
1 package fudge-striped cookies, crumbled

PREPARATION

In a serving bowl, combine the oranges, pineapple, bananas, pudding and Cool Whip. (Do not make the pudding; just use the pudding powder.) Add the crumbled cookies just before serving.

corn salad

Jason Lawler > *Garland, Texas*

Serves 2 to 6

INGREDIENTS

1 (15.25-ounce) can whole kernel corn, drained
1/2 white onion, chopped
1 green bell pepper, chopped
1 to 2 tablespoons of mayonnaise
2 cups grated cheddar cheese
1 (12-ounce) bag of Chili Cheese Fritos, crumbled

PREPARATION

In a medium-sized bowl, combine the corn, onion, and bell pepper. Add mayonnaise to taste. Add the grated cheese (use more if the mixture seems too thin). Stir to combine. Add the Fritos just before serving.

APPETIZERS

BREADS

BREAKFAST &
BRUNCH

ENTRÉES

VEGETABLES &
SIDE DISHES

SALADS

SOUPS

DESSERTS

country mustard red potato salad

Sharon Sveningson > *San Diego, California*

Serves 4 to 6

INGREDIENTS

2 1/2 pounds red-skinned potatoes, peels on, cut into 1/2-inch cubes
1 cup mayonnaise
1/3 cup whole grain mustard
2 tablespoons cider vinegar
1 (2.2-ounce) can sliced olives
4 green onions, thinly sliced
3 to 4 tablespoons chopped parsley
Kosher salt and freshly ground black pepper

PREPARATION

Steam the potato chunks in a steamer basket for approximately 13 minutes or until tender. Drain. While the potatoes are steaming, mix the mayonnaise, mustard, and vinegar in a bowl. Add the mayonnaise mixture to the potatoes while they are still hot. Add the olives, green onions, and parsley. Mix thoroughly. Add salt and pepper to taste. Either serve warm immediately or put into a shallow dish and refrigerate thoroughly.

crispy chicken salad

Karen Hood > *St. Louis, Missouri*

Serves 6 to 8`

INGREDIENTS

1 to 2 heads lettuce
1/2 bag crispy chicken tenders
3 or 4 medium tomatoes cut into small pieces
1 (16-ounce) package bacon
1 (8-ounce) bag cheddar/mozzarella blend cheese
Ranch dressing or dressing of your choice

PREPARATION

Cook the chicken tenders according to the package directions and place on a paper towel to cool. While the chicken is cooling, fry the bacon until crisp and drain on a paper towel. Once the chicken is cool, cut it into small pieces. To prepare salad, wash the lettuce and tear it into small pieces. Place the lettuce in a large bowl. Layer the lettuce first, then add chicken, tomatoes, and bacon, and top with cheese. Add dressing to taste.

SALADS

" I WAS LOOKING FOR A GOOD SALAD TO TAKE TO A SUMMER PICNIC THAT HAD TO SERVE ABOUT 15 TO 20 PEOPLE. I DOUBLED THE RECIPE. EVERYONE LOVED THIS CRISP SUMMER SALAD. "

> Karen

craisin salad

Stacy Jacoby > *Lakeland, Florida*

Serves 6 to 8

INGREDIENTS FOR SALAD MIX

2 bags Italian mixture lettuce
3/4 cup sliced almonds
1 cup **Craisins** (dried cranberries)
1 1/2 cups Chinese noodles
4 green onions, sliced

INGREDIENTS FOR DRESSING

1/2 cup oil
1/2 cup granulated sugar
1/4 cup white distilled vinegar
1/4 teaspoon pepper
1 1/2 teaspoon poppy seeds
1 tablespoon seasoning salt

PREPARATION

Mix the oil, sugar, vinegar, pepper, poppy seeds, and seasoning salt. Refrigerate dressing. Combine the lettuce, almonds, Craisins, Chinese noodles, and onions in a serving bowl. Add the dressing just before serving.

fresh cranberry salad

Alan Gutwald > *Weirton, West Virginia*

Serves 10 to 12

INGREDIENTS

2 to 3 boxes cranberry gelatin (or another red flavor)
1 1/2 cups boiling water
1 (20-ounce) **can crushed pineapple** (drain and retain 1 cup of juice)
1 pound fresh cranberries
1 apple, peeled and cored
1 orange, peeled
1/2 cup granulated sugar

PREPARATION

Dissolve the gelatin in the boiling water. Refrigerate until gelatin is semi-set. In a food processor, chop the cranberries, pineapple, apple, and orange separately. In a large bowl, combine the processed fruit and add the sugar. Fold the fruit mixture into the semi-set gelatin. Refrigerate until firm.

APPETIZERS

BREADS

BREAKFAST & BRUNCH

ENTRÉES

VEGETABLES & SIDE DISHES

SALADS

SOUPS

DESSERTS

especially for you salad

Merrie Eads > *Peoria, Arizona*

Serves 6 to 8

INGREDIENTS

3 small packages lemon gelatin (may be sugar-free)
1 (20-ounce) **can crushed pineapple in syrup** (not in juice)
4 **medium carrots, peeled and diced**
4 **stalks celery, diced**
1 **large bell pepper** (green, red, or yellow)**, diced**
1 cup **Miracle Whip** (do not substitute mayonnaise)
2 cups **sharp cheddar cheese, shredded**

PREPARATION

Prepare the gelatin according to the package directions, but subtract one cup of water. In a 9 by 13-inch glass pan, place the carrots, celery, bell pepper, and crushed pineapple with the syrup. Pour the gelatin over the mixture and chill overnight or until firm. Just before serving, spread a thin layer of Miracle Whip on top of the gelatin mixture and sprinkle with shredded cheddar cheese. Cut into medium-sized squares and serve.

fruit and cookie salad

Phyllis Rotert > *Layton, Utah*

Serves 6 to 8

INGREDIENTS

1 (20-ounce) **can pineapple chunks, drained**
1 (20-ounce) **can crushed pineapple, drained**
3 (8-ounce) **cans mandarin oranges, drained**
1 (6 to 7-ounce) **large box instant vanilla pudding mix**
2 cups **buttermilk**
1 (12-ounce) **tub whipped topping**
1 package Keebler Fudge Stripe cookies, broken into chunks
3 cups mini marshmallows

PREPARATION

In a large bowl, mix the pudding and buttermilk with a spoon. Carefully add the pineapple and oranges to the mixture and mix well. Add the cookies and marshmallows no more than 1 hour before serving.

freezer slaw

Charlotte Anderson > *Oklahoma City, Oklahoma*

Yields 6 cups

INGREDIENTS

1 1/2 cups granulated sugar
1 cup cider vinegar
3 (10-ounce) packages shredded cabbage slaw
1 small package shredded carrots
1 small green pepper, diced
1 teaspoon celery salt
1 teaspoon mustard seed

PREPARATION

In a small saucepan, bring the sugar and vinegar to a boil, stirring until the sugar dissolves; cool. In a bowl, combine the cabbage, carrots, pepper, celery salt, and mustard seed. Pour the vinegar mixture over the vegetables, tossing to coat. Place the salad in a large heavy-duty resealable plastic bag or an airtight container, and freeze for up to 3 months. Thaw in refrigerator before serving.

grandma roseberry's glazed fruit salad

Kate Clemmons > *Tecumseh, Kansas*

Serves 6 to 8

INGREDIENTS

1 (20-ounce) can apricot pie filling
1 (15 to 20-ounce) can pineapple chunks, drained
2 (11-ounce) cans or 1 (15 to 20-ounce) can mandarin oranges, drained
2 bananas, sliced in bite-sized pieces

PREPARATION

Combine the apricot filling, pineapple, oranges, and bananas. Chill and serve.

> THERE ARE FEW DISHES QUITE AS COMFORTING AS THE RECIPES MY MOM HANDED DOWN TO ME AND MY SISTERS. THEY'RE THE KIND OF FOOD TRADITIONS THAT CONJURE UP FOND MEMORIES OF FAMILY MEALS GONE BY. WITH FOUR CHILDREN AND ALL OF OUR ACTIVITIES, SHE WAS ALWAYS LOOKING FOR WAYS TO SAVE TIME. THIS RECIPE ALLOWED HER TO MAKE SLAW AHEAD OF TIME AND KEEP IT IN THE FREEZER. WHEN UNEXPECTED COMPANY DROPPED BY OR SHE NEEDED A QUICK SALAD, IT WAS JUST THAW AND SERVE! THE FLAVOR AND TEXTURE IS ABSOLUTELY DELICIOUS...AND OH SO EASY!
>
> > Charlotte

> MY GRANDMA USED TO MAKE THIS RECIPE. I FOUND HER RECIPE BOOK AND MADE THIS FOR THANKSGIVING ONE YEAR. MY DAD WAS SO SURPRISED AND PLEASED TO HAVE THIS SALAD ON THE TABLE AGAIN. IT'S SO EASY THAT I MAKE IT SEVERAL TIMES DURING THE YEAR.
>
> > Kate

APPETIZERS

BREADS

BREAKFAST & BRUNCH

ENTRÉES

VEGETABLES & SIDE DISHES

SALADS

SOUPS

DESSERTS

"golly" fruit salad

Paula Henry > *Salem, Virginia*

Serves 8 to 10

INGREDIENTS FOR SALAD

1 (20-ounce) **can pineapple chunks** (drain and retain juice)
1 cup Tokay grapes, sliced
3 to 4 bananas, sliced
1 cup nuts (walnuts preferred)
1 package mini marshmallows (optional)

INGREDIENTS FOR DRESSING

1 1/2 cups pineapple juice plus retained juice from pineapple chunks
1/4 cup lemon juice
4 teaspoons granulated sugar
4 teaspoons cornstarch
1/2 teaspoon salt
2 egg yolks
1 tablespoon butter

PREPARATION FOR DRESSING

In a saucepan, combine the pineapple juice, lemon juice, sugar, cornstarch, and salt. Heat 8 to 10 minutes over low to medium heat until the sugar and cornstarch dissolve. Add the egg yolks and cook for another 3 minutes, stirring constantly. Remove from heat and add the butter; stir until the butter melts.

PREPARATION FOR SALAD

In a serving bowl, combine the pineapple chunks, grapes, bananas, nuts, and marshmallows. Pour the dressing over the fruit and fold to mix. Chill until serving.

> "I'M NOT SURE WHAT THIS SALAD IS ACTUALLY CALLED. ALL I REMEMBER IS MY YOUNGER SISTER ALWAYS SAYING, 'GOLLY, GRANDMA, THIS IS GOOD!'"
>
> > Paula

grandma's carrot salad

Susan Polk > *Nokesville, Virginia*

Serves 6 to 8

INGREDIENTS

1 pound carrots, grated
1 lemon, with peel, grated, seeds and membrane removed
1 cup granulated sugar

PREPARATION

In a medium bowl combine the whole lemon, carrots, and sugar. Stir to combine, and let stand for at least an hour before serving.

> "GRANDMA ORIGINALLY GOT THIS RECIPE AS A HOME DEMONSTRATION CLUB MEMBER IN THE 1940s. RAISINS WERE INCLUDED IN THE ORIGINAL RECIPE, BUT SHE NEVER USED THEM BECAUSE MY FATHER DID NOT LIKE THEM. THIS HAS BEEN A FAVORITE IN OUR FAMILY SINCE THEN AND IS INCLUDED WITH EVERY SPECIAL FAMILY DINNER. IT IS LIGHT AND VERY REFRESHING, AND CAN BE MADE WITH A SUGAR SUBSTITUTE IF DIETS REQUIRE."
>
> > Susan

APPETIZERS

BREADS

BREAKFAST &
BRUNCH

ENTRÉES

VEGETABLES &
SIDE DISHES

SALADS

SOUPS

DESSERTS

green salad

Carol Snyder > *Pearl, Mississippi*

Serves 2 to 4

INGREDIENTS FOR SALAD

Equal mix of iceberg lettuce and escarole, torn into bite-size shreds (1/2
head each)
1 tomato, cut into wedges
1/2 green pepper, seeded and diced
1/2 red onion, sliced translucent-thin
8 Kalamata olives
2 ounces feta cheese, thickly crumbled
4 anchovy fillets

INGREDIENTS FOR DRESSING

1/4 cup olive oil
1 tablespoon red wine vinegar
1/2 teaspoon salt
1/2 teaspoon coarse ground black pepper
1/4 teaspoon dry mustard
1/2 teaspoon oregano
1 clove garlic, crushed
Pinch of granulated sugar

PREPARATION

Arrange the lettuce, escarole, tomato, pepper, onion, olives, and cheese on a
wide oval plate, laying the anchovy fillets in a parallel pattern across the top.
Prepare the dressing by combining the oil, vinegar, salt, pepper, mustard, oregano, garlic, and sugar in a separate bowl. Pour dressing over salad and serve.

hawaiian chicken salad

Jo Massie > *Salem, Missouri*

Serves 12

INGREDIENTS

4 (3-ounce) **packages of cream cheese**
2/3 cup Miracle Whip
2 (8-ounce) **cans pineapple chunks** (drain, reserving 2 tablespoons of juice)
6 (5-ounce) **cans chicken chunks, drained**
1 cup celery, diced
1 cup red bell pepper, chopped
3 cups seedless grapes, halved
1 cup mandarin oranges, halved
2 cups blanched slivered almonds
1 cup toasted coconut

PREPARATION

In large bowl, beat the cream cheese until fluffy. Mix in the Miracle Whip and the reserved pineapple juice. Stir in the pineapple, chicken, celery, bell pepper, grapes, and mandarin oranges until evenly coated. Chill. Just before serving, mix in the almonds and coconut.

holiday white salad

Kathy Ward > *Overland Park, Kansas*

Serves 4 to 6

INGREDIENTS

1 tablespoon mayonnaise
1 (20-ounce) **can chunk or crushed pineapple** (drain, reserving 2 tablespoons of juice)
1 (3-ounce) **package cream cheese**
2 cups mini marshmallows
1 cup seedless red grapes
1 cup Cool Whip

PREPARATION

With a hand mixer, cream the pineapple juice, mayonnaise, and cream cheese together in a mixing bowl. Fold in the marshmallows, grapes, pineapple, and Cool Whip. Chill. This salad can also be frozen.

"THIS SALAD HAS BEEN A PART OF EVERY WARD CHRISTMAS EVE DINNER FOR AS LONG AS I CAN REMEMBER. AND I'VE BEEN AROUND FOR A VERY LONG TIME! ONCE, THERE WAS A LACK OF COMMUNICATION AND I MISTAKENLY EXCLUDED IT FROM THE MENU. A RIOT NEARLY ENSUED FROM 22 FAMILY MEMBERS! AS ALWAYS, MOM CAME TO THE RESCUE; SHE HAD ALL THE INGREDIENTS ON HAND. WITH ALL HANDS ON DECK, THE SALAD WAS ASSEMBLED MOMENTS BEFORE THE SERVING LINE STARTED."

> Kathy

italian pasta salad

Mark Eggerding > *Rosemont, Illinois*

Serves 6 to 8

INGREDIENTS

1 pound spiral pasta
1 green pepper, chopped
1/2 pound mushrooms, sliced
1 basket cherry tomatoes, halved
1 bunch broccoli, cut in small pieces
1 small purple onion, sliced
1/4 cup parsley, chopped
1/2 cup pepperoni, sliced
1 (2.25-ounce) can sliced black olives
1/2 pound mozzarella cheese, cubed
1/4 cup parmesan cheese
1 large bottle Italian dressing

PREPARATION

Cook the pasta to desired firmness; drain and set aside to cool. When the pasta has cooled, transfer it to a serving bowl and combine it with the pepper, mushrooms, tomatoes, broccoli, onion, parsley, pepperoni, olives, cheese, and dressing. Refrigerate for 4 to 6 hours before serving.

layered salad

Lee Nybo > *Las Vegas, Nevada*

Serves 8 to 10

INGREDIENTS

6 cups iceberg lettuce, torn into bite-sized pieces
1 cup celery, chopped
1 (16-ounce) can cut green beans, drained
4 hard-cooked eggs, sliced
1 cup green pepper, chopped
1/3 cup onion, thinly sliced
1 (17-ounce) can small peas, drained
2 cups mayonnaise
1 cup cheddar cheese, grated

PREPARATION

In a large bowl, layer the lettuce, celery, green beans, egg, green pepper, onion rings, and peas in order given. Spread the mayonnaise over the top of the salad. Sprinkle with grated cheese. Cover well and let stand 8 hours or overnight.

APPETIZERS

BREADS

BREAKFAST & BRUNCH

ENTRÉES

VEGETABLES & SIDE DISHES

SALADS

SOUPS

DESSERTS

mandarin salad

Doug Ricketts > *Cleveland, Ohio*

Serves 8

INGREDIENTS FOR SALAD

1/4 cup sliced almonds
3 teaspoons granulated sugar
1/4 head iceberg lettuce, torn into bite-sized pieces
1/4 bunch romaine lettuce, torn into bite-sized pieces
2 medium stalks celery, chopped (about 1 cup)
2 green onions with tops, thinly sliced (about 2 tablespoons)
1 (11-ounce) can mandarin orange segments, drained

INGREDIENTS FOR SWEET-SOUR DRESSING

1/4 cup vegetable oil
2 tablespoons granulated sugar
2 tablespoons vinegar
1 tablespoon snipped parsley
1/2 teaspoon salt
Freshly ground pepper
Pinch of red pepper sauce

PREPARATION FOR DRESSING

Combine the oil, sugar, vinegar, parsley, salt, pepper, and red pepper sauce in a tightly covered jar and shake to combine. Refrigerate until needed.

PREPARATION FOR SALAD

Cook the almonds and sugar over low heat, stirring constantly, until the sugar is melted and the almonds are coated. Let cool and break apart. Store at room temperature. Place the iceberg and romaine lettuce in a large resealable plastic bag, and add the celery and onions. Pour the dressing into the bag, and add the orange segments. Close the bag tightly and shake until the greens and orange segments are well coated. Add the sugared almonds and shake again to coat.

For pineapple salad, substitute 1 (13 1/4 ounce) can pineapple chunks, drained, for the mandarin orange segments, and substitute snipped mint leaves for the parsley.

marie's tomato
and black olive salad

Steve Afflitio > *Lakeland, Florida*

Serves 4 to 6

INGREDIENTS

2 pounds ripe tomatoes, cut into 3/4-inch thick wedges
2 cups pimentos, broken in pieces
2 cups black olives
1/2 cup green onions, diced
1 cup celery, diced
1 teaspoon oregano
1/4 cup red vinegar
1/2 cup olive oil
Salt and freshly ground black pepper

PREPARATION

Combine the tomatoes, pimentos, olives, onions, celery, oregano, vinegar, and oil, and gently mix. Season with salt and pepper to taste. Drain excess liquid as needed.

mom's best taco salad

Crystal Hendershot > *Houston, Texas*

Serves 6

INGREDIENTS FOR SALAD

1 pound ground beef
2 cups Monterey Jack cheese, shredded
1 head iceberg lettuce, chopped
2 large tomatoes, diced
1 (12-ounce) bag nacho cheese tortilla chips, crushed

INGREDIENTS FOR DRESSING

1 cup light Miracle Whip
1 cup chunky salsa

PREPARATION

Brown the ground beef in a large nonstick skillet over medium-high heat, and drain. Prepare the dressing by mixing the Miracle Whip with salsa until well blended, and set aside. In a large serving bowl, toss the cooked ground beef with the lettuce, tomatoes, and cheese. Add the dressing and mix evenly. Right before serving, add the crushed tortilla chips and stir gently. Note: If the salad mixture is too dry, add more salsa as needed.

> "GROWING UP, THIS SALAD WAS A FAVORITE IN OUR HOUSE. MY SISTERS AND I WOULD BEG MY MOM TO MAKE THIS FOR DINNER! NOW THAT I AM PREPARING MY OWN MEALS, THIS IS STILL ONE OF MY FAVORITE DISHES BECAUSE IT IS SO SIMPLE TO PREPARE AND TASTES AMAZING. IF YOU ARE COMING TO MY HOUSE FOR DINNER, CHANCES ARE THIS TACO SALAD WILL BE ON THE MENU."
>
> > Crystal

APPETIZERS

BREADS

BREAKFAST & BRUNCH

ENTRÉES

VEGETABLES & SIDE DISHES

SALADS

SOUPS

DESSERTS

> "MY GRANDMOTHER, OR NANA AS WE AFFECTIONATELY REFERRED TO HER, CAME TO THIS COUNTRY FROM GERMANY AS A CHILD. THIS IS A DISH THAT WAS BROUGHT FROM THE OLD COUNTRY. NANA SERVED HER FAMOUS POTATO SALAD ON THOSE UNFORGETTABLE WEEKENDS THAT WE SPENT AT OUR FAMILY CABIN. THIS RECIPE BRINGS BACK GREAT CHILDHOOD MEMORIES SPENT WITH NANA, MY COUSINS, AND EXTENDED FAMILY."

> Fara

> "MY PATERNAL GRANDMOTHER FOUND THIS RECIPE. IT WAS ORIGINALLY INTENDED AS A TOPPING FOR ICE CREAM BUT SHE SAW ITS POTENTIAL AS A WONDERFUL SALAD AND DECIDED TO TRY IT OUT ON THE FAMILY ONE THANKSGIVING. WE ALL LOVED IT. IT HAS BEEN A DINNER STAPLE AT ALL OF OUR HOLIDAY GATHERINGS SINCE. I KEEP BAGS OF CRANBER-RIES IN THE FREEZER SO I CAN MAKE THIS DISH THROUGHOUT THE YEAR."

> Roxanne

nana's german potato salad

Fara Bone > *Salt Lake City, Utah*

Serves 4

INGREDIENTS

4 to 6 small potatoes
4 slices bacon
Bacon drippings
1 teaspoon salt
1/4 cup vinegar
1/2 teaspoon granulated sugar
5 tablespoons water
2 tablespoons oil
1/4 cup onion, minced (optional)
Freshly ground black pepper
Chives or parsley for garnish

PREPARATION

Boil, peel, and slice the potatoes. In a heavy frying pan, cook the bacon; drain, crumble, and set aside, reserving the bacon drippings. To the reserved drippings, add the salt, vinegar, sugar, water, oil, and minced onion. Heat the dressing and slowly add the potatoes and bacon. Heat thoroughly to serving temperature. Add black pepper to taste, and garnish with chives or parsley.

not your usual cranberry salad

Roxanne Jueckstock > *Phoenix, Arizona*

Serves 8 to 10

INGREDIENTS

1 bag fresh cranberries
2 medium apples, diced
2 bananas, diced
1/2 to 3/4 cup granulated sugar

PREPARATION

Chop the cranberries in a food processor. Combine the chopped cranberries, diced apples and bananas, and sugar. Refrigerate overnight for best flavor.

oriental cole slaw

Marilyn Cuber > *Chicago, Illinois*

Serves 14 (1/2 cup servings)

INGREDIENTS

1 (3-ounce) package ramen noodles, crushed
6 cups cabbage, shredded
4 green onions, sliced
1/2 cup toasted sunflower seeds
1/2 cup slivered almonds
1/2 cup olive oil
3 tablespoons vinegar
2 tablespoons granulated sugar
Seasoning packet from noodles
Salt and freshly ground black pepper

PREPARATION

In a serving bowl, combine the crushed ramen, cabbage, onions, sunflower seeds, almonds, oil, vinegar, sugar, the seasoning packet, and salt and pepper to taste. Cover and refrigerate until noodles have softened. Can be prepared one day before serving.

oriental noodle salad

Cindy Perkins > *Columbia, Maryland*

Serves 6 to 8

INGREDIENTS FOR SALAD

2 packages beef ramen noodles
Boiling water in large pot
2 bunches scallions, chopped
1 cup sliced toasted almonds
1 cup sunflower seeds
1 (16-ounce) bag coleslaw

INGREDIENTS FOR DRESSING

1 cup oil
1 cup balsamic vinegar
1/2 cup granulated sugar
2 packets seasoning from ramen noodles

PREPARATION

In a large bowl, crumble the ramen noodles (setting aside the seasoning packets). Reconstitute with boiling water and drain, then let cool. When cool, add the scallions, almonds, sunflower seeds, and coleslaw. Prepare dressing by combining oil, vinegar, sugar, and the beef seasoning, and pour over the salad when ready to serve.

APPETIZERS

BREADS

BREAKFAST & BRUNCH

ENTRÉES

VEGETABLES & SIDE DISHES

SALADS

SOUPS

DESSERTS

peanut salad

Alan Myers > *Los Angeles, California*

Serves 4

INGREDIENTS

4 egg yolks
3 tablespoons granulated sugar
Pinch of salt
1 (20-ounce) can crushed pineapple, drained
1/2 pint whipping cream
1 pound mini marshmallows (for holidays, use colored marshmallows)
1 cup salted peanuts

PREPARATION

In a double boiler, mix the egg yolks, sugar, and salt over boiling water to form a thick mixture. Let it cool. Add the pineapple to the cooled mixture, then whip the cream and fold it into to the cooled mixture. Mix in the marshmallows and refrigerate. Add peanuts just before serving.

pretzel salad

Sandee Chaffino > *Tracy, California*

Serves 8

INGREDIENTS

1 (6-ounce) package strawberry gelatin
Boiling water in large pot
1 (10-ounce) box frozen strawberries, thawed
1 (8-ounce) box cream cheese, softened
1 (8-ounce) tub Cool Whip
1/2 cup plus 1/4 cup granulated sugar
3/4 cup salted pretzels, crushed
1/4 cup plus 2 tablespoons butter, melted
Pinch of cinnamon or nutmeg for garnish

PREPARATION

Dissolve the gelatin in boiling water according to the package directions. Add the strawberries. Pour the mixture into a serving dish and refrigerate until firm. Using a hand mixer, thoroughly combine the softened cream cheese, Cool Whip, and sugar. Spread the mixture carefully on top of the firm gelatin.

For pretzel topping, preheat oven to 350°F. In a bowl, combine the sugar and melted butter and pour mixture over the pretzels. Toss to combine, spread the pretzels on a cookie sheet, and bake for 10 minutes. Crumble and sprinkle the pretzels on top of the creamy layer. Garnish with cinnamon or nutmeg. Keep chilled until ready to serve.

raspberry pecan salad

Justine Sierzega > *DeLand, Florida*

Serves 4

INGREDIENTS

2 cups pecans
1/2 cup granulated sugar
1 head romaine lettuce,
1 head iceberg lettuce, torn or shredded
1 bag gourmet mixed field greens
3 stalks celery, thinly sliced
1 bunch parsley, chopped
2 rolls Montrachet (soft goat cheese), broken into chunks
2 pints fresh raspberries
Raspberry vinaigrette dressing

PREPARATION

Heat the pecans with the sugar in a skillet until very brown. Spread the mixture on wax paper to cool. Then break it apart. To prepare salad, arrange the lettuce, greens, celery, parsley, and cheese on individual salad plates and chill. To serve, top the salad with the raspberries and candied pecans, and drizzle raspberry vinaigrette over all. Serve very cold.

strawberry salad

Joan Miller > *Battleboro, North Carolina*

Serves 6 to 8

INGREDIENTS

2 (3-ounce) boxes strawberry gelatin
1 cup boiling water
2 (10-ounce) containers frozen strawberries in syrup, partially thawed
1 (15-ounce) can crushed pineapple, drained
1 cup chopped pecans
2 cups (1 pint) sour cream

PREPARATION

Dissolve the gelatin in boiling water. Add the strawberries and stir until the all the frozen lumps have dissolved. Add the pineapple and nuts. Pour half of the gelatin mixture into a 9- by 13-inch baking dish and refrigerate until set. Spread the sour cream over the set mixture and pour the remaining gelatin mixture over the sour cream. Refrigerate until set.

> "THIS IS PROBABLY A VERY COMMON RECIPE, BUT WHEN MY AUNT SERVED IT AT THANKSGIVING ONE YEAR, MY DADDY FELL IN LOVE WITH IT. THAT WAS AT LEAST 30 YEARS AGO. HE ALWAYS REQUESTED THIS SALAD AT SPECIAL FAMILY GATHERINGS. MY DADDY PASSED AWAY IN 1996, BUT WE CONTINUE THE TRADITION OF SERVING THIS SALAD AT SPECIAL MEALS, ESPECIALLY THANKSGIVING. MY MAMMA PASSED AWAY IN 2000, AND NOW MY SISTERS AND I MAKE SURE WE SERVE SOME TRADITIONAL FOODS THAT MAMMA AND DADDY LOVED TO KEEP THEM CLOSE IN OUR HEARTS. WE HOPE OUR CHILDREN WILL CONTINUE THESE TRADITIONS AFTER WE ARE GONE. THIS SALAD IS ONE OF THOSE FOODS."
>
> > Joan

APPETIZERS

BREADS

BREAKFAST & BRUNCH

ENTRÉES

VEGETABLES & SIDE DISHES

SALADS

SOUPS

DESSERTS

sesame seed salad

Sandee Chaffino > *Tracy, California*

Serves 4

INGREDIENTS FOR SALAD

8 cups cabbage, julienned
2 tablespoons slivered almonds
2 green onions, chopped (green stems only)
2 tablespoons sesame seeds
1 package ramen noodles, crumbled

INGREDIENTS FOR DRESSING

2 tablespoons granulated sugar
2 tablespoons vegetable oil
1/4 cup sesame oil
1/2 teaspoon freshly ground black pepper
3 tablespoons vinegar
1/2 teaspoon MSG (optional)

PREPARATION

In a large bowl, combine the cabbage, almonds, onions, sesame seeds, and ramen noodles. The moisture from the cabbage will rehydrate the ramen noodles. In a jar, combine the sugar, vegetable and sesame oils, pepper, vinegar, and MSG and shake well. Pour dressing on salad just before serving.

texas salad

Linda Sharp > *Greenville, South Carolina*

Serves 4

INGREDIENTS

2 (15.75-ounce) cans pork and beans, drained
1 tomato, chopped into bean-sized pieces
1 medium onion, chopped into bean-sized pieces
Mayonnaise

PREPARATION

Combine the pork and beans, tomato, and onion. Add mayonnaise to desired consistency. Stir all ingredients. Refrigerate at least 2 hours. Serve cold.

taco salad

Cindy Harrod > *Phoenix, Arizona*

Serves 4 to 6

INGREDIENTS

1 pound hamburger
1 can chopped green chilies
1 1/2 pounds Velveeta cheese, cubed
1/2 cup milk
1 head of lettuce, chopped
1 bunch of green onions, chopped
1 avocado, peeled and chopped
2 jalapeño peppers (optional)
1 (20-ounce) package corn chips

PREPARATION

Brown the hamburger and add the chopped green chilies. Drain well and set aside. In a separate saucepan, combine the Velveeta and milk and cook over very low heat until completely melted.

In a serving bowl, combine the lettuce, onions, avocado, and jalapeño peppers and toss together until mixed. Add the hamburger to the salad and toss, then add the corn chips and toss again. Pour the cheese mixture over the entire salad and toss well before serving.

tortellini caesar salad

Christine Kakolewski > *Winter Haven, Florida*

Serves 10

INGREDIENTS

1 (19-ounce) package frozen cheese tortellini
1/2 cup mayonnaise
1/4 cup milk
1/4 cup plus 1/3 cup shredded parmesan cheese
2 tablespoons lemon juice
2 garlic cloves, minced
8 cups romaine lettuce, torn
1 cup seasoned salad croutons
Halved cherry tomatoes for garnish

PREPARATION

Cook the tortellini according to package directions. Meanwhile, in a small bowl, combine the mayonnaise, milk, 1/4 cup parmesan cheese, lemon juice, and garlic. Drain the tortellini and rinse in cold water; transfer to a large bowl. Add the romaine and remaining 1/3 cup parmesan cheese. Just before serving, drizzle with the mayonnaise mixture and toss to coat. Top with croutons and tomatoes.

> "WE USED TO HAVE VERY LARGE FAMILY REUNIONS (70 TO 80 PEOPLE) EVERY SUMMER WHEN I WAS GROWING UP. I LOVED IT WHEN WE ALL GOT TOGETHER. THIS WAS ONE OF THE MEALS MY GRANDMOTHER ALWAYS PLANNED FOR US. THERE WERE SO MANY OF US, AND THIS SALAD WAS FAST AND EASY TO MAKE. EVERYONE LOVED IT. SHE WOULD MAKE ONE SALAD HOT FOR THE ADULTS AND ONE WITHOUT THE PEPPERS FOR THE KIDS. SHE WAS A WONDERFUL GRANDMOTHER, AND I MISS HER TERRIBLY!"
>
> > Cindy

> "THIS SALAD WAS SERVED AT SEVERAL OF OUR ITALIAN HOLIDAY PARTIES. IT WAS A GREAT SUCCESS. EVERYONE WANTED MORE OF THIS TASTY SALAD."
>
> > Christine

APPETIZERS
BREADS
BREAKFAST & BRUNCH
ENTRÉES
VEGETABLES & SIDE DISHES
SALADS
SOUPS
DESSERTS

the absolute cranberry fruit salad

Christine Brown > *Greensburg, Pennsylvania*

Serves 12 to 18

INGREDIENTS

1 1/2 cups chopped walnuts
1 1/2 to 2 large cans of mandarin oranges, drained
2 to 3 Gala apples, cored and cubed
1 1/2 to 2 cans pineapple chunks, drained
2 (16-ounce) cans whole cranberry sauce
1 (3-ounce) package of cherry gelatin
1 (3-ounce) package of orange gelatin
4 cups water
Whipped cream for garnish

PREPARATION

Cover the bottom of 9 by 13-inch baking dish with the chopped walnuts. Layer the oranges, apples, and pineapples on the walnuts, and top with the cranberry sauce.

Boil 2 cups of water. In a bowl, dissolve both packages of gelatin in the boiling water. Add remaining 2 cups of cold water. Pour the gelatin mixture over the fruit and nuts until the pan is almost full. Refrigerate overnight or until firm. Serve with a dollop of whipped cream.

trees and raisins

Linda Sharp > *Greenville, South Carolina*

Serves 6

INGREDIENTS

1 large head broccoli, cut into small florets
10 to 12 strips bacon, fried crisp and crumbled
1/2 cup regular or golden raisins
1/2 to 3/4 cup chopped red onion
1 cup mayonnaise
1/2 cup granulated sugar
2 tablespoons vinegar

PREPARATION

In a large bowl, combine the broccoli, bacon, raisins, and onion. In a separate bowl, blend the mayonnaise, sugar, and vinegar. Pour the mayonnaise mixture over the broccoli mixture and stir to coat well. Cover and marinate for at least 1 hour.

vinaigrette potato salad

Linda Chirash > *Rosemont, Illinois*

Serves 8 to 12

INGREDIENTS

6 pounds potatoes (red-skinned or Yukon gold)
2/3 cup dry white wine
4 shallots, minced
1/2 cup red wine vinegar
1 tablespoon Dijon mustard
2 teaspoons salt
1 teaspoon pepper
1 cup olive oil
1/2 cup chopped fresh parsley

PREPARATION

Boil the potatoes until fork-tender. After somewhat cool, peel and slice potatoes. Put potatoes in a large bowl and add the white wine while the potatoes are still warm. Add the shallots and toss to mix. In a separate medium bowl, whisk together the vinegar, mustard, salt, and pepper. Gradually whisk in olive oil. Pour the vinaigrette over the potatoes and toss to coat. Toss with the parsley shortly before serving. This recipe can be doubled, and it can be prepared ahead of time and refrigerated overnight.

> "A DEAR FRIEND MADE THIS RECIPE FOR A PARTY YEARS AGO. IT CAME FROM ONE OF THE MANY OLD COOKBOOKS SHE HAD. I REMEMBER THINKING IT WAS SUCH A NICE CHANGE FROM MAYONNAISE-STYLE POTATO SALAD AND TASTED SO GOOD THAT I JUST HAD TO HAVE THE RECIPE. HOPE YOU LIKE IT AS MUCH AS I DO. ENJOY!"
>
> > Linda

wvu tailgate salad

Rick Wilson > *Morgantown, West Virginia*

Serves 12

INGREDIENTS

1 pound cheese tortellini
1 small green pepper, diced
1 small red pepper, diced
1 to 1 1/2 red onion, diced
1 (12 to 16-ounce) package fresh broccoli florets
1 (1-pound) bag matchstick carrots
1 pint grape tomatoes
1 (16-ounce) bottle red French dressing
1 (16-ounce) bottle zesty Italian dressing
1 small (2.62-ounce) **bottle Salad Supreme** (spice)

PREPARATION

Cook the tortellini as directed. Drain and cool completely. Combine the green and red peppers, onion, broccoli, carrots, and tomatoes. Add the vegetable mix to the tortellini. Add equal parts of French and Italian dressing to taste (approximately half a bottle of each). Add half bottle (more if desired) of Salad Supreme. Mix well and refrigerate. More dressing may be added before serving.

APPETIZERS

BREADS

BREAKFAST & BRUNCH

ENTRÉES

VEGETABLES & SIDE DISHES

SALADS

SOUPS

DESSERTS

wild rice salad

Maggie Goldsborough > *Columbia, Maryland*

Serves 4 to 6

INGREDIENTS FOR SALAD

2 (6-ounce) boxes wild rice
1/3 cup scallions, chopped
1 pint cherry tomatoes, halved

INGREDIENTS FOR DRESSING

1 cup olive oil
2 tablespoons lemon juice
2 tablespoons wine vinegar
1 teaspoon dry mustard
1 teaspoon basil
2 cloves garlic, minced
1 teaspoon salt
1/2 teaspoon pepper
1/4 to 1/3 cup chopped parsley for garnish

PREPARATION

Prepare the wild rice according to the directions on the package. When the rice is cooked and cooled, combine the scallions and tomatoes with the rice. In a jar, combine the oil, lemon juice, vinegar, mustard, basil, garlic, salt, and pepper. Cover the jar; shake and chill. Before serving, pour the dressing over the rice mixture and toss to combine. Add parsley and serve.

soups

APPETIZERS

BREADS

BREAKFAST &
BRUNCH

ENTREES

VEGETABLES &
SIDE DISHES

SALADS

SOUPS

DESSERTS

anna lou's gumbo

Rick Nafzinger > *Stockton, California*

Serves 4 to 6

INGREDIENTS

1 whole chicken or pheasant, boiled, meat cut into bite-sized pieces
8 cups water
1 cup corn or peanut oil
1 cup all-purpose flour
1 stalk celery, finely chopped
2 medium yellow onions, finely chopped
1 bunch parsley, finely chopped
8 cloves garlic, mashed and chopped
1 large bell pepper, chopped
1 bay leaf
1/2 teaspoon cayenne pepper
1 teaspoon white or black pepper
1 pound andouille or smoked sausage, browned and sliced into bite-sized pieces
2 tablespoons gumbo filé powder

PREPARATION

In a large pot, boil the chicken or pheasant in 8 cups water. Cook for about an hour. Remove the meat and de-bone it. Reserve the stock. In a cast-iron skillet, heat the oil over medium heat. Slowly add the flour. Cook and stir constantly until the oil and flour form a chocolate-colored roux. Transfer the roux to a large stockpot and add the celery, onions, parsley, garlic, pepper, and seasonings. Cook until the vegetables are tender. Add the stock slowly, stirring until well blended. Cover and simmer for about 45 minutes. Add the meat. Cover and cook over low heat for at least 1 hour, stirring occasionally. Stir in the gumbo filé until you can taste it. Serve immediately.

"MY MOTHER WAS BORN AND RAISED IN BEAUREGARD PARISH IN CENTRAL LOUISIANA, BUT MOVED TO COLORADO AFTER MARRYING MY DAD. SHE NEVER TIRED OF SHARING HER GOOD COOKING WITH FRIENDS AND NEIGHBORS. THIS GUMBO HAD MANY VARIATIONS, AND EVERY ONE DREW RAVE REVIEWS FROM ALL WHO TRIED IT. THIS RECIPE IS AS MUCH A PART OF ME AS THE PRAIRIE I GREW UP ON IN EASTERN COLORADO."

> Rick

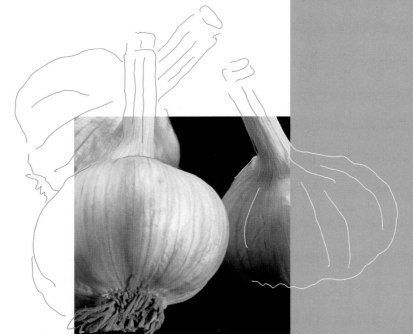

beef carbonade soup

Ron Thaden > *Grand Forks, North Dakota*

Serves 6 to 8

INGREDIENTS

2 pounds stew beef
1/4 cup all-purpose flour
1 tablespoon vegetable oil
5 cups beef broth
4 cups spicy Bloody Mary mix
12 ounces dark beer
1 cup onion, chopped
1 cup celery, sliced
2 teaspoons chili powder
1 teaspoon dried basil
2 cloves garlic, sliced
2 bay leaves
1 cup carrots, sliced
1 cup frozen green beans, thawed
1 cup mushrooms, sliced
1 (10-ounce) **package dry dumpling noodles**

PREPARATION

Trim excess fat from the meat. Shake the meat in a plastic bag with the flour until all pieces are coated. In 5-quart Dutch oven (or large kettle), heat the oil over medium heat and brown the meat. Stir in the broth, Bloody Mary mix, beer, onion, celery, chili powder, basil, garlic, and bay leaves. Bring to a boil. Reduce heat, cover, and simmer for 2 to 3 hours until the meat is tender. Stir in the carrots. Bring to a boil. Reduce heat, simmer for 15 minutes or until carrots are crisp-tender. Add the green beans, mushrooms, and noodles. Cover and simmer an additional 10 minutes until vegetables are tender.

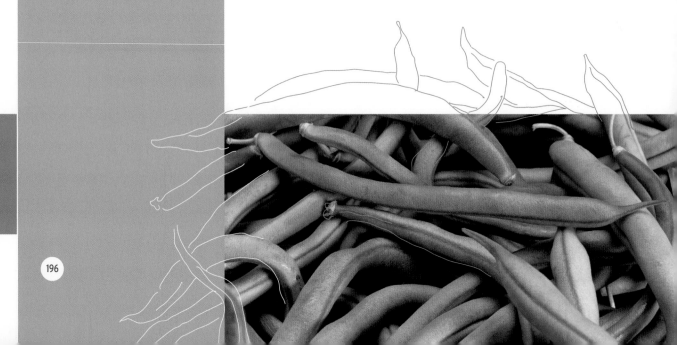

beer cheese soup

Linda Gooden > *Minneapolis, Minnesota*

Serves 6 to 8

INGREDIENTS

1/2 cup butter
1 cup all-purpose flour
6 (14.75-ounce) cans chicken broth
1 1/2 cups half and half
24 ounces Cheez Whiz
12 ounces beer
1 tablespoon Worcestershire sauce
1/2 teaspoon yellow food coloring
1 tablespoon chicken bouillon grains
1/4 cup dehydrated chives
Popcorn for garnish

PREPARATION

Set the Cheez Whiz jars in hot water to soften the contents. In a heavy 5-quart pot, melt the butter and mix with the flour over very low heat until blended, about 5 minutes, stirring constantly. Add the chicken broth and half and half. Stir until smooth and thick. Add the Cheez Whiz and stir on very low heat until all the cheese is melted and the soup is smooth. Add the beer and Worcestershire sauce. Stir in the coloring, bouillon, and chives. Simmer 15 minutes. Sprinkle with popcorn and serve.

> "THIS IS A CHRISTMAS TRADITION ON MY HUSBAND'S SIDE OF THE FAMILY. I EVEN INHERITED THE BOWLS TO USE. THEY DON'T GET HOT, SO YOU CAN STAND AND HOLD YOUR BOWL AND EAT. GREAT FOR OPEN HOUSES WHERE PEOPLE DON'T ALWAYS SIT DOWN."
>
> > Linda

broccoli cheese soup

Diane Wheeler > *Virginia Beach, Virginia*

Serves 6

INGREDIENTS

2 tablespoons butter
1/2 onion, diced
4 medium potatoes, diced
1 (10-ounce) package frozen broccoli, thawed
1 1/2 cups vegetable broth
2 cups milk
1 pound Mexican Mild Velveeta cheese, cubed
1 (10.75-ounce) can cream of celery soup

PREPARATION

In a saucepan, heat the butter; sauté the onion and potatoes. Add the broccoli and broth. Cook until the broccoli is tender. Mix in the milk, cheese, and soup. Simmer until the cheese melts.

> "THIS ONE IS A HIT WITH MY FAMILY!"
>
> > Diane

APPETIZERS

BREADS

BREAKFAST & BRUNCH

ENTREES

VEGETABLES & SIDE DISHES

SALADS

SOUPS

DESSERTS

butternut squash soup

Jeff Bland > *Roanoke, Virginia*

Serves 4

INGREDIENTS

4 tablespoons butter
1 small yellow onion, diced
1 medium butternut squash, roasted and cooled
1/4 cup all-purpose flour
3 cups chicken broth
1 cup heavy cream
Pinch cayenne pepper
1 tablespoon honey
Parsley or chives, chopped, sour cream or crème fraîche, candied pecans
for garnish

PREPARATION

Preheat the oven to 350°F. Cut the squash in halves, place cut sides down on a pan or cookie sheet, and roast for 45 minutes to 1 hour until tender. Let the squash cool, then scoop out the flesh with an ice cream scoop. Set aside. In a large pot, sauté the onion in the butter for 10 minutes until golden brown. Season with salt and pepper. Add the roasted squash and the flour and stir until well blended. Mix in the broth, bring to a boil, reduce to a simmer, and cook for 20 minutes. Puree the mixture with an immersion blender or a standard blender until smooth. Add the cream, cayenne pepper to taste, and honey and simmer until the desired consistency has been reached. Taste and adjust seasoning if necessary. Garnish with chopped parsley or chives, sour cream or crème fraîche, or candied pecans.

cabbage stew italiano

Stanley Bristol > *Centennial, Colorado*

Serves 4

INGREDIENTS

1 medium cabbage, cut into chunks
2 (14.5-ounce) large cans of whole tomatoes
1 pound Italian sausage, ground or links
5 russet potatoes, peeled and cut into chunks

PREPARATION

Steam the cabbage. In a frying pan, cook the sausage and drain the fat. Boil the potatoes until almost tender. Mix the cabbage, tomatoes, sausage, and potatoes in a large cooking pot. Simmer for 25 to 30 minutes and taste. Add garlic powder, black pepper, or other seasonings as desired.

chilled plum
and berry soup

Dometta Blacka > *Cleveland, Ohio*

Serves 6 to 8

INGREDIENTS

6 ripe plums, halved and pits removed
1/4 cup sugar
8 ounces blackberries, divided
6 ounces red raspberries, divided
3/4 cup Sauternes (sweet dessert wine)
2 cups water
1/4 teaspoon salt
6 small brioches (or one large loaf brioche)
1 cup mascarpone cheese
1 ounce heavy cream

PREPARATION

Set a large skillet over medium heat. Add 5 plums, cut side down; sear until the plums start to blister, 8 to 10 minutes. Stir the plums skin side down with a wooden spoon. Sprinkle the plums with sugar and add 1/3 of the blackberries and 1/3 of the raspberries. Cook until the fruit begins to release juice, about 10 minutes.

Add the wine, water, and salt. Stir well. Bring the mixture to a boil, reduce heat to medium low, and let simmer until the fruit begins to break down and the liquid is very flavorful, 10 to 12 minutes. Remove from heat. Puree the mixture through a food mill set over a bowl and discard the remaining solids. Slice the remaining plum into thin slivers and add it to the soup. Add another third of the blackberries and another third of the raspberries to the soup. Refrigerate the soup until chilled.

Preheat oven to 350°F. Slice small brioche in half (if using a loaf, slice into 1/2-inch-thick slices). Place the brioche on a baking sheet and toast 10 to 12 minutes, until golden. Remove from the oven and set aside. Combine the mascarpone and heavy cream in a small mixing bowl. Fold together by hand. Spoon the mixture over the toasted brioche. Arrange the remaining third of the berries over the mascarpone, and place two slices of toast in each bowl. Pour the chilled soup into bowls and serve.

APPETIZERS
BREADS
BREAKFAST & BRUNCH
ENTREES
VEGETABLES & SIDE DISHES
SALADS
SOUPS
DESSERTS

corn and crab chowder

Bob and Pam Crawford > *Pahrump, Nevada*

Serves 4 to 6

INGREDIENTS

1 tablespoon vegetable oil or extra-virgin olive oil
2 tablespoons butter
2 all-purpose potatoes, diced
2 stalks celery, chopped
1 medium yellow onion, chopped
1 small red bell pepper, diced
1 bay leaf, fresh or dried
1 tablespoon Old Bay seasoning blend
3 tablespoons all-purpose flour
2 cups vegetable or chicken stock or broth
1 quart whole milk
3 cups corn kernels, scraped fresh from the cob, or frozen kernels
8 to 12 ounces lump crabmeat
4 small bread loaves hollowed into bowls (preferably sourdough)
Oyster crackers, hot cayenne pepper sauce, and scallions, sliced, for garnishes

PREPARATION

Heat a deep pot over moderate heat. Add the oil and butter. Add the potatoes, celery, onion, red bell pepper, and bay leaf. Season the vegetables with salt, pepper, and Old Bay seasoning. Sauté the vegetables for 5 minutes, then sprinkle in the flour. Cook a further 2 minutes, stirring constantly. Stir in the broth and combine, then stir in the milk and combine. Bring the soup to a boil. Add the corn and crabmeat and simmer for 5 minutes. Add salt and pepper to taste. Remove the bay leaf. Ladle the soup into bread bowls or soup bowls and top with oyster crackers, hot sauce, and sliced scallions as desired.

cream of carrot soup

Linda Gooden > *Minneapolis, Minnesota*

Serves 6

INGREDIENTS

2 tablespoons margarine or butter
3 cups carrots, diced
1/2 cup onions, chopped
3 1/2 cups water
5 teaspoons chicken bouillon granules
1 bay leaf
1 1/2 cups evaporated milk

PREPARATION

In a medium to large saucepan, melt the margarine over medium heat. Add the carrots and onions. Cook 5 minutes, stirring frequently. Add the water, bouillon, bay leaf, and salt and pepper to taste. Cover, reduce heat to low, and simmer 30 minutes, until carrots are soft. Remove the bay leaf. Place the soup in a blender container, reserving about 1/4 cup of the carrots and onions. Blend until smooth. Return the soup to the saucepan and add the reserved carrots and onions. Stir in the milk. Heat the soup, but do not boil.

creamy reuben soup

Karen James > *Grand Forks, North Dakota*

Serves 8 to 10

INGREDIENTS

2 tablespoons butter
1 medium onion, diced
3 tablespoons all-purpose flour
1 teaspoon white pepper
2 (32-ounce) cans chicken broth
1 (16-ounce) jar sauerkraut, drained well
1 pound deli-sliced corned beef, cut into bite-sized pieces
1 cup half and half
1 cup fresh parsley, chopped
Grated Swiss cheese and rye croutons for garnishes

PREPARATION

Heat the butter in a large saucepan over medium heat. Sauté the onion until soft. Add the flour and pepper and cook for 2 to 3 minutes, stirring. Stir in the chicken broth; add the sauerkraut and corned beef. Heat to boiling. Reduce heat, then stir in the half and half and parsley, but do not boil. Serve sprinkled with grated Swiss cheese and rye croutons.

APPETIZERS

BREADS

BREAKFAST & BRUNCH

ENTREES

VEGETABLES & SIDE DISHES

SALADS

SOUPS

DESSERTS

curried butternut squash soup

Cathy Wofford > *Fayetteville, Georgia*

Serves 6 to 8

INGREDIENTS

3 tablespoons extra-virgin olive oil or vegetable oil
1 cup onions, chopped
4 cloves garlic, minced
1 tablespoon curry powder
1 teaspoon ground cumin
Red (cayenne) pepper to taste
2 1/2 pounds butternut squash, peeled, seeded, halved, and sliced thin
3 cups chicken or vegetable broth
3 cups water
1 pound tart apples, peeled, cored, and chopped
2 cups whipping cream (optional)
Salt and fresh ground pepper

PREPARATION

In a large soup pot over medium heat, heat the oil. Add onion and sauté until golden brown. Add garlic, curry powder, cumin, and cayenne pepper. Cook, stirring constantly, for 30 seconds. Add the squash, broth, water, and apples. Bring to a boil; reduce heat and simmer, covered, 25 minutes or until the squash is tender. Remove from heat and cool 15 to 20 minutes. Puree the mixture in a food processor or blender and transfer back into the soup pot. Season with salt and pepper to taste. Add the cream and stir.

garden fresh tomato soup

Doug Ricketts > *Cleveland, Ohio*

Serves 6 to 8

INGREDIENTS

4 cups fresh tomatoes, chopped
1 onion, diced
4 whole cloves
2 cups chicken broth
2 tablespoons butter
2 tablespoons all-purpose flour
1 teaspoon salt
2 tablespoons white sugar

PREPARATION

In a stockpot, over medium heat, combine the tomatoes, onion, cloves, and chicken broth. Bring to a boil and boil gently for about 20 minutes to blend the flavors. Remove from heat and run the mixture through a food mill into a large bowl or pan. Discard anything left over in the food mill. In the now-empty stockpot, melt the butter over medium heat. Stir in the flour to make a roux, cooking and stirring until the roux is a medium brown. Gradually whisk in a bit of the tomato mixture, so that no lumps form, then stir in the rest. Season with sugar and salt to taste.

lynn's baked potato soup

Clare Whitlock > *Atlanta, Georgia*

Serves 12

INGREDIENTS

Pulp of 4 large baked potatoes
2/3 cup margarine or butter
2/3 cup all-purpose flour
6 cups milk
3/4 teaspoon salt
1/2 teaspoon pepper
6 green onions, chopped
1 pound bacon, cooked, drained, and crumbled
1 1/2 cups sharp cheddar cheese
1 cup (8 ounces) **sour cream**

PREPARATION

In a large pot, melt margarine and stir in flour until mixed. Add the milk, salt, and pepper and stir until blended. Add the potato pulp and stir until heated. Add half the onions, half the bacon, half the cheese, and all of the sour cream. Cook until blended and warm. Garnish with the remaining onions, bacon, and cheese.

"LYNN SWEET SHARED THIS RECIPE WITH ME ONE YEAR WHILE SPENDING THE WEEKEND IN THE NORTH GEORGIA MOUNTAINS. LYNN WAS A DEAR FRIEND OF MINE WHO LOST HER BATTLE WITH CANCER IN 2005. HER SWEET SPIRIT LIVES ON AS THIS RECIPE HAS BECOME A TRADITION TO SERVE ON CHRISTMAS EVE WITH SANDWICHES FOLLOWING THE CHRISTMAS EVE SERVICE AT OUR CHURCH."

> Clare

APPETIZERS

BREADS

BREAKFAST & BRUNCH

ENTREES

VEGETABLES & SIDE DISHES

SALADS

SOUPS

DESSERTS

hearty meatball spinach soup

Boneita Page > *Charlotte, North Carolina*

Serves 6 to 8

INGREDIENTS

1/2 pound lean ground beef
1 cup chopped onion, divided
3 cloves garlic, minced, divided
2 teaspoons dried oregano leaves, divided
20 saltine crackers, finely crushed
1 egg, lightly beaten
1 tablespoon vegetable oil
2 (14-ounce) cans reduced-sodium beef broth
1 (14 1/2-ounce) can stewed tomatoes
1 (10-ounce) package frozen chopped spinach, thawed, well drained

PREPARATION

Combine the beef, 1/4 cup of the onion, 1/3 of the garlic, and 1/2 teaspoon of the oregano in a large bowl. Add the crushed crackers and egg; mix well. Shape into 1-inch balls; set aside. In a Dutch oven or large saucepan, heat the oil. Cook the remaining 3/4 cup onion and remaining garlic in the hot oil on medium-high heat, stirring, 3 to 5 minutes, or until the onion is tender. Add beef broth, tomatoes with their liquid, spinach, and the remaining oregano; bring to a boil. Add the meatballs. Reduce the heat to low; cover. Simmer 20 to 25 minutes or until the meatballs are cooked through.

hot 'n' sour soup

Rod Chinery > *Woodinville, Washington*

Serves 12

INGREDIENTS

2 tablespoons sesame oil
1-inch slice fresh ginger, peeled and grated
1/2 tablespoon red chili paste
1 pint fresh shiitake mushrooms
1 small can bamboo shoots, drained and slivered
1/4 pound barbecued pork, diced
1/2 cup soy sauce
1/2 cup rice vinegar
1 teaspoon salt
1 teaspoon ground white pepper
1/2 teaspoon sugar
4 cups (2 quarts) chicken stock
1 square of firm tofu (preferably smoked), diced
3 tablespoons cornstarch
1/4 cup cold water
1 large egg, beaten
Green onions or cilantro, chopped, for garnish

PREPARATION

In a wok or large pot, heat the oil over medium-high heat. Add the ginger, chili paste, shiitakes, bamboo shoots, and pork. Cook down for 1 to 2 minutes. In a medium bowl, combine the soy sauce, vinegar, salt, pepper, and sugar, then pour it into the pot. Add the chicken stock. Bring the mixture to a boil and simmer for 10 minutes. Add the tofu and cook for 3 more minutes. Dissolve the cornstarch in water, then mix the combination into the soup and simmer until thickened.

Remove the soup from heat. Stir in one direction, and slowly pour in the beaten egg in a steady stream – it quickly cooks and feathers out into the soup. Garnish with cilantro or green onion.

APPETIZERS
BREADS
BREAKFAST & BRUNCH
ENTREES
VEGETABLES & SIDE DISHES
SALADS
SOUPS
DESSERTS

mac 'n' cheese soup

Christine Kakolewski > *Winter Haven, Florida*

Serves 8

INGREDIENTS

1 (14-ounce) package deluxe macaroni and cheese dinner mix
9 cups of water, divided
1 cup fresh broccoli florets
2 tablespoons onion, finely chopped
1 (10 3/4-ounce) can condensed cheddar cheese soup, undiluted
2 1/2 cups milk
1 cup fully cooked ham, chopped

PREPARATION

In a large saucepan, bring 8 cups of water to a boil. Add macaroni; cook for 8 to 10 minutes or until tender. Meanwhile, in another large saucepan, bring the remaining 1 cup of water to a boil. Add the broccoli and onion; cook for 3 minutes. Stir in the soup, milk, ham, and contents of the cheese sauce packet; heat through. Drain the macaroni, add it to the soup mixture, and stir.

microwave french onion soup

Susan Yusko > *Streator, Illinois*

Serves 4 to 5

INGREDIENTS

2 medium onions, thinly sliced
1/4 cup butter
2 (10-ounce) cans beef consommé
2 soup cans (20 ounces) water
1 loaf French bread, sliced
1 package sliced mozzarella cheese
1 tablespoon Worcestershire sauce
1 teaspoon celery salt
1/2 teaspoon black pepper

PREPARATION

Place onion and butter in a 2 1/2-quart microwaveable bowl. Microwave 6 to 8 minutes on high. Add the beef consommé and water and microwave for an additional 10 to 13 minutes. Toast French bread slices on both sides. Pour onion soup into individual bowls. Top each bowl of soup with one slice of toast topped with a cheese slice. Microwave for approximately 3 minutes on high, or until the cheese melts.

maryland crab and corn chowder

Charles Aboyoun > *Columbia, Maryland*

Serves 4

INGREDIENTS

2 tablespoons olive oil
2 tablespoons butter
2 potatoes, chopped
1 medium onion, chopped
1 red pepper, chopped
12 baby Bella mushrooms, chopped
1 teaspoon thyme
2 tablespoons Old Bay seasoning
3 tablespoons all-purpose flour
1 (8-ounce) can chicken broth
4 cups (1 quart) 1 percent milk
1/4 teaspoon Worcestershire sauce
2 cups corn kernels
8 ounces lump crabmeat
Chives, chopped, for garnish
Salt and fresh ground pepper

PREPARATION

In a Dutch oven or large pot, heat the olive oil and butter over moderate heat. Add the potatoes, onion, red pepper, mushrooms, thyme, and Old Bay seasoning, along with salt and pepper to taste. Sauté 5 minutes. Add the flour and stir for 2 minutes. Add the chicken broth, milk, and Worcestershire sauce and bring to a boil. Add the corn and crabmeat and simmer for 5 minutes. Ladle into bowls and garnish with chopped chives.

"THIS WAS MY WIFE'S COLD WINTER DAY CREATION IN OUR NEW HOUSE. AS I SPENT THE DAY PAINTING OUR LIVING ROOM AND USING OUR FIREPLACE FOR THE FIRST TIME, SHE WHIPPED THIS UP FOR US TO ENJOY."

> Charles

APPETIZERS

BREADS

BREAKFAST & BRUNCH

ENTREES

VEGETABLES & SIDE DISHES

SALADS

SOUPS

DESSERTS

really easy meatball soup

Debra Migliorisi > *Chicago, Illinois*

Serves 4 to 6

> "I GREW UP WITH MY GRANDPARENTS WHO IMMIGRATED FROM ITALY. MY MOTHER WAS A FIRST-GENERATION AMERICAN WHO WAS ALWAYS TRYING TO BECOME MORE AMERICAN. SHE WOULD CALL THIS HER AMERICAN SOUP SINCE SHE USED A PACKAGED SOUP MIX. SHE COULD NEVER COOK ANY DISH THAT DID NOT INCLUDE SOME FORM OF TOMATO."
>
> > Debra

INGREDIENTS

1 pound ground round beef
2 eggs
1/2 cup Italian seasoned bread crumbs
1/4 cup parmesan cheese, grated
1 package dry onion soup mix
4 cups water
1 (8-ounce) **can tomato sauce**
1 stalk celery, chopped
1 carrot, sliced
2 cloves garlic, chopped
1/4 cup fresh parsley, chopped
1/2 cup **small pasta** (such as orzo, elbow, or bow ties)

PREPARATION

Put beef, eggs, bread crumbs, and parmesan cheese in a bowl. Mix well and form into meatballs about the size of a golf ball. In a large saucepan, combine the onion soup mix, water, and tomato sauce, and bring to a simmer. When the soup is simmering, add the meatballs, celery, carrot, and garlic. Simmer for about 30 minutes until the meatballs are cooked.

At the same time, boil water in a large pot, add the pasta, and cook for approximately 10 to 15 minutes. Drain the pasta and add it to the soup, along with the parsley. Heat to serving temperature.

rosa's potato soup

Mark Wenzel > *Plymouth, Minnesota*

Serves 8

INGREDIENTS

1/4 cup butter
1 large onion, diced
6 to 8 large potatoes, diced
16 ounces mushrooms, sliced
2 (8-ounce) packages frozen spinach, thawed
1 sprig fresh thyme
8 cups chicken broth
2 cups heavy cream
1/4 teaspoon nutmeg

PREPARATION

In a soup pot, melt the butter over medium heat. Add the onions and potatoes. When the onions are translucent, add the mushrooms and spinach. Gently toss the vegetables. Add the thyme and broth. Bring to a rapid boil. Lower the heat and simmer until the potatoes are fully cooked. Season with salt and pepper to taste, then add heavy cream and nutmeg. Heat but do not boil.

taco soup

Tina Parker > *Charlotte, Carolina*

Serves 6 to 8

INGREDIENTS

2 pounds hamburger
1 bunch celery, chopped
1 large onion, chopped
2 (15.25-ounce) cans whole corn
2 (15.5-ounce) cans kidney beans
2 (15-ounce) cans pinto beans
1 (15-ounce) can black beans
2 cans beef broth
2 (15-ounce) cans diced tomatoes
1 package taco seasoning
Jalapeño pepper (optional)
Shredded cheese and corn chips for garnish

PREPARATION

In a large pan, brown the hamburger along with the celery and onion and drain. Add the corn, beans, broth, tomatoes, taco seasoning, and jalapeño pepper. Simmer for 15 to 30 minutes. Garnish with shredded cheese and corn chips. To make a really eye-catching soup, use light and dark beans and white and yellow corn.

APPETIZERS

BREADS

BREAKFAST & BRUNCH

ENTREES

VEGETABLES & SIDE DISHES

SALADS

SOUPS

DESSERTS

satin chicken cream soup

Rob Wolfe > *Platte City, Missouri*

Serves 6 to 8

INGREDIENTS

1/2 cup (4 ounces) **salted butter**
1 cup onion, diced
1 cup carrot, finely diced
1 cup celery, finely diced
1/4 cup garlic, minced
2 1/2 pounds chicken meat, precooked, diced into 1/2-inch pieces
1 tablespoon salt
1 1/2 teaspoons white pepper
2 3/4 cups chicken broth
1 pound cream cheese
1 bay leaf
Stale pumpernickel bread cubes for garnish

PREPARATION

In a 2-gallon pot, melt the butter over medium heat. When melted, add the onion, carrots, celery, garlic, and bay leaf, and lower the heat. Stir the vegetables until the onions are translucent and the carrots have slightly softened. Add the chicken, salt, and pepper. Raise the heat and slowly add the chicken broth. Whisk over heat until simmering. While waiting for simmer, place the cream cheese in a microwave dish and soften it. (The cream cheese should be warm, but not melted, before it is added to the broth.) When the broth reaches a simmer, lower the heat and whisk in the cream cheese 1/4 pound at a time until fully incorporated. Add the bay leaf. Bring the soup up to medium high (145°F) and immediately place it in a double boiler or other form of indirect heat to keep it from separating. Serve garnished with pumpernickel cubes.

smoked turkey leg and rice soup

Linda Kull > *Cabot, Arkansas*

Serves 2 to 4

INGREDIENTS FOR BROTH

2 quarts water
2 smoked turkey legs
3 stalks celery, coarsely chopped
1 large onion, chopped
1 carrot, sliced
1 teaspoon kosher salt
1/2 to 1 teaspoon freshly ground black pepper

INGREDIENTS FOR SOUP

5 slices of smoked bacon, chopped
1 large onion, chopped
2 large stalks celery, chopped
3 or 4 andouille sausages, sliced thinly
1 cup of white or brown rice, uncooked
4 (14.75-ounce) **cans chicken broth** (as needed)
1 teaspoon kosher salt
1 teaspoon freshly ground black pepper
1 teaspoon Creole seasoning
1 cup white wine

PREPARATION FOR BROTH

In a large pot, bring the water to a boil, add the turkey legs, celery, onion, carrot, salt, and pepper. Simmer for at least 1-1/2 hours, covered. Strain the broth into a large bowl and set aside. Reserve the turkey meat; dispose of the bones and vegetables.

PREPARATION FOR SOUP

In a soup pot, sauté the bacon over medium heat until crisp. Add the onion and celery and cook until softened. Strain off the bacon fat and add the turkey meat, sausage, rice, salt, pepper, Creole seasoning, wine, and previously prepared turkey broth. (If there is not enough broth, add 1 or 2 cans of chicken broth, as the rice will absorb the liquid — the soup should be thick, almost like a gumbo.) Bring the soup to a boil, cover, and reduce to low heat. Simmer for 2 hours, checking regularly to be sure there is enough broth, and add chicken broth as needed.

> " WE ARRIVED HOME EXHAUSTED FROM A TRIP WITH NOTHING IN THE FRIDGE BUT SOME SMOKED TURKEY LEGS. MY HUSBAND DECIDED THAT RATHER THAN GO TO THE STORE, HE'D INVENT A SOUP. HE HAD NO RECIPE TO FOLLOW AND SIMPLY ADDED INGREDIENTS AS HE WENT ALONG. IT TURNED OUT TO BE DELICIOUS, AND WITH SOME PIECES OF FRENCH BREAD TAKEN OUT OF THE FREEZER, IT WAS A PERFECT DINNER. THE SOUP ALSO CREATES A WONDERFUL AROMA. WE SPENT THE AFTERNOON WITH THAT AROMA KEEPING US IN HIGH ANTICIPATION OF DINNER! "
>
> > Linda

APPETIZERS

BREADS

BREAKFAST & BRUNCH

ENTREES

VEGETABLES & SIDE DISHES

SALADS

SOUPS

DESSERTS

southwest chicken soup

Cheryl Humphreys > *Prospect, Kentucky*

Serves 4 to 6

INGREDIENTS

4 tablespoons butter
2 teaspoon olive oil
1 small red pepper, diced
1 small to medium onion, chopped
2 carrots, sliced
1 (48-ounce) can great northern beans, with liquid
1 (16-ounce) jar salsa
1 cup pepper jack cheese, grated
1 (14-ounce) can mixed greens
6 cups reduced-sodium chicken broth
6 cups cooked chicken, shredded
Fresh parsley, chopped, for garnish
Salt and fresh ground pepper

PREPARATION

In a large soup pot, melt the butter and olive oil. When sizzling, add the red pepper, onion, and carrots. Sauté until softened, 6 to 8 minutes. Add the beans, salsa, grated cheese, greens, broth, and chicken. Bring to a boil. Reduce heat and cook for 20 to 30 minutes. Adjust the seasonings with salt and pepper if needed. Garnish with chopped parsley.

tomato soup

Michelle Dry > *Austin, Texas*

Serves 4 to 6

INGREDIENTS

12 fresh tomatoes, cored and quartered
6 onions, cut in half
3 cloves garlic, chopped
1 tablespoon olive oil to coat
1 quart milk, cream, or half and half

PREPARATION

Preheat the oven to 350°F. Place the tomatoes and onions in a shallow baking dish. Sprinkle with garlic and a little olive oil. Bake for 45 minutes until soft. Remove from oven and blend in food processor until smooth. Transfer to a large cooking pot and add the milk, cream, or half and half (depending on how rich you would like your soup). Season with salt and pepper to taste. Heat slowly until hot, but do not boil.

"WHEN I WAS A TERRITORY MANAGER, I WOULD WATCH THE CHEF AT ONE OF MY CUSTOMER'S RESTAURANTS MAKE WONDERFUL SOUPS. HE WOULD LET ME TASTE IT AS WE WERE DOING THE ORDER. HE GAVE ME THE LIST OF INGREDIENTS FOR THIS SOUP, AND I WENT HOME AND MADE IT. IT IS SO GOOD, AND THE AMOUNTS DO NOT HAVE TO BE EXACT DEPENDING ON AVAILABILITY OF THE INGREDIENTS."

> Michelle

SOUPS

tortellini in brodo

Lori Goodbody > *Salisbury, Maryland*

Serves 4 to 6

INGREDIENTS

1 tablespoon olive oil
1 pound meat-filled tortellini pasta (chicken or beef)
2 stalks celery with leaves, chopped
2 carrots, chopped
1 small onion, chopped
2 links Italian sausage, skin removed, broken into small pieces
4 cups water
1 cup beef or chicken stock
1/4 cup parmesan cheese, grated, and fresh parsley, chopped, for garnishes

PREPARATION

Heat olive oil in large stock pan. Sauté celery, carrots, and onions in olive oil for approximately 5 minutes. Add the sausage and brown it. Add the water and stock, and bring to a low boil. Add the tortellini and reduce heat to simmer until tortellini is cooked. Serve topped with parsley and parmesan cheese.

" WE USED TO CALL THIS 'ITALIAN-STYLE WONTON SOUP.' THIS IS A VERY QUICK, EASY, AND DELICIOUS SOUP THAT IS TYPICALLY SERVED AT THE HOLIDAY SEASON BUT CAN BE ENJOYED ANY TIME OF YEAR. "

> Lori

tomato veggie soup

Marla Kitzan > *Bismarck, North Dakota*

Serves 8

INGREDIENTS

1 pound ground beef
4 cups water
1 package onion soup mix
2 (15-ounce) cans stewed tomatoes
1 small potato, chopped
2 (8-ounce) cans tomato sauce
Chili powder
2 carrots, chopped
1 green pepper, chopped
1 medium onion, chopped
1/2 head cabbage, chopped
4 ounces spaghetti

PREPARATION

Brown the hamburger in a Dutch oven over medium heat and drain. Add the water, soup mix, tomatoes, potato, tomato sauce, chili powder to taste, carrots, green pepper, onion, and cabbage. Cook until the vegetables are soft. Add the spaghetti about 15 minutes before serving, and boil until the spaghetti is cooked.

APPETIZERS

BREADS

BREAKFAST & BRUNCH

ENTREES

VEGETABLES & SIDE DISHES

SALADS

SOUPS

DESSERTS

tummy warming vegetable soup

Kristen Forsman > *Mantua, New Jersey*

Serves 12 to 14

INGREDIENTS

1 to 2 pounds beef, cut into small cubes
1 tablespoon olive oil
2 tablespoons beef base or 10 beef bouillon cubes
8 cups (2 quarts) water
1 small cabbage, chopped
1 large onion, chopped
2 (1-pound) bags mixed frozen vegetables
4 large potatoes cut into small pieces
1 (20-ounce) can crushed tomatoes
2 tablespoons dry or fresh parsley
Salt and fresh ground pepper

PREPARATION

In a large stock pot, heat the olive oil over medium heat and braise the beef cubes. Add the beef base or bouillon cubes to taste. Add the water, cabbage, onion, mixed vegetables, potatoes, tomatoes, and parsley; add salt and pepper to taste. Bring to a boil. Simmer, covered, for 45 minutes.

wild rice soup

Linda Sharp > *Greenville, South Carolina*

Serves 4

INGREDIENTS

1/2 cup wild rice
3 1/2 cups water, divided
2 tablespoons butter
1 medium onion, minced
4 cups (1 quart) milk
2 (10.75-ounce) cans cream of potato soup
1 pound Velveeta cheese, cubed
2 chicken breasts, cooked and diced
10 strips bacon, cooked and crumbled

PREPARATION

Wash the wild rice and add to 1-1/2 cups boiling water in a heavy saucepan. Return to boil; stir. Cover, reduce heat, and simmer 30 to 45 minutes or until kernels pop open. Uncover, fluff with a fork, and simmer 5 more minutes. In a separate pan, sauté the onion in butter until tender. Stir in the milk, potato soup, and remaining 2 cups water. Increase heat to medium and stir occasionally. When the mixture is hot, add the cheese. When the cheese is melted, add the cooked wild rice, chicken, and bacon.

APPETIZERS
BREADS
BREAKFAST & BRUNCH
ENTREES
VEGETABLES & SIDE DISHES
SALADS
SOUPS
DESSERTS

winter vegetable soup

Linda Sharp > *Greenville, South Carolina*

Yields 10 servings

INGREDIENTS

3 tablespoons butter
1 medium head green cabbage (about 2 pounds), cut into bite-sized pieces
4 medium carrots, diced
2 large celery stalks, diced
1 medium leek, diced
1 tablespoon all-purpose flour
2 1/2 teaspoons salt
1/2 teaspoon pepper
1 (13 3/4 to 14 1/2-ounce) can chicken broth
1 (10-ounce) package frozen baby lima beans
6 cups water
1/2 cup regular long-grain rice
1 (10-ounce) package frozen chopped spinach
1/2 cup heavy cream

PREPARATION

In a 5-quart Dutch oven over medium-high heat, melt the butter. Sauté the cabbage, carrots, celery, and leek about 15 minutes until lightly browned, stirring occasionally. Stir in the flour, salt, and pepper and cook 1 minute, stirring frequently. Add the broth, lima beans, water, and rice to the vegetable mixture. Heat to boiling over high heat. Reduce the heat to low; cover, and simmer 35 minutes. Add the frozen spinach and gradually break up the spinach with a fork. Stir in the heavy cream and heat through, but do not boil.

desserts

andy's suspension cookies

Andy Travers > *Roanoke, Virginia*

Yields 5 dozen cookies

INGREDIENTS

1 cup granulated sugar
1 cup brown sugar
2 eggs, lightly beaten
1/2 cup (4 ounces/1 stick) butter, at room temperature
1 cup applesauce
1 teaspoon vanilla extract
1 cup all-purpose flour
1 teaspoon salt
1 teaspoon baking soda
1 cup flaked coconut
4 to 5 cups regular rolled oats
1 bag chocolate chips

PREPARATION

Preheat the oven to 375°F. Grease 2 cookie sheets. In a mixing bowl, combine the granulated sugar, the brown sugar, eggs, butter, applesauce, and vanilla. In another bowl, combine the flour, salt, and baking soda. Fold the flour mixture into the butter mixture. Add the coconut, oats, and chocolate chips.

Drop the dough by tablespoons onto the cookie sheets. Bake the cookies for about 8 minutes. I like to take them out when they do not look quite done. If your wife asks, "Are you sure they are done?" Then take them out and eat them. I often eat them for breakfast with coffee.

> **WHEN I WOULD GET INTO TROUBLE IN SCHOOL, I WOULD BREAK THE NEWS TO MY PARENTS OVER THESE COOKIES. THE TACTIC SEEMED TO MAKE THINGS GO DOWN A LITTLE EASIER FOR ALL. I HAVE SINCE PASSED THIS RECIPE ONTO MY KIDS, WHO NOW KNOW IT BY HEART.**
>
> > Andy

APPETIZERS

BREADS

BREAKFAST & BRUNCH

ENTRÉES

VEGETABLES & SIDE DISHES

SALADS

SOUPS

DESSERTS

annie's pumpkin bars

Kurt Nelson > *Champlin, Minnesota*

Yields 1 pan of bars

INGREDIENTS FOR BARS

2 cups pumpkin purée
2 cups all-purpose flour
1 2/3 cups sugar
1 cup vegetable oil
4 eggs
2 teaspoons ground cinnamon
2 teaspoons baking powder
1 teaspoon baking soda

INGREDIENTS FOR FROSTING

3 to 4 cups confectioners' sugar
4 ounces cream cheese, at room temperature
1/2 cup (4 ounces/1 stick) salted butter, at room temperature
1 tablespoon heavy cream
1 teaspoon vanilla extract

PREPARATION FOR BARS

Preheat the oven to 350°F. Grease a 10 by 15-inch baking pan. In a large mixing bowl, stir together the pumpkin purée, flour, sugar, oil, eggs, cinnamon, baking powder, and baking soda, and mix until smooth. Spoon into the pan. Bake for 20 minutes, or until the top is firm. Set aside to cool.

PREPARATION FOR FROSTING

Meanwhile, in a large mixing bowl, combine the sugar, cream cheese, butter, cream, and vanilla, and mix until well combined with a sturdy wooden spoon. Frost the cooled bars.

apple bars

Amy Pittman > *Inver Grove Heights, Minnesota*

Yields 24 bars

INGREDIENTS

2 cups all-purpose flour
3/4 cup shortening
1/2 cup regular rolled oats
1 teaspoon salt
1 cup firmly packed brown sugar
1 cup water
1 cup granulated sugar
3 tablespoon cornstarch
1 teaspoon vanilla extract
2 1/2 cups quartered and sliced apples

PREPARATION

Preheat the oven to 350°F. Grease a 9 by 13-inch baking pan. In a large mixing bowl, combine the flour, shortening, oats, salt, and brown sugar. Mix well with a sturdy spoon. Press three-quarters of the mixture into the prepared pan.

In a saucepan, heat the water and granulated sugar over medium heat, and bring to a boil. Dissolve 1 tablespoon of the cornstarch in 2 tablespoons cold water; mix this slurry into the sugar mixture, and stir in the remaining cornstarch. Stir until the mixture thickens, and remove from the heat. Add the vanilla and apples. Spread this evenly over the mixture in the pan, and top with the remaining oat-flour mixture.

Bake for 40 minutes, or until the top is evenly browned.

APPETIZERS

BREADS

BREAKFAST &
BRUNCH

ENTRÉES

VEGETABLES &
SIDE DISHES

SALADS

SOUPS

apple crumb pie

Jodie Bergey > *Mohrsville, Pennsylvania*

Yields 1 9-inch Pie

INGREDIENTS

6 apples (such as Cortland or Gala)
1 cup sugar
1 teaspoon ground cinnamon
1 (9-inch) piecrust, unbaked
3/4 cup all-purpose flour
1/3 cup salted butter

PREPARATION

Preheat the oven to 425°F. Peel apples, and cut into thin slices. Mix 1/2 cup of the sugar and the cinnamon together, and sprinkle over the apples; mix well. Put the apple mixture into the piecrust. Combine the remaining 1/2 cup sugar and the flour. Add the butter, and mix with a fork until crumbs form. Sprinkle the crumb mixture over the apples. The crust will be very full, but the filling will shrink as it bakes.

Bake for 10 minutes. Decrease the oven temperature to 350°F, and bake for 35 minutes longer.

betty's banana wonderful

Keith Ellis > *Fort Mill, South Carolina*

Serves 15 to 20

INGREDIENTS

2 large boxes instant vanilla pudding mix
4 cups whole milk
1 cup sour cream
1 large container Cool Whip
15 to 20 ripe bananas, peeled and sliced
2 boxes vanilla wafers

PREPARATION

In a large mixing bowl, combine the pudding mix, milk, and sour cream. Mix by hand with a sturdy wooden spoon, or mix with a portable electric mixer on the lowest setting for 2 minutes. Stir in the Cool Whip.

In a large serving bowl, alternate layers of the pudding mixture, bananas, and the vanilla wafers, ending with a layer of whole or crushed wafers.

apple walnut cake

Robert Thompson > *Vista, California*

Serves 20

INGREDIENTS

2 cups sugar
1 cup (8 ounces/2 sticks) salted butter, at room temperature
3 eggs
3 cups all-purpose flour, sifted
1 1/2 teaspoons baking soda
1 teaspoon ground cinnamon
Pinch of nutmeg
2 teaspoons vanilla extract
3 cups peeled and chopped Granny Smith apples
2 cups finely chopped walnuts

PREPARATION

Preheat the oven to 325°F. Grease and flour a 9 by 13-inch baking pan. In a large mixing bowl, cream the sugar and butter with a portable mixer until smooth. Add the eggs, one at a time, beating well after each addition.

In a separate bowl, combine the flour, baking soda, cinnamon, and nutmeg. Gradually add the dry ingredients into the butter mixture. Stir in the vanilla, and fold in the apples and walnuts. The batter will be thick. Pour into the prepared pan. Spread the batter out evenly in the pan with a wooden spoon or spatula.

Bake for 1 hour, 15 minutes. The cake is done if a toothpick inserted in the middle comes out clean. If not, continue cooking and check every 10 minutes until the toothpick comes out clean.

> "MY PATERNAL GRANDMA HAS HAD THIS RECIPE SINCE MY DAD WAS A LITTLE BOY. WHEN SHE PASSED AWAY, WE INHERITED HER RECIPE BOX. MY MOM MAKES THIS A COUPLE TIMES A YEAR, AND IT IS A REAL TREAT."
>
> > Robert

APPETIZERS

BREADS

BREAKFAST & BRUNCH

ENTRÉES

VEGETABLES & SIDE DISHES

SALADS

SOUPS

banana pudding

Vivian Pryor > *Salem, Missouri*

Serves 12 to 15

INGREDIENTS

2 large boxes instant vanilla pudding
6 ripe bananas, peeled and sliced
1 can "white" soda, such as Sprite or 7-Up
1 box vanilla wafers
1 small container Cool Whip
1 (14-ounce) can condensed milk
6 cups of milk

PREPARATION

Prepare the pudding as directed on the box. Put the banana slices in a large bowl, and cover with the white soda. This prevents the bananas from turning black. Crush almost all the vanilla wafers, setting aside 4 or 5 whole wafers for garnish. Once pudding has thickened, fold in the Cool Whip and condensed milk. Mix well. Drain the bananas and discard the liquid. Layer the bananas, crushed wafers, and pudding in a large bowl. Garnish with the whole wafers. Refrigerate until you are ready to serve.

banana split cake

Bonnie Hoffman > *Baltimore, Maryland*

Serves 12

INGREDIENTS

1 box yellow cake mix
1 large box vanilla instant pudding mix
1 (16-ounce) can crushed pineapple
3 bananas, peeled and sliced
1 large container Cool Whip
1 cup nuts, chopped
1 small jar cherries

PREPARATION

Grease and flour a 9 by 13-inch baking pan. Prepare and bake the yellow cake mix according to package directions. While the cake is cooling, make the pudding, and spread it on top of the cake. Spread the crushed pineapple on top of the pudding. Layer the banana slices on top of the pineapple. Spread Cool Whip on the bananas, sprinkle nuts on the Cool Whip, and garnish with the cherries.

best ever sugar cookies

Rita Otten > *Rockford, New Mexico*

Yields 6 dozen cookies

INGREDIENTS

1 cup granulated sugar
1 cup confectioners' sugar
1 cup vegetable oil
1 cup (8 ounces/2 sticks) butter, at room temperature
2 eggs
4 cups plus 4 tablespoons all-purpose flour
1 teaspoon cream of tartar
1 teaspoon baking soda
1 teaspoon vanilla extract
Pinch of salt
Colored sugar for sprinkling, if desired

PREPARATION

In a large mixing bowl, beat together the sugars, the oil, and the butter with a portable mixer until creamy. Beat in the eggs, flour, cream of tartar, baking soda, vanilla, and salt. Blend the mixture just until all the ingredients are incorporated. Wrap the dough in plastic wrap or wax paper. Chill it for several hours or overnight.

Preheat the oven 350°F. Pinch off pieces of the dough, and roll them into balls the size of walnuts. Place the balls 2 inches apart on the baking sheet. Press each down with the bottom of a glass. Sprinkle with the colored sugar, if using. Bake for 10 minutes.

> "THESE COOKIES ARE GREAT FOR CHRISTMAS OR AT ANY TIME AND ARE FUN TO DECORATE."
>
> > Rita

APPETIZERS

BREADS

BREAKFAST & BRUNCH

ENTRÉES

VEGETABLES & SIDE DISHES

SALADS

SOUPS

big mom's sweet potato pie

Philip Jones > *Columbia, Maryland*

Serves 10

INGREDIENTS

1 1/2 cups cooked mashed sweet potatoes, warm
1/2 cup (4 ounces/1 stick) butter, at room temperature
1 1/2 cups sugar
1 teaspoon ground cinnamon
1 teaspoon ground nutmeg
1/2 teaspoon salt
Pinch of allspice (optional)
1 teaspoon vanilla extract
2 eggs, well beaten
1 cup evaporated milk
1 (9-inch) pie shell, unbaked

PREPARATION

Preheat the oven to 350°F. In a large mixing bowl, put the mashed sweet potatoes, add the butter, and mix well. In a separate mixing bowl, combine the sugar, cinnamon, nutmeg, salt, and allspice, if using. Blend them together. Stir in the vanilla. Then add the sweet potatoes and the eggs, stirring well. Stir in the evaporated milk, a little at a time. (You don't want your mixture to be too soupy.) Pour the mixture into the pie shell. Bake for about 35 minutes, or until the center is firm.

Optional: Serve with a small scoop of whipped cream on top of each slice. Better yet, have a warm slice of pie and a small serving of French vanilla ice cream on the side. It's the perfect way to end a meal.

bittersweet molten chocolate cake with coffee ice cream

Debbie Anderson > *Raleigh, North Carolina*

For best results, use a dark baking chocolate with high cocoa butter content (about 30 percent).

Serves 8

INGREDIENTS

12 teaspoons plus 5 tablespoons sugar
8 ounces bittersweet or semisweet chocolate, chopped
3/4 cup (6 ounces/1 1/2 sticks) **unsalted butter**
3 eggs
3 egg yolks
1 tablespoon all-purpose flour
1 quart coffee ice cream

PREPARATION

Preheat the oven to 425°F. Generously butter eight 1/2-cup soufflé dishes or custard cups. Sprinkle the inside of each dish with 1 1/2 teaspoons sugar. Set aside.

In a heavy medium saucepan, melt the chocolate and butter over low heat, stirring until smooth. Remove from the heat, and set aside to cool. In a large bowl, using an electric hand mixer, beat the eggs, egg yolks, and the remaining 5 tablespoons sugar until thick and pale yellow, about 8 minutes. Fold one-third of the chocolate into the egg mixture, and then fold in the remaining chocolate. Fold in flour. Divide batter among prepared dishes. You can prepare this dessert a day ahead. Cover in plastic, and refrigerate. Before continuing, bring the dessert to room temperature.

Place soufflé dishes on baking sheet. Bake uncovered until edges are puffed and slightly cracked but center-1-inch of each moves slightly when dishes are shaken gently, about 13 minutes. Top each cake with scoop of coffee ice cream. Serve immediately.

Hint: Before serving, scoop the ice cream ahead of time into 8 balls onto a cookie sheet and freeze in freezer until ready to serve.

APPETIZERS

BREADS

BREAKFAST & BRUNCH

ENTRÉES

VEGETABLES & SIDE DISHES

SALADS

SOUPS

DESSERTS

black magic chocolate cake

Susan Bossung > *Greensburg, Pennsylvania*

Serves 20

INGREDIENTS

2 cups sugar
1 3/4 cups all-purpose flour
3/4 cups cocoa powder
2 teaspoons baking soda
1 teaspoon baking powder
2 eggs, lightly beaten
1 cup strong black coffee
1 cup buttermilk
1/2 cup vegetable oil
1 teaspoon vanilla extract

PREPARATION

Preheat the oven to 350°F. Grease and flour a 9 by 13-inch baking pan. In a large mixing bowl, combine the sugar, flour, cocoa powder, baking soda, and baking powder. Add the eggs, coffee, buttermilk, oil, and vanilla, mixing with a sturdy wooden spoon until smooth. (The batter will be thin, but don't worry.) Pour into the prepared pan. Bake for 35 to 40 minutes, or until a toothpick inserted in the center comes out clean.

Note: To curdle milk to resemble buttermilk, add 1 tablespoon vinegar to 1 cup milk.

caramel chocolate bars

Joni Fauchald > *Grand Rapids, Minnesota*

Yields 24 bars

INGREDIENTS

1 package caramels
1 (5.3-ounce) can evaporated milk
1 package German chocolate cake mix
3/4 cup (6 ounces/1 1/2 sticks) **salted butter, melted**
1 cup chopped nuts (optional)
1 cup chocolate chips

PREPARATION

In a microwaveable dish, melt the caramels with 1/3 cup evaporated milk (1/2 can), stirring often. Set aside. Preheat the oven to 350°F. Grease and flour a 9 by 13-inch baking pan. In a large bowl, combine the cake mix, the remaining 1/3 cup evaporated milk, and the butter. Using a sturdy wooden spoon, stir by hand until the mixture holds together. Press half of the dough into the prepared pan.

Bake for 6 to 8 minutes. Remove from the oven, sprinkle with the chocolate chips, and spread the caramel mixture over the top. Drop by spoonfuls the remainder of the dough over the caramel. Bake 15 to 18 minutes more. Cool in the refrigerator for 30 minutes or overnight. Yummy!

APPETIZERS

BREADS

BREAKFAST & BRUNCH

ENTRÉES

VEGETABLES & SIDE DISHES

SALADS

SOUPS

DESSERTS

cheesecake brownie bites

Jennifer Adams-Delph > *Rockwell, North Carolina*

Yields 24 medium muffins or 75 mini muffins

INGREDIENTS

1 (8-ounce) package cream cheese, at room temperature
1 egg
1/3 cup plus 1 cup sugar
Pinch of salt plus 1/2 teaspoon salt
6 ounces mini chocolate chips
1 cup chopped pecans
1 1/2 cups all-purpose flour
1/4 cup cocoa powder
1 teaspoon baking soda
1 cup water
1/3 cup vegetable oil
1 teaspoon vinegar
1 teaspoon vanilla extract

PREPARATION

Preheat the oven to 350°F. Line the muffin cups with paper liners. In a large mixing bowl, beat together the cream cheese, egg, 1/3 cup sugar, and pinch of salt, using a sturdy wooden spoon. Fold in the chocolate chips and the pecans. Set aside.

In a separate bowl, combine the flour, the remaining 1 cup sugar, cocoa powder, baking soda, and the remaining salt.

In a separate bowl, beat the water, oil, vinegar, and vanilla together, using a sturdy wooden spoon. Add the liquid to the dry ingredients, stirring well. (The mixture will be loose.) Fill each muffin cup one-third full with the batter. Top with a tablespoonful of the cream cheese mixture. Bake for 20 to 25 minutes. Do not let cheesecake mixture brown. Store in the refrigerator.

Note: These freeze well.

cheesecake

Barb Gotch > *Hudson, Ohio*

Serves 20

INGREDIENTS

2 cups graham cracker crumbs
1 cup plus 12 tablespoons sugar
1/2 cup (4 ounces/1 stick) salted butter, melted
3 (8-ounce) packages cream cheese, at room temperature
5 eggs
2 1/2 teaspoons vanilla extract
1 pint sour cream

PREPARATION

In a 9 by 13-inch baking pan, stir together the crumbs and 6 tablespoons of the sugar. Pour the melted butter over the crumb mixture and mix well. Using a fork, spread the mixture evenly over the bottom and up the sides of the pan. Set aside.

Preheat the oven to 325°F. In a large mixing bowl, beat the cream cheese until smooth with a hand-held electric mixer. Add the eggs, one at a time, beating well after each addition. Scrape the sides of the bowl as needed to blend the eggs and cream cheese. Slowly add 1 cup of the sugar. Add 1 1/2 teaspoons of the vanilla. Beat until the mixture is smooth and well blended. Pour the mixture over crust.

Bake for 40 minutes. Remove from the oven and cool for 10 minutes. Meanwhile, stir together the sour cream, the remaining 6 tablespoons of sugar, and the remaining 1 teaspoon vanilla. Pour the mixture over the cooled crust, and spread evenly with a spatula. Bake 10 minutes more, or until firm in the center. Remove from oven and cool. Refrigerate several hours or overnight before serving. Store leftovers in the refrigerator.

APPETIZERS

BREADS

BREAKFAST & BRUNCH

ENTRÉES

VEGETABLES & SIDE DISHES

SALADS

SOUPS

231

DESSERTS

cherry berry on a cloud

Mark Eggerding > *Rosemont, Illinois*

You should make the meringue crust the day before serving this dessert.

Serves 20

INGREDIENTS FOR MERINGUE

6 egg whites, at room temperature
1/2 teaspoon cream of tartar
1/4 teaspoon salt
1 3/4 cup sugar

INGREDIENTS FOR FILLING

8 ounces cream cheese, at room temperature
3/4 cup sugar
1 teaspoon vanilla extract
2 cups Cool Whip
2 cups marshmallows

INGREDIENTS FOR TOPPING

1 can cherry pie filling
2 cups fresh strawberries, hulled
1 tablespoon lemon juice

PREPARATION

Preheat the oven to 275°F. Grease a 9 by 13-inch baking pan. In the work bowl of an upright mixer and using the whisk attachment, beat the egg whites, cream of tartar, and salt until stiff peaks form. Gradually add the sugar, a few tablespoons at a time. Beat for 15 minutes. Spread the mixture into the prepared pan to form the crust. Bake for 1 hour. Turn off the oven, and leave the pan in the oven over-night. Sounds crazy but it makes a hard crust.

To make the filling, in a large mixing bowl, cream together the cream cheese, sugar, and vanilla with a portable mixer. Fold in the Cool Whip and marshmal-lows. Spread this mixture over the crust.

In a separate bowl, mix together the pie filling, strawberries, and lemon juice, and spread over the cream cheese layer. Refrigerate for 2 hours before serving.

cherry cheesecake

Debi Coonce > *Ypsilanti, Michigan*

Serves 8

INGREDIENTS

1 (8-ounce) **package cream cheese, softened**
1/2 cup sugar
2 cups Cool Whip, thawed
1 (9-inch) **graham cracker piecrust**
1 can cherry pie filling

PREPARATION

Beat together the cream cheese and sugar until creamy. Blend in Cool Whip. Pour into the unbaked graham cracker piecrust. Top with cherry pie filling. Chill for at least 3 hours before serving.

butterscotch cake

Dawn Stone > *Riverside, California*

Serves 20

INGREDIENTS

1 package butterscotch pudding
1 box spice cake mix
1 (12-ounce) **package butterscotch morsels**
1 cup chopped walnuts

PREPARATION

Preheat the oven to 325°F. Grease and flour a 9 by 13-inch baking pan. Cook the pudding according to package directions. In a large mixing bowl, mix the pudding with the cake mix, using a sturdy wooden spoon to stir until blended well. Pour the batter into the prepared pan. Sprinkle the butterscotch morsels on top of the batter, spread the chopped nuts over the top.

Bake for 30 to 35 minutes, or until a toothpick inserted in the center comes out clean.

> "MY MOM IS A WONDERFUL COOK AND BAKER. SHE ALWAYS ASKS WHAT DESSERT WE WOULD LIKE FOR OUR BIRTHDAY EACH YEAR. THIS CHEESECAKE HAS BEEN MY BIRTHDAY PICK FOR SO LONG THAT SHE DOESN'T EVEN ASK ANYMORE."
>
> > Debi

APPETIZERS

BREADS

BREAKFAST & BRUNCH

ENTRÉES

VEGETABLES & SIDE DISHES

SALADS

SOUPS

cherry confetti cake

Maureen McDade > *Cumberland, Rhode Island*

Serves 12

INGREDIENTS

3 cups all-purpose flour
2 teaspoons baking powder
1 teaspoon salt
1 cup shortening (may use 1/2 cup shortening and 1/2 cup butter)
1 (16 ounce) box confectioners' sugar
1 teaspoon vanilla extract
4 eggs
1 cup milk
1/2 cup chopped nuts
1 cup maraschino cherries, thinly sliced
Butter, cinnamon, and sugar for garnish

PREPARATION

Preheat the oven to 350°F. Grease and lightly flour a 10-inch tube pan. Sift together the flour, baking powder, and salt; set aside. In a large mixing bowl, cream the shortening using a portable mixer. Gradually add the confectioners' sugar, beating to cream well. Stir in the vanilla. Beat in the eggs one at a time, blending well after each addition. Beat the mixture for 1 minute.

To the creamed mixture, add alternately the dry ingredients and the milk, beginning and ending with the dry ingredients. Blend thoroughly after each addition, using the portable mixer on low speed. Fold in the chopped nuts and the maraschino cherries. Pour into the prepared pan. Cut gently through batter with a knife to break up large air bubbles.

Bake for 60 to 65 minutes, or until the center feels firm. While still warm, spread the top with the butter, and sprinkle with cinnamon and sugar. Let cool.

" THIS RECIPE IS ABOUT 40 YEARS OLD. MY MOTHER MADE THIS AROUND THE HOLIDAY TIME AS LONG AS I CAN REMEMBER. SHE ALWAYS LOVED TO BAKE AND COOK AND HAS A COLLECTION OF MORE THAN 500 COOKBOOKS.

AT 83 YEARS OLD, SHE IS STILL READING AND RE-READING HER COOKBOOKS, HIGHLIGHTING RECIPES SHE WOULD LIKE TO MAKE; HOWEVER, HER HEALTH HAS LIMITED HER ABILITY TO DO SO. SOMEHOW SHE STILL FINDS THE STRENGTH TO DO SOME LIMITED BAKING AT CHRISTMAS TIME WITH HER YOUNGEST GRANDCHILD, MELISSA, WHO AT AGE 11 LOVES TO WATCH THE COOKING SHOWS. "

> Maureen

chocolate applesauce cookies

Jennifer Rice > *Lenexa, Kansas*

Yields 5 dozen

INGREDIENTS

2 cups flour
1 cup sugar
1 teaspoon baking soda
1/2 teaspoon baking powder
1 teaspoon cinnamon
1/2 teaspoon nutmeg
1/4 teaspoon cloves
2 tablespoon cocoa powder
1/2 cup shortening
2 eggs
1 cup thick applesauce

PREPARATION

Preheat oven to 325ºF. Sift the dry ingredients together. Add the shortening and blend. Next add the eggs. Mix well. Last, stir in the applesauce and mix well. Drop by tablespoons on an ungreased cookie sheet and bake for 8 minutes.

cherry cake

Joanne Adams > *Mesa, Arizona*

Serves 20

INGREDIENTS

1 package Devils Food cake mix
2 eggs
1 (21-ounce) can cherry pie filling
3/4 cup finely chopped pecans
3/4 cup chocolate chips
1/2 cup firmly packed brown sugar

PREPARATION

Preheat oven to 350ºF. Grease and flour a 9 by 13-inch baking pan. In a large mixing bowl, beat together the cake mix, eggs, and pie filling with a portable mixer on low speed. Pour the batter into the prepared pan. Sprinkle the top with the nuts, chocolate chips, and brown sugar. Bake for about 35 minutes, or until the center feels firm.

> "I AM PART OF THE NATIONAL SIS GROUP AT THE SHARED SERVICE CENTER IN PHOENIX. I ENJOY BAKING FOR MY TEAM AND TRYING OUT NEW RECIPES ON THEM. HOPE YOU ENJOY THIS AS MUCH AS THEY DID!"
>
> > Joanne

APPETIZERS

BREADS

BREAKFAST & BRUNCH

ENTRÉES

VEGETABLES & SIDE DISHES

SALADS

SOUPS

DESSERTS

chocolate chip pie

Robert Wright > *Lake City, Tennessee*

Serves 8

INGREDIENTS

2 eggs
1/2 cup granulated sugar
1/2 cup firmly packed brown sugar
1 teaspoon vanilla extract
1 cup butter, at room temperature
1/2 cup flour
1 cup semisweet chocolate chips
1 cup chopped walnuts
1 (9-inch) piecrust, unbaked

PREPARATION

Preheat oven to 325°F. In a large mixing bowl, beat the eggs with a portable mixer until frothy; add the granulated and brown sugars, and vanilla.

In a small saucepan, melt the butter, and stir it into the sugar mixture. Stir in the flour with a sturdy wooden spoon. Stir in the chocolate chips and nuts. Pour the mixture into the crust. Bake 1 hour, or until set.

cookie dough truffles

Melissa Husband > *Greenville, South Carolina*

Yields 5 1/2 dozen

INGREDIENTS

1/2 cup (4 ounces/1 stick) butter, at room temperature
3/4 cup firmly packed brown sugar
2 cups all-purpose flour
1 (14-ounce) can sweetened condensed milk
1 teaspoon vanilla extract
1/2 cup miniature semisweet chocolate chips
1 1/2 pounds (24 ounces) semisweet chocolate candy coating

PREPARATION

In a large mixing bowl, cream the butter and brown sugar with a portable mixer until light and fluffy. Add the flour, milk, and vanilla, and mix well. Stir in chocolate chips with a sturdy wooden spoon. Shape the dough into balls, and place them on wax paper. Refrigerate the balls for 1 to 2 hours, or until firm. Melt candy coating, and dip the balls one at a time into it. Store in the refrigerator.

chocolate cream pie

Glen Dusina > *Lexington, North Carolina*

Serves 16

INGREDIENTS

2 (9-inch) pie shells, unbaked
2 eggs
2 cups whole milk
1 can evaporated milk
1/2 cup (4 ounces/1 stick) butter or margarine, melted
2 cups sugar
4 1/2 tablespoons cocoa powder
8 tablespoons self-rising flour
Pinch of salt
1 tablespoon vanilla extract
Cool Whip for serving

PREPARATION

Bake the pie shells according to package directions. Set aside. In a large sauce-pan, mix together the eggs, milks, and butter. In a separate bowl, mix together sugar, cocoa powder, flour, and salt. Take 1/3 cup of the egg mixture, and combine with the dry ingredients. Pour this mixture into the saucepan and cook slowly, stirring constantly until thickened, letting the mixture come to a boil.

Take off the heat and stir in the vanilla extract. Pour at once into the pie shells. Chill for 1 hour before serving. To serve, top with Cool Whip.

> "MY SISTER USED THIS RECIPE FOR YEARS AND GAVE IT TO MY WIFE AFTER WE WERE MARRIED. SINCE MY DAUGHTERS AND I DO NOT LIKE PUMPKIN PIE, WE INSIST THAT THIS PIE BE SERVED ON THANKSGIVING AND CHRISTMAS. IT IS THE BEST CHOCOLATE PIE I HAVE EVER TASTED."
>
> > Glen

APPETIZERS

BREADS

BREAKFAST & BRUNCH

ENTRÉES

VEGETABLES & SIDE DISHES

SALADS

SOUPS

237

chocolate easter eggs

Flossie Raybold > *Mullica Hill, New Jersey*

You can shape the mixture, dip the shapes in chocolate, and decorate them for Easter.

Yields about 5 dozen

INGREDIENTS

2 cups sugar
6 tablespoons cocoa powder
1 1/2 teaspoons vanilla extract
About 1/2 cup milk
1/4 pound (1 stick) margarine
3 1/2 cups quick-cooking rolled oats

PREPARATION

In a large saucepan, stir together the sugar and cocoa powder, and set aside. Pour the vanilla into a measuring cup, and fill with the milk to make 1/2 cup. Add the milk to the pan. Add the margarine, and heat the mixture over medium heat, stirring constantly, until it boils. Boil for exactly 2 minutes. Cool for 1 minute. Slowly add the oats, and stir vigorously. Cool slightly to handle and shape, or drop by teaspoonfuls on wax paper.

"MY GRANDCHILDREN KNOW THIS AS THE 'CENTER EGG' CANDY. WHEN I MADE MY CHILDREN'S EASTER BASKET, I DECORATED THESE EGGS WITH THEIR NAMES ON THEM AND PLACED THEM IN THE CENTER OF THEIR BASKETS. IT WAS A TRADITION THEIR 'INDIAN GRANDMA' (MY MOM, A NATIVE AMERICAN) DID FOR OUR BASKETS WHEN I WAS GROWING UP. IT IS NOW IN ITS FOURTH GENERATION STILL MAKING THE ROUNDS! THE EGGS TASTE GREAT DIPPED OR NOT. ENJOY AS A HOMEMADE CANDY ANY TIME OF THE YEAR."

> Flossie

gooey butter cake

Sherri Turner > *Rocky Mount, North Carolina*

Serves 15

INGREDIENTS

1 box yellow cake mix
3 eggs
1/2 cup (4 ounces/1 stick) butter
1 (8-ounce) package cream cheese, at room temperature
1 box confectioners' sugar plus extra for dusting
1 teaspoon vanilla extract

PREPARATION

Preheat the oven to 350°F. Grease a 9 by 9-inch cake pan. In a large mixing bowl, beat the cake mix with 1 egg and the butter with a portable mixer, and pat into the prepared cake pan. (This takes a few minutes; the batter will eventually get stiff and be thick.) In another bowl, beat the cream cheese, confectioners' sugar, the remaining 2 eggs, and the vanilla together and pour over the cake. Bake for 30 to 35 minutes, or until a toothpick inserted in the center comes out clean. Dust the top with confectioners' sugar.

"I MAKE THIS CAKE FOR WORK AND FAMILY FUNCTIONS ALL THE TIME. EVERYONE LOVES IT AND THERE IS NEVER ANY LEFT OVER."

> Sherri

chocolate pie

Michelle Dry > *Bertram, Texas*

Serves 8

INGREDIENTS

1/3 cup cocoa powder
1 cup sugar
3 tablespoons cornstarch
Pinch salt
2 cup evaporated milk
3 eggs separated
1 teaspoon margarine or butter
1 (9-inch) pie crust, baked
1/3 cup sugar
1 teaspoon vanilla extract
Pinch of cream of tartar

PREPARATION

Preheat the oven to 400°F. In a medium saucepan, mix the cocoa powder, sugar, cornstarch, and salt. Stir to blend. Add the evaporated milk and cook over medium heat until thick and slightly boiling, stirring continually. Take off the burner. Beat the egg yolks with a fork; add a little of the hot pudding to the egg yolks then transfer to hot pudding mixture. Put back on the burner and cook a few minutes more to cook egg yolks. Add margarine and stir to blend. Pour pudding into baked pie shell.

Make sure the egg whites are room temperature. Pour into a large, dry and clean mixing bowl. Beat with the cream of tartar and vanilla, adding the sugar a little at a time at the highest speed with an electric mixer. Top the pie with the meringue making sure to touch all sides of the crust. Bake for 10 minutes at 400°F till top is golden brown.

"THIS IS MY FAMILY'S FAVORITE PIE."

> Michelle

APPETIZERS

BREADS

BREAKFAST & BRUNCH

ENTRÉES

VEGETABLES & SIDE DISHES

SALADS

SOUPS

chocolate sheet cake

Suzanne Milton > *Silver Spring, Maryland*

Serves 10 to 12

INGREDIENTS FOR CAKE

2 cups sugar
2 cups all-purpose flour
1 cup (2 sticks) **butter**
1 cup water
1/2 cup buttermilk
4 tablespoons cocoa powder
2 eggs
1 teaspoon baking soda
1 teaspoon vanilla extract

INGREDIENTS FOR ICING

1/4 cup (4 ounces/1/2 stick) **salted butter**
1/4 cup cocoa powder
1/4 cup buttermilk
2 cups confectioners' sugar

PREPARATION

Preheat the oven to 350°F. Grease and flour a 9 by 13-inch baking pan. To make the cake, in a large mixing bowl, stir together the sugar and the flour with a sturdy wooden spoon. In a saucepan, heat the butter, water, buttermilk, and cocoa powder over low heat. Combine the butter mixture with the flour mixture. Beat in the eggs, one at a time, and stir in the baking soda and vanilla. Mix the batter until smooth, and pour into the prepared pan.

Bake for 30 minutes, or until a toothpick inserted in the center comes out clean. Cool slightly before icing.

To make the icing, heat the butter, cocoa powder, and buttermilk over low heat. Take the mixture off the heat, and beat in the confectioners' sugar with a portable mixer. Mix until smooth. Pour the icing over the cake.

> "MY MOM ALWAYS LET US CHOOSE WHAT KIND OF CAKE WE WANTED HER TO BAKE FOR OUR BIRTHDAYS, BUT MY BROTHER AND SISTER AND I VERY OFTEN CHOSE THIS BASIC CHOCOLATE SHEET CAKE – OUR OLD STANDBY. THIS IS THE FIRST CAKE I LEARNED TO BAKE WITH MY MOM, AND WHENEVER I MAKE IT, I THINK OF HER IN A SUNNY KITCHEN SERVING ME A WARM PIECE WITH A COLD GLASS OF MILK. AND GUESS WHAT? MY SON AND DAUGHTER ASK FOR IT MORE OFTEN THAN ANY OTHER THING I BAKE. THANKS, MOM!"
>
> > Suzanne

christmas cookies

Beth Rasmussen > *Livermore, California*

Yields about 3 dozen cookies

INGREDIENTS FOR COOKIE DOUGH

3 1/2 cups all-purpose flour
2 teaspoons baking powder
1 teaspoon ground nutmeg
1/2 teaspoon salt
1 cup (8 ounces/2 sticks) **butter, at room temperature**
1 cup sugar
2 eggs
1 teaspoon vanilla extract

INGREDIENTS FOR FROSTING

About 3/4 cup confectioners' sugar
About 1/4 stick margarine, at room temperature
About 2 tablespoons whole milk
About 1 teaspoon vanilla extract
Few drops green and/or red food coloring, for light green and pink colors

PREPARATION FOR DOUGH

In a large mixing bowl, stir together the flour, baking powder, nutmeg, and salt. In a second bowl, beat together the butter, sugar, eggs, and vanilla with a portable mixer. Slowly add the flour mixture to the egg mixture, blending well with a sturdy wooden spoon. Roll the dough in a large ball, put into a bowl, cover it with a damp towel, and refrigerate overnight.

Preheat the oven to 375ºF. Lightly flour a work surface, and roll out the dough. Using favorite cookie cutter shapes, cut out cookies, and place them on baking sheets. Repeat until all the dough is used up.

Bake 7 to 10 minutes, or until golden. Cool before icing or decorating.

PREPARATION FOR FROSTING

We always made 3 frosting colors: pink, green, and white (no food coloring for white). The frosting recipe was always eyeballed so I don't have exact measurements of the ingredients.

> "THIS FAMILY RECIPE HAS BEEN PASSED DOWN FROM MY GREAT-GRANDMOTHER WHO LIVED IN IOWA. I HAVE FOND MEMORIES OF DECORATING THESE CHRISTMAS COOKIES WITH MY MOM, SISTERS, AND BROTHER. THE WHOLE PROCESS TOOK AN ENTIRE DAY, BUT MADE GREAT GIFTS AND TREATS DURING THE HOLIDAY. MY MOM WAS ALWAYS MUCH MORE 'EFFICIENT' AT DECORATING WHILE WE TRIED TO BE MORE ELABORATE WITH ALL THE DECORATIONS AND FROSTING. I SWEAR SHE WOULD DECORATE 1 DOZEN COOKIES TO OUR 1 'FANCY' COOKIE!"
>
> > Beth

APPETIZERS

BREADS

BREAKFAST & BRUNCH

ENTRÉES

VEGETABLES & SIDE DISHES

SALADS

SOUPS

DESSERTS

coconut clouds

Nick Intagliata > *Palm Beach, Florida*

Yields 5 1/2 dozen cookies

INGREDIENTS FOR COOKIES

1/4 cup (1/2 stick) **butter, at room temperature**
1/4 cup shortening
1 cup granulated sugar
1/2 cup firmly packed brown sugar
2 eggs
1 teaspoon coconut extract
1 cup sour cream
2 3/4 cups all-purpose flour
1 teaspoon salt
1/2 teaspoon baking soda
1 cup flaked coconut, toasted

INGREDIENTS FOR FROSTING

1/3 cup butter, cubed
3 cups confectioners' sugar
3 tablespoons evaporated milk
1 teaspoon vanilla extract
1 teaspoon coconut extract
2 cups flaked coconut, toasted

PREPARATION FOR COOKIES

Preheat the oven to 375°F. Lightly grease 2 baking sheets. In a large mixing bowl, cream the butter, shortening, and sugars with a portable mixer until light and fluffy. Beat in the eggs and the coconut extract, and stir in the sour cream.

In a separate bowl, sift together the flour, salt, and baking soda. Gradually stir the flour mixture into the butter mixture, and mix well with a sturdy wooden spoon. Fold in the coconut. Drop the dough by tablespoonfuls 2 inches apart onto the prepared baking sheets. Bake for 8 to 10 minutes, or until set. Remove to wire racks to cool.

PREPARATION FOR FROSTING

In a small heavy saucepan, heat the butter over medium heat for 5 to 7 minutes, or until golden brown. Pour the butter into a small mixing bowl. Beat in the confectioners' sugar, a little at a time with a portable mixer, adding the milk and the vanilla and coconut extracts. Frost the cookies, and dip each in the coconut. Let stand until completely dry. Store in an airtight container.

concord grape pie

Kimberly Cook > *Mount Airy, Maryland*

Serves 8

INGREDIENTS

1 1/2 pounds (4 cups) Concord grapes
3/4 plus 1/2 cups sugar
1/3 cup plus 1/2 cup all-purpose flour
1/4 teaspoon salt
2 tablespoons margarine, melted
1 tablespoon lemon juice
1 (9-inch) piecrust, unbaked
1/4 cup margarine

PREPARATION

Preheat the oven to 375°F. Skin the grapes; if the grapes are ripe, you should be able to squeeze the skins right off. Set the skins aside in a separate bowl.

In a large pot, heat the grape pulp over medium heat until it boils. Reduce the heat to low, and cook, uncovered, for 5 minutes. Strain the pulp to remove the seeds, and add the skins to the pulp. In a large bowl, mix together 3/4 cup of the sugar, 1/3 cup of the flour, and salt. Stir in the grape mixture, margarine, and lemon juice. Pour the mixture into the piecrust. Cover the edges with aluminum foil. Bake for 20 minutes.

Meanwhile, stir together the remaining 1/2 cup flour and 1/2 cup sugar. Cut in the margarine until the mixture resembles coarse crumbs. Remove the foil from the pie, and sprinkle the crumb mixture over the pie. Bake 25 minutes more, or until the topping is golden. Cool on wire rack.

APPETIZERS

BREADS

BREAKFAST & BRUNCH

ENTRÉES

VEGETABLES & SIDE DISHES

SALADS

SOUPS

DESSERTS

" I BOUGHT A HOUSE IN THE COUNTRY WITH MY MOM IN 2004. I WAS EXCITED TO FIND THAT THE PREVIOUS OWNERS HAD PLANTED GRAPES ALONG AN ARCHWAY ARBOR IN THE BACKYARD. THE GRAPES WERE SO GOOD AND SWEET I ATE THEM RIGHT OFF THE VINE. MY MOM WANTED ME TO MAKE A PIE WITH THE GRAPES WHEN THE NEXT SEASON CAME. EACH SEPTEMBER MY MOM AND I CLIMBED UP ON LADDERS WITH THE BIGGEST BOWLS WE HAD TO PICK THE GRAPES. EVERY YEAR OUR VINES YIELDED ENOUGH GRAPES TO MAKE AT LEAST THREE PIES. WE STARTED PUTTING SOME ASIDE IN THE FREEZER TO SERVE AT CHRISTMAS. WE DID THIS EVERY YEAR WE LIVED IN THAT HOUSE. MY MOM LOVED THIS PIE. BECAUSE THIS PIE IS SO DIFFERENT, IT WAS A REAL TREAT TO SERVE. MY MOM PASSED AWAY IN APRIL 2007, AND I MOVED AWAY FROM OUR HOUSE IN THE COUNTRY. I WILL ALWAYS REMEMBER THE JOY WE HAD PICKING THE GRAPES, MAKING THE PIES, AND ENJOYING THEM THROUGH THE HOLIDAY SEASON. "

> Kimberly

243

crazy carrot cake

Jason Benton > *Dallas, Texas*

Serves 20

INGREDIENTS FOR CAKE

4 eggs
1 1/4 cups vegetable oil
2 cups sugar
2 teaspoons vanilla extract
2 cups all-purpose flour
2 teaspoons baking soda
2 teaspoons baking powder
2 teaspoons ground cinnamon
1 teaspoon ground nutmeg
1/2 teaspoon salt
3 cups grated carrots
1 1/2 cups chopped walnuts
8 ounces raisins
2 ounces shredded coconut

INGREDIENTS FOR FROSTING

8 ounces cream cheese, at room temperature
1/2 cup (4 ounces/1 stick) unsalted butter, at room temperature
1 teaspoon vanilla extract
Splash lemon juice
10 ounces confectioners' sugar
1 1/2 cups walnuts
3 ounces shredded coconut

PREPARATION FOR CAKE

Preheat the oven to 350°F. Grease and flour a 9 by 13-inch baking pan. In a large bowl, beat together the eggs, oil, sugar, and vanilla with a portable mixer. Mix in the flour, baking soda, baking powder, cinnamon, nutmeg, and salt with a sturdy wooden spoon. Fold in the carrots, walnuts, raisins, and coconut. Pour into the prepared pan. Bake for 50 to 55 minutes, or until a toothpick inserted into the center comes out clean. Let cool for about 20 minutes, then frost the cake.

PREPARATION FOR FROSTING

In a large mixing bowl, cream together the cream cheese and butter with a portable mixer on low until just combined. Add the vanilla and lemon juice. With the mixer on low, add the confectioners' sugar in batches, and beat until creamy. Fold in the walnuts and coconut. Refrigerate the frosting for about 10 minutes before using. Frost the cake, and serve.

creamy dreamy crème brûlée

Dawne Wood > *Salem, Missouri*

Serves 6

INGREDIENTS

8 egg yolks
1/3 cup granulated sugar
2 cups half-and-half (or heavy whipping cream for those days when calories don't scare you)
2 teaspoons vanilla extract
1/4 cup thinly sliced almonds
1/4 cup firmly packed brown sugar (for the caramelized tops)

PREPARATION

Preheat the oven to 300°F. In a large mixing bowl, whisk together the egg yolks and granulated sugar until the sugar has dissolved. When the mixture becomes pale yellow, whisk in the half-and-half and vanilla. Blend well. Skim off any foam or bubbles that have formed on top. Divide your mixture among 6 ramekins, and set them into a large baking pan with high sides. Pour in 1 to 2 inches of water for a water bath. Carefully place each cup into the bath, and bake for 55 minutes. The edges will be set, but the centers will still appear loose. Slowly remove the baking pan, leaving the ramekins in the water bath until the water cools. Remove the ramekins, cover with aluminum foil, and refrigerate for 2 hours. (You can safely keep each dessert covered in your refrigerator for up to 2 days.)

When ready to serve, sprinkle on each an equal amount of almonds, and then brown sugar. If you have a handheld kitchen torch, use it to caramelize the sugar. If not, place the ramekins under the broiler to caramelize. Refrigerate the ramekins, uncovered, for 10 minutes. Serve and enjoy!

APPETIZERS
BREADS
BREAKFAST & BRUNCH
ENTRÉES
VEGETABLES & SIDE DISHES
SALADS
SOUPS
DESSERTS

"THE VERY FIRST TIME I TRIED CRÈME BRÛLÉE I WAS HOOKED. TO ME IT WAS THE BEST THING I'D EVER TASTED. I BECAME A WOMAN ON A MISSION – I HAD TO LEARN TO PREPARE THIS MYSELF. I TRIED SEVERAL DIFFERENT RECIPES USING MY FAMILY AS GUINEA PIGS. MANY SPECIAL TIMES HAVE BEEN SHARED OVER HELPINGS OF THIS WARM, BUBBLY HEAVEN. WE DON'T NEED A SPECIAL OCCASION TO CELEBRATE WITH IT, BUT REST ASSURED, IF ONE COMES UP, IT'S MOST LIKELY ON THE MENU. NOT TOO LONG AGO, I WAS HAVING AN ABSOLUTELY AWFUL DAY AND MENTIONED THIS TO MY DAUGHTER BEFORE COMING HOME. WHEN I GOT HOME, SHE LET ME KNOW THAT SHE'D MADE US A BATCH. TALK ABOUT AN ANGEL! THE REST OF MY EVENING WAS SHEER DELIGHT AS MY DAUGHTER AND I SPENT IT DIVING INTO THAT DELICIOUS CONCOCTION AND GOOFING AROUND."

> Dawne

245

date pinwheel cookies

Shane Guilliams > *Phoenix, Arizona*

Yields 5 dozen

INGREDIENTS

1 cup (8 ounces/2 sticks) **butter, at room temperature**
2 cups firmly packed brown sugar
3 eggs
4 1/2 cups all-purpose flour
1 teaspoon ground cinnamon
1/2 teaspoon baking soda
1/4 teaspoon salt
1 teaspoon vanilla extract
8 ounces dates, pitted and chopped
1 cup chopped pecans
1/2 cup water
1/2 cup granulated sugar

PREPARATION

In a large mixing bowl, cream together the butter and brown sugar with a portable mixer. Add the eggs, one at a time, beating well after each addition.

In a separate bowl, sift together the flour, cinnamon, baking soda, and salt. Fold the dry ingredients into the egg mixture slowly, mixing well with a sturdy wooden spoon. Stir in the vanilla. Divide the dough into three portions, and wrap them in waxed paper. Chill until the dough becomes firm. Meanwhile, preheat the oven to 350°F. Grease 2 baking sheets.

To make the filling, in a saucepan, heat the dates, pecans, water, and granulated sugar over low heat, and cook until the mixture becomes pastelike. On a lightly floured surface, roll out one portion of the chilled dough to make a thin layer. Place one-third of the filling on the dough and roll up. Repeat the process with the remaining ingredients. (You can bake the dough right away, or freeze the rolls until ready to use.) Cut the rolls into 1/4-inch-thick slices with a sharp knife. Place slices on the prepared sheet, and bake for 15 minutes.

> "THIS RECIPE IS FROM MY PARTNER'S MOTHER. NO CHRISTMAS EVE WOULD BE COMPLETE WITHOUT DATE PINWHEEL COOKIES AND PEPPERMINT ICE CREAM SERVED AT MIDNIGHT!"
>
> > Shane

dawnitra's special peanut butter cookies

Josie Smith > *Bowie, Maryland*

Yields 3 dozen cookies

INGREDIENTS

1/2 cup shortening
1/2 cup (4 ounces/1 stick) **butter or margarine**
1 cup granulated sugar
1 cup firmly packed brown sugar
2 eggs
1 cup peanut butter
2 1/2 cups all-purpose flour, sifted
1 1/2 teaspoon baking soda
1 teaspoon baking powder
1/4 teaspoon salt

PREPARATION

Preheat the oven to 350°F. Lightly grease a baking sheet. In a large mixing bowl, cream the shortening and butter with a portable mixer. Add the sugars, and cream thoroughly. Add the eggs, and blend thoroughly. Fold in the peanut butter and blend.

In a separate bowl, sift together the flour, baking soda, baking powder, and salt. Fold the flour mixture gradually into the butter mixture, blending well. Form the dough into soft balls, and place them about 3 inches apart on the prepared sheet. Flatten each with a fork dipped in flour, making a crisscross pattern. (If dough is a little too soft to flatten without sticking to fork, chill dough.) Repeat until all the dough is used up. Bake 10 to 12 minutes, or until the cookies feel firm.

"THIS IS A RECIPE THAT I SHARED WITH MY DAUGHTER, DAWNITRA, WHEN SHE WAS ABOUT 9 YEARS OLD. SHE HAS BECOME AN EXPERT AT MAKING THE BEST PEANUT BUTTER COOKIES EVER. SHE IS NOW 35 YEARS OLD AND HAS TWO DAUGHTERS OF HER OWN. SHE IS TEACHING HER DAUGHTER (ARABIA) WHO IS 9 YEARS OLD TO MAKE THESE DELICIOUS COOKIES. WE FELL IN LOVE WITH HER COOKIES AND HOPEFULLY, ARABIA (MY GRANDDAUGHTER) WILL SHARE THEM WHEN SHE HAS DAUGHTERS OF HER OWN."

> Josie

APPETIZERS

BREADS

BREAKFAST & BRUNCH

ENTRÉES

VEGETABLES & SIDE DISHES

SALADS

SOUPS

DESSERTS

dolores eggerding's cut-out cookies

Mark Eggerding > *Rosemont, Illinois*

Look for meringue powder in baking stores or specialty groceries.

Yields 3 dozen

INGREDIENTS FOR COOKIES

3/4 cup (6 ounces/1 1/2 sticks) **butter, at room temperature**
2/3 cup sugar
1/4 teaspoon salt
2 egg yolks
1 tablespoon heavy cream
1 teaspoon vanilla extract
2 cups all-purpose flour

INGREDIENTS FOR ROYAL ICING

1 pound confectioners' sugar
5 tablespoons meringue powder
1/2 cup water
Gel-paste food coloring (optional)

PREPARATION FOR COOKIES

In a large mixing bowl, cream the butter and sugar with a portable mixer. Add the salt, egg yolks, cream, and vanilla. Gradually add the flour, beating the mixture at low speed. Shape the dough into a ball, and wrap it in wax paper. Refrigerate for 1 hour.

Preheat the oven to 325°F. Lightly flour a work surface, and roll out the dough to 1/4-inch thick. Use your favorite cookie cutters. Place the cookies on a baking sheet. Bake for 12 minutes, or until the edges turn brown. Set aside to cool before decorating with Royal Icing.

PREPARATION FOR ROYAL ICING

In a large mixing bowl, beat together all the ingredients with a portable mixer on low speed. Beat until fluffy, about 8 minutes. Add food coloring, if using. Spread the icing on with a spatula, or pipe it on with a pastry bag. Use the icing immediately because it hardens quickly.

"THIS RECIPE IS A TRADITIONAL HOLIDAY FAVORITE IN THE EGGERDING FAMILY. THIS DELICIOUS BUTTER COOKIE RECIPE WAS MY MOTHER-IN-LAW'S, PASSED DOWN BY HER MOTHER, WHO IMMIGRATED TO THE UNITED STATES IN THE LATE 1800s. SHE LOVINGLY MADE THESE COOKIES EVERY YEAR FOR HER FAMILY. WHEN SHE PASSED AWAY, WE CONTINUED THE TRADITION FOR OUR ENTIRE FAMILY, NOW NUMBERING 100 STRONG EACH HOLIDAY SEASON. ENJOY!"

> Mark

diet banana pudding

Steven Keeling > *Paducah, Kentucky*

Serves 12

INGREDIENTS

2 small boxes sugar-free vanilla pudding mix
4 cups skim milk
1 can fat-free sweetened condensed milk
1 (16-ounce) container light whipped topping
3 to 5 bananas, peeled and sliced
Reduced fat graham crackers

PREPARATION

In a large mixing bowl, combine the pudding and skim milk, beating with a portable mixer. Add sweetened condensed milk and half the whipped topping. Beat until smooth and slightly fluffy. Layer the pudding mixture, bananas, and graham crackers in a trifle dish or bowl, reserving 2 crackers for garnish. Repeat the layers until the ingredients are used up. Spread the remaining whipped topping over the top. Crush 2 crackers, and sprinkle over the whipped topping. Refrigerate 1 hour.

Optional: You can also change the pudding mix to another sugar-free flavor, such as chocolate or butterscotch, and omit the bananas, if you like, for a different fancy pudding dessert.

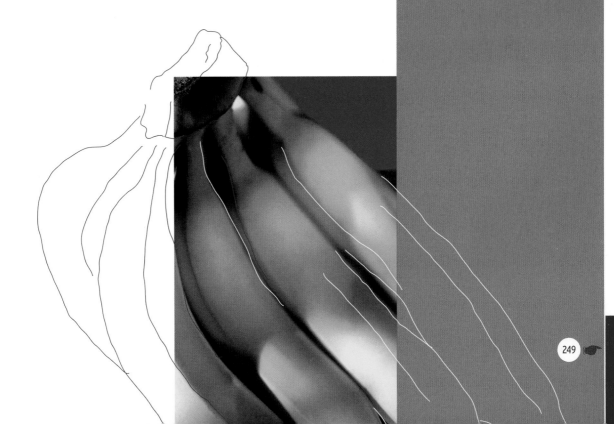

APPETIZERS

BREADS

BREAKFAST &
BRUNCH

ENTRÉES

VEGETABLES &
SIDE DISHES

SALADS

SOUPS

DESSERTS

divinity

Leslie Needham > *Austin, Texas*

Serves 8 to 10

INGREDIENTS

2 egg whites, at room temperature
4 cups sugar
1 cup light corn syrup
1 cup boiling water
1 tablespoon vanilla extract
1 cup diced pecans

PREPARATION

In a large mixing bowl, beat the egg whites with a portable mixer on high until stiff peaks form. In a large saucepan, heat the sugar, corn syrup, and water over medium heat, and bring to a boil. Cook to the soft ball stage (234 to 238°F). Pour half the mixture over the stiffly beaten egg whites.

Boil the remaining sugar mixture to the brittle stage (265 to 270°F). Pour the remaining syrup over the egg white mixture, and beat on high. Add the vanilla and pecans, and continue to beat with a sturdy wooden spoon until the mixture loses its shiny gloss. Using a tablespoon, drop scoops immediately onto wax paper.

"MY FATHER'S NEIGHBOR USED TO MAKE THIS CANDY AND BRING IT TO HIM DURING THE HOLIDAYS. IT WAS MY FATHER'S FAVORITE. MY FATHER TRACKED DOWN THE RECIPE, AND HE AND MY MOTHER STARTED MAKING IT FOR CHRISTMAS TIME RIGHT AFTER THEY GOT MARRIED. WE (MY MOM, DAD, SISTER, AND MYSELF) STILL MAKE IT TOGETHER EVERY CHRISTMAS. IT BECOMES VERY DIFFICULT TO STIR, SO WE ALL TAKE TURNS.

> Leslie

dot's brownie cupcakes

Melinda Freeman > *Salem, Missouri*

Yields 24

INGREDIENTS

1 pound (4 sticks) **butter**
12 ounces semi-sweet chocolate chips
3 1/2 cups sugar
2 cups flour
8 eggs, slightly beaten
2 teaspoons vanilla
1 teaspoon salt
4 cups pecans
7 ounces flaked coconut

PREPARATION

Preheat the oven to 325ºF. Line muffin tins with paper cups. In a large sauce-pan, heat the butter and chocolate chips over low heat until melted. Set aside to cool.

In a large mixing bowl, beat the sugar, flour, eggs, vanilla, and salt together with a portable mixer. Add the cooled butter/chocolate mixture, and stir until well blended. Stir in the pecans and coconut. Fill the muffin cups two-thirds full. Bake for 30 to 35 minutes, or until the tops feel firm.

APPETIZERS

BREADS

BREAKFAST &
BRUNCH

ENTRÉES

VEGETABLES &
SIDE DISHES

SALADS

SOUPS

DESSERTS

durgin park baked indian pudding

Patricia Rothrock > *Knoxville, Tennessee*

Serves 8

> MY MOM IS FROM NEW YORK CITY. AS A CHILD, HER FAMILY WOULD GO TO A RESTAURANT NAMED DURGIN PARK IN BOSTON WHERE THEY WOULD GET THIS TREAT. WHEN THE RESTAURANT CLOSED, A RELATIVE GOT THE RECIPE FOR THEM. SHE HAS BEEN BLESSING OUR FAMILY WITH IT EVERY CHRISTMAS SINCE.

> Patricia

INGREDIENTS

1 cup coarse yellow cornmeal
1/2 cup black molasses
1/4 cup sugar
1/4 cup (2 ounces/1/2 stick) butter, at room temperature
1/2 teaspoon salt
1/4 teaspoon baking soda
1/4 teaspoon ground ginger
1/4 teaspoon ground cinnamon
2 eggs, lightly beaten
1 1/2 quarts HOT (not boiling) milk
Raisins (optional)
Ice cream or whipped cream for topping

PREPARATION

Preheat the oven to 350°F. Grease well a 3-quart stone crock or baking dish.

In a large mixing bowl, stir the cornmeal, molasses, sugar, butter, salt, baking soda, ginger, cinnamon, and eggs with 3 cups of the hot milk. Pour into a 3-quart baking dish, and bake until the mixture just begins to boil. Stir in the remaining 3 cups hot milk, decrease the heat to 300°F, and bake for 3 to 5 hours (1/2 recipe equals 2 to 3 hours). The surface will crust over, but insert a knife to test. (Recipe can be halved). Serve topped with ice cream or whipped cream.

easy southern apple crisp

Wendy Johnson > *Norwich, Connecticut*

Serves 10

INGREDIENTS FOR APPLE CRISP

3 large baking apples
3 ounces cream cheese, at room temperature
3/4 cup sour cream
3/4 cup sugar
2 tablespoons flour
1 egg, lightly beaten
1/2 teaspoon vanilla extract
1 unbaked (9-inch) piecrust, at room temperature

INGREDIENTS FOR TOPPING

1/4 cup quick-cooking rolled oats
1/4 cup flour
1/4 cup sugar
1 teaspoon ground cinnamon
1/4 cup butter, melted

PREPARATION

Preheat the oven to 350°F. Peel, core and slice the apples; set aside. In a large mixing bowl, beat the cream cheese, sour cream, sugar, flour, egg, and vanilla with a portable mixer on low speed until blended. Stir the apples into the cream cheese mixture. Place the piecrust into a 9-inch round casserole dish. Pour the apple mixture into the crust.

To make the topping, in a large bowl, stir together the oats, flour, sugar, and cinnamon. Sprinkle the topping over the apple mixture. Drizzle the butter over the topping. Bake 30 to 40 minutes, or until firm in the center. Serve warm with your favorite ice cream.

APPETIZERS

BREADS

BREAKFAST & BRUNCH

ENTRÉES

VEGETABLES & SIDE DISHES

SALADS

SOUPS

easy chocolate pie

David Rose > *Piedmont, South Carolina*

Serves 12

INGREDIENTS

6 Hershey bars
1 container of Cool Whip
1 (9-inch) graham cracker piecrust

PREPARATION

Melt 5 Hershey bars in a microwave and stir well. Add Cool Whip and stir well. Pour into crust. Grate the remaining Hershey bar on top.

easy peach crisp

Robert Wright > *Lake City, Tennessee*

Serves 12

INGREDIENTS

1 (29-ounce) can sliced peaches with juice
1 cup sugar
1 teaspoon ground cinnamon
1 (18.25-ounce) box yellow cake mix
1/2 cup butter

PREPARATION

Preheat the oven to 350°F. Pour the peaches into a 9 by 13-inch baking pan, making sure the juice covers the peaches; if not, add a little water to cover. Mix peaches with 1/2 cup of the sugar, and sprinkle with cinnamon to taste. Sprinkle the cake mix evenly over the peaches. Cut the stick of butter into small pats, placing on top of the cake mix. Sprinkle with the remaining 1/2 cup sugar and a light dusting of cinnamon. Bake 25 to 30 minutes, or until the juice is bubbly and top is golden brown.

éclair

Denny Confort > *Greensburg, Pennsylvania*

Serves 18

INGREDIENTS

1/2 cup (4 ounces/1 stick) butter
1 cup boiling water
1 cup all-purpose flour
4 eggs
1 (8-ounce) package cream cheese, at room temperature
5 cups whole milk
3 (3-ounce) packages vanilla instant pudding
2 (8-ounce) containers Cool Whip
Chocolate syrup

PREPARATION

Preheat the oven to 350°F. Grease a baking sheet. In a saucepan, melt the butter in the boiling water. Remove from the heat, and stir in the flour. Set aside to cool for 5 minutes. Beat the eggs in by hand, one at a time. Pour or spread the mixture onto the prepared sheet. Bake for 25 minutes, or until golden brown.

Meanwhile, in a large mixing bowl, beat the cream cheese with 1 cup milk for 2 minutes with a portable mixer on medium. Add the pudding and the remaining milk, and beat for 2 minutes. Spread the mixture over the cooled crust. Cover with Cool Whip. Drizzle chocolate syrup over all before serving.

ellie's brownies

Dometta Blacka > *Mt. Pleasant, Pennsylvania*

Serves 10 to 12

INGREDIENTS

1 box devils food chocolate cake mix
1 box instant chocolate pudding mix
2 cups 1% milk
Chocolate chips or peanut butter chips

PREPARATION

Mix cake mix, pudding mix, and milk in mixer at medium speed. Grease and flour a 13 by 9-inch jelly roll sheet pan. Pour batter into coated pan. Sprinkle with chocolate chips or peanut butter chips. Bake at 350°F for 25 to 30 minutes. Cool well. Ice with chocolate icing (or vanilla for a change). Enjoy with milk!

> "THIS IS A CONSTANT REQUEST FOR EVERY FAMILY PICNIC. ELLIE (MY MOM) HAS EVEN WON A RECIPE CONTEST WITH THESE MOIST, CHEWY TREATS."
>
> > Dometta

APPETIZERS

BREADS

BREAKFAST & BRUNCH

ENTRÉES

VEGETABLES & SIDE DISHES

SALADS

SOUPS

DESSERTS

english toffee

Peggy Arvin > *Olathe, Kansas*

Serves 8 to 10

INGREDIENTS

14 tablespoons butter
1 cup sugar
2 tablespoons cold water
1/2 cup chopped pecans
1 teaspoon vanilla extract
Pinch of salt
6 ounces semisweet chocolate chips

PREPARATION

Generously butter an 8 by 10-inch baking dish. In a large saucepan, heat the butter, sugar, and water over medium-high heat. Bring to a bubbling boil, stirring constantly with a sturdy wooden spoon. Remove the spoon from the pan, and cook to the brittle stage (300 to 310°F on a candy thermometer). Remove from the heat. To avoid splattering, carefully add the nuts, vanilla, and salt. Pour the mixture into the prepared baking dish, and spread it to 1/4 inch thickness. Let cool slightly, and sprinkle the chocolate chips over top. Spread the chocolate chips out as they melt. Cool completely, and break into pieces. Store in an air-tight container.

gold rush bars

Glenn Sutton > *Prospect Heights, Illinois*

Serves 16

INGREDIENTS

1 (14-ounce) can sweetened, condensed milk
1 2/3 cup graham cracker crumbs
1 cup (6 ounces) semisweet chocolate chips
1 cup pecans

PREPARATION

Preheat oven to 350°F. Grease an 8 by 8-inch baking pan. In a large bowl, combine all the ingredients, and mix thoroughly with a sturdy wooden spoon. Spread the mixture into the prepared pan evenly. Bake 26 minutes. Cool on a wire rack for 20 minutes before cutting it into squares.

escalloped pineapple

James P. Meiners Sr. > *Streator, Illinois*

Serves 6 to 8

INGREDIENTS

1 (20-ounce) can pineapple chunks or tidbits, drained
4 cups fresh breadcrumbs
3 eggs, lightly beaten
1 cup whole milk
1 1/2 cups granulated sugar
1 teaspoon vanilla extract
1/2 cup (4 ounces/1 stick) butter or margarine, melted and cooled slightly

PREPARATION

Preheat the oven to 350°F. Grease a 3-quart ovenproof baking dish. Use a food processor to grind the dried bread up into crumbs. If you have an immersion blender with a grinding blade this works equally well. Place all the ingredients in a large bowl and mix together very well with a sturdy wooden spoon. Pour into the prepared baking dish. Bake for 1 hour, or until golden brown and puffy. Serve this dish either warm or cold. If you like more pineapple you can add an extra can.

> "THIS RECIPE WAS GIVEN TO MY WIFE BY FRIENDS OF OURS FROM STAPLETON, GEORGIA. WE ENJOY THIS DISH SO MUCH IT HAS BECOME A TRADITION IN OUR HOUSEHOLD TO SERVE IT AT THANKSGIVING AND CHRISTMAS. THIS CAN BE USED AS A SIDE DISH OR AS A DESSERT AND IS DELICIOUS BOTH WARM AND COLD."
>
> > James

APPETIZERS

BREADS

BREAKFAST & BRUNCH

ENTRÉES

VEGETABLES & SIDE DISHES

SALADS

SOUPS

DESSERTS

famous fudge

Susan Clark > *Columbia, South Carolina*

Yields 100 1-inch squares

INGREDIENTS

1 cup (8 ounces/2 sticks) **unsalted butter**
1 (12-ounce) **can evaporated milk**
4 cups sugar
1 (12 ounce) **package semisweet chocolate chips**
2 ounces unsweetened chocolate (optional)
1 jar marshmallow cream
8 ounces walnuts or pecans, coarsely chopped
2 teaspoons vanilla extract
Pinch of salt

PREPARATION

Butter a 9 by 13-inch baking pan, and set aside. In a heavy large saucepan, combine the butter, evaporated milk, and sugar. Heat over medium heat, stirring constantly, until it reaches the soft ball stage (238°F on a candy thermometer). Remove from the heat and, working quickly, add the marshmallow cream, nuts, vanilla, and salt. Stir until smooth. Pour into the prepared pan, and set aside to cool at room temperature until firm. Store in an airtight container at room temperature. Cut into squares as needed.

" THIS IS THE FUDGE THAT I LOOK FORWARD TO SHARING EACH CHRISTMAS WITH MY COWORKERS AT THE U.S. FOODSERVICE COLUMBIA DIVISION. UNSWEETENED CHOCOLATE IS THE INGREDIENT THAT MAKES THE RECIPE SPECIAL, BUT IT WILL BE JUST AS DELICIOUS IF YOU OMIT IT. "

> Susan

easy chocolate fudge

Lee Nybo > *Las Vegas, Nevada*

Serves 12

INGREDIENTS

1 (12-ounce) **package** (2 cups) **of semi-sweet chocolate bits**
1 (14-ounce) **can sweetened condensed milk**
1 1/4 cup chopped walnuts
1 teaspoon vanilla extract

PREPARATION

Line a baking pan with waxed paper.

In a large glass measuring cup, combine the chocolate and condensed milk. Microwave on high for 3 minutes, and remove. Stir until the morsels melt and mixture is smooth. Stir in the walnuts and vanilla. Pour the mixture into the prepared pan, and cover. Refrigerate overnight to firm.

french cherry dessert

Jack Blackburn > *Sayre, Oklahoma*

Serves 12

INGREDIENTS

3 egg whites
1 cup sugar
20 square saltine crackers, crushed
1 teaspoon baking powder
1 teaspoon vinegar
1 teaspoon plus 1 1/2 teaspoons vanilla
1/2 cup pecans finely chopped
1 (8-ounce) package cream cheese
1/2 cup powdered sugar
1 12-ounce tub Cool Whip
1 can cherry pie filling

PREPARATION

Beat the egg whites until foamy, gradually add sugar while beating. Beat until stiff peaks form when beater is pulled up. Fold the crackers, baking powder, vinegar, 1 teaspoon vanilla, and pecans into the egg white mixture. Spoon into a greased 13 by 9 by 2-inch baking dish. Bake at 325°F for 20 minutes or until done. Cool thoroughly. Combine the cream cheese, powdered sugar, 1 1/2 teaspoons vanilla, and Cool Whip and beat until smooth. Spread over the cooled egg white mixture. Spoon cherry pie filling over the cheese mixture. Chill 2 to 3 hours before serving.

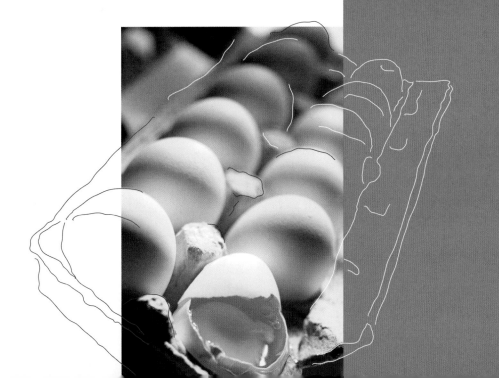

APPETIZERS

BREADS

BREAKFAST & BRUNCH

ENTRÉES

VEGETABLES & SIDE DISHES

SALADS

SOUPS

fresh apple cake

Shane Guilliams > *Phoenix, Arizona*

This recipe works great with pears in place of the apples. It is super easy and moist! Serve it warm with vanilla ice cream!

Serves 20

INGREDIENTS

3 cups all-purpose flour
2 cups sugar
1 teaspoon baking soda
1 teaspoon salt
1 teaspoon ground cinnamon
1 cup vegetable oil
2 eggs
1 teaspoon vanilla extract
3 cups diced apples
1 cup chopped walnuts or pecans

PREPARATION

Preheat the oven to 300°F. Grease and flour a 9 by 13-inch cake pan. Into a large bowl, sift the flour, sugar, baking soda, salt, and cinnamon. Add the oil, eggs, and vanilla, beating well with a portable mixer.

Fold in the apples and nuts. Pour into the prepared pans. Bake for 50 minutes, or until a toothpick inserted in the center comes out clean.

fresh peach pie

Kevin Maher > *Rapid City, Dakota*

Serves 8

INGREDIENTS FOR FILLING

3 1/2 cups sugar
1/2 cup plus 2 tablespoons minute tapioca
1 teaspoon salt
2 teaspoons fruit fresh ascorbic acid
1/4 to 1/3 cup lemon juice (depending on your taste)
4 quarts peeled sliced peaches

INGREDIENTS FOR CRUST

4 cups flour
2 cups shortening
1 egg
1 tablespoon sugar
1/2 teaspoon baking powder
1/2 teaspoon salt
2 tablespoons lemon juice
1/2 cup very cold water add last

PREPARATION FOR FILLING

Mix sugar, tapioca, salt, ascorbic acid, and lemon juice. Mix into the peaches. To freeze, line pie tins with foil and divide peaches into the 4 tins. Wrap well and freeze. These stack well. Or, you can use quart containers if you have time to thaw the filling before baking. To bake, unwrap the filling and place between a double crust and bake 1 hour at 425°F.

PREPARATION FOR CRUST

Mix all the ingredients very well. Refrigerate for 12 hours then divide into 5 parts to use or freeze. You can make ahead and freeze to use anytime. To bake unfilled, bake 7 minutes at 450°F. Otherwise fill and bake according to directions in the previous paragraph. May be sticky, so use more flour as necessary.

APPETIZERS
BREADS
BREAKFAST & BRUNCH
ENTRÉES
VEGETABLES & SIDE DISHES
SALADS
SOUPS

glorified brownies

Gary Hinson > *North Augusta, South Carolina*

Serves 10 to 12

INGREDIENTS FOR BROWNIES

3/4 cup all-purpose flour
1 heaping tablespoon cocoa powder
1 cup sugar
Pinch of salt
1 stick margarine, at room temperature
2 eggs
1/2 teaspoon vanilla
3/4 cup pecans (optional)
1/2 bag miniature marshmallows

INGREDIENTS FOR ICING

1 stick margarine
1 box powdered sugar
3 tablespoons cocoa powder, heaping
3 tablespoons warm milk
1 teaspoon vanilla

PREPARATION FOR BROWNIES

Sift flour, cocoa powder, sugar, and salt. Add soft margarine, eggs, and vanilla to dry ingredients. Fold in nuts. Bake in a 7 by 11-inch pan at 350°F for 20 to 25 minutes. Mix icing while brownies are baking. As soon as brownies come out of the oven, cover the top with the miniature marshmallows.

PREPARATION FOR ICING

Combine all the ingredients in a saucepan. Mix on low heat until combined. Keep icing warm so that you can pour it easily over top of the marshmallows.

google custard

Cecilia Farrell > *Ormond Beach, Florida*

Serves 4

INGREDIENTS

1 bag of egg noodles
3 whole eggs
1/2 cup of sugar
1 teaspoon of vanilla
1 large jar of applesauce
Cinnamon

PREPARATION

Cook egg noodles slightly. Beat the eggs with the sugar, vanilla, and applesauce. Add the egg noodles and mix well. Put into a flat casserole dish and sprinkle cinnamon on the top. Bake uncovered at 350°F for 30 minutes or until golden brown.

grand marnier fudge cake

Doug Ricketts > *Cleveland, Ohio*

Serves 6 to 8

INGREDIENTS

1 pound bittersweet chocolate, broken into small pieces
1 1/2 cups sugar
1 cup strong coffee
1 pound (4 sticks) unsalted butter, at room temperature
8 eggs, lightly beaten
2 ounces Grand Marnier

PREPARATION

Preheat the oven to 350°F. Line a springform pan with aluminum foil. In a food processor, process the chocolate and sugar until well combined. Add the coffee, and continue to process. Add the butter and eggs, and process until well combined. Add the Grand Marnier, and process for 3 to 4 seconds. Pour into the prepared pan. Bake for 1 hour.

> **I HAD INVITED MY FRIENDS DORIS AND BILL LAST YEAR FOR OUR NEW YEAR'S DINNER, FOR WHICH I MADE FRESH PORK AND SAUERKRAUT. NOW DORIS CALLS THIS RECIPE GOOGLE, WHICH SHE SAID WAS A DESSERT THAT YOU SERVE WITH PORK. SO WE MADE THIS TOGETHER AND HAD A WONDERFUL NEW YEAR'S DINNER.**
>
> > Cecilia

APPETIZERS

BREADS

BREAKFAST & BRUNCH

ENTRÉES

VEGETABLES & SIDE DISHES

SALADS

SOUPS

DESSERTS

grandma clayton's chocolate snowballs

Lisa Powers > *Streator, Illinois*

Yields 3 dozen

INGREDIENTS

1 1/4 cups (2 1/2 sticks) margarine
2/3 cup sugar
2 teaspoons vanilla extract
2 cups sifted all-purpose flour
1/2 cup cocoa powder
Pinch of salt
2 cups finely chopped pecans
Confectioners' sugar for rolling

PREPARATION

Preheat the oven to 350°F. In a large mixing bowl, beat the margarine with a portable mixer until fluffy, and gradually add the sugar. Beat until light and fluffy. Add the vanilla. Into another bowl, sift the flour, cocoa powder, and salt and add to the creamed mixture. Fold in the pecans. Form the mixture into marble-sized balls. Bake for 20 minutes. Cool, and roll in confectioners' sugar. Enjoy!

ma maw dorsey's pecan pie

Fran Rackley > *Dallas, Georgia*

Serves 6 to 8

INGREDIENTS

1 cup sugar
1 cup light corn syrup
1/2 teaspoon salt
3 large eggs, beaten
1 (9-inch) unbaked piecrust
1 1/2 to 2 cups chopped pecans
1 tablespoon chopped butter

PREPARATION

Preheat the oven to 325°F. In a large mixing bowl, beat the sugar, syrup, and salt together with a portable mixer until the sugar is dissolved. Fold the eggs into the mixture. Line the piecrust with the nuts, and pour the filling over the top. Top with the butter. Bake for 1 hour, or until the center of the pie is set. Let cool for at least 45 minutes to 1 hour before serving.

> "MY MOM MAKES US KIDS A 'GOODY' BASKET TO TAKE HOME EVERY YEAR AT CHRISTMAS. WE ALWAYS LOOK FORWARD TO HER CHOCOLATE SNOWBALLS!"
> > Lisa

> "MY GRANDMOTHER, MARY DORSEY, USED TO MAKE THIS WITH FRESH PECANS FROM THE TREES ON HER FARM. WE WOULD GO OUT AND PICK UP THE PECANS AND SOMETIMES I'D HELP HER PICK THEM OUT OF THE SHELLS. MY FAVORITE MEMORY IS OF THE MOST LOVING 'MA MAW' IN THE WORLD, WHO WOULD COOK THESE HUGE DINNERS FOR ALL OF US TO ENJOY. DELICIOUS AND FILLING BUT ALWAYS FILLED WITH HER LOVE. SHE LIVED IN JEFFERSONVILLE, GEORGIA. SHE HAD A LONG TABLE THAT COULD SIT 10 TO 12 PEOPLE. WE WOULD ALL GATHER AROUND AND EAT TOGETHER AS ONE BIG HAPPY FAMILY. WE MISS HER, BUT SHE TAUGHT US TO LOVE AND SHOW LOVE THROUGH THE FOOD YOU PREPARE."
> > Fran

264

DESSERTS

grandma susie's chocolate pound cake

Lynn Hall > *Columbia, Maryland*

Serves 16

INGREDIENTS

3 cups all-purpose flour
4 heaping tablespoons cocoa powder
1 1/2 teaspoons baking powder
1 teaspoon salt
1 1/2 cups shortening
3 cups sugar
5 large eggs
1 teaspoon vanilla extract
1 1/4 cups whole milk

PREPARATION

Preheat the oven to 325°F. Grease and flour a 10-inch tube pan. Into a large bowl, sift the flour, cocoa powder, baking powder, and salt; sift three times. Set aside. In another bowl, add the shortening, and beat well with a portable mixer. Add the sugar gradually, and continue beating. Add the eggs, one at a time, beating in well after each addition. Add the vanilla. Add the milk and flour mixtures alternately, beating well. The batter will resemble a mousse in consistency. Bake for 1 1/2 hours, or until a toothpick inserted in the middle comes out clean.

> "MY SOUTHERN GRANDMOTHERS AND MY MOTHER WERE INSTRUMENTAL IN DEVELOPING MY LOVE FOR COOKING. THIS RECIPE (AS WITH ALL OF THEIR RECIPES) WAS OBTAINED BY SITTING IN HER KITCHEN WITH PEN AND PAPER AS SHE MADE THE CAKE. MEASUREMENTS WERE CHALLENGING SINCE THESE COOKS NEVER MEASURED. THE ORIGINAL RECIPE CALLED FOR 'MEDIUM EGGS' AND 'SWEET MILK' (AS OPPOSED TO BUTTERMILK). I CHANGED IT OVER THE YEARS TO LARGE EGGS (THESE WERE MEDIUM EGGS IN HER DAY) AND JUST MILK AS 'SWEET MILK' TENDS TO BE CONFUSING TO US NORTHERNERS."

> Lynn

APPETIZERS

BREADS

BREAKFAST & BRUNCH

ENTRÉES

VEGETABLES & SIDE DISHES

SALADS

SOUPS

DESSERTS

grandma's apple strudel

James E. Hanson > *Omaha, Nebraska*

Serves 6 to 8

INGREDIENTS

2 cups flour
4 tablespoons butter
1/2 teaspoon salt
2 eggs, lightly beaten
Milk to thin
Peeled and sliced Jonathan apples or cooking apples
Sugar to taste
Ground cinnamon to taste

PREPARATION

Preheat oven to 375°F. Grease a cookie sheet. Into a large bowl, combine the flour, butter, and salt. Mix until crumbly with your fingers. Add the eggs and enough milk so that the mixture can be rolled out on a floured board like a piecrust. After rolling, cover with apple slices, and sprinkle with sugar and cinnamon. Roll up jellyroll style, and pinch ends closed. Place on the prepared cookie sheet. Bake for 1 hour, or until browned.

grandma's pound cake

Rhonda Boutte > *Oklahoma City, Oklahoma*

Serves 10 to 12

INGREDIENTS

3 cups sugar
1/2 pound (2 sticks) butter
5 eggs
3 1/3 cups all-purpose flour, sifted
1 cup whole milk
1 teaspoon baking powder
1 teaspoon vanilla extract

PREPARATION

Preheat the oven to 325°F. Grease and flour a Bundt or 10-inch tube pan.

In a large mixing bowl, beat together the sugar and butter with a portable mixer. Beat in the eggs, 1 at a time, beating for 1 minute after each addition. Stir in the flour, milk, baking powder, and vanilla. Beat well. Pour into the prepared pan.

Bake for 1 hour and 20 minutes, or until a toothpick inserted into the center comes out clean.

grandma's
banana muffins

Cindy Rosinski > *Buffalo, New York*

Serves 16 to 18

INGREDIENTS

2 cups all-purpose flour
2 teaspoons baking powder
1 teaspoon salt
1/2 teaspoon baking soda
1/4 teaspoon nutmeg
1/4 teaspoon cinnamon
1 egg, lightly beaten
1 cup mashed bananas (about 2)
1/2 cup sugar
1/3 cup margarine, melted
1/3 cup whole milk
1/2 cup jelly, such as strawberry or grape

PREPARATION

Preheat the oven to 375ºF. Line regular-sized muffin cups with muffin papers. In a large mixing bowl, combine the flour, baking powder, salt, baking soda, nutmeg, and cinnamon. In a second bowl, combine the egg, bananas, sugar, margarine, and milk. Stir the dry ingredients into the wet ingredients just until moistened. Spoon the batter into muffin cups until each is two-thirds full. Using a small spoon, place a dab of jelly in the center of each muffin, tucking it down a bit so it doesn't overflow. Bake 15 to 20 minutes.

" THESE MUFFINS ARE A TRADITION IN OUR FAMILY. MY GRANDMOTHER MADE THEM FOR MY MOM, WHO THEN MADE THEM FOR ME, AND NOW I MAKE THEM WITH MY SON. HE ENJOYS HELPING TO MAKE THEM, JUST AS I DID — MASHING THE BANANAS, MEASURING THE SPICES. IT'S A GREAT WAY FOR US TO SPEND TIME TOGETHER, AND HE ALSO LEARNS HOW TO MEASURE AND BAKE SOMETHING THAT HE LOVES. OUR BANANA MUFFINS ARE A REAL, TANGIBLE LINK BETWEEN PAST AND FUTURE BAKERS IN THE FAMILY. "

> Cindy

APPETIZERS

BREADS

BREAKFAST & BRUNCH

ENTRÉES

VEGETABLES & SIDE DISHES

SALADS

SOUPS

DESSERTS

grandmother benton's scrumptious chocolate cake

Fran Rackley > *Dallas, Georgia*

Serves 10 to 12

THIS CAKE IS SO SPECIAL TO MY COUSINS AND ME. MY GRAND-MOTHER MADE THIS CAKE FOR EVERY SPECIAL OCCASION FROM OUR BIRTHDAYS TO CHRISTMAS. HER NAME WAS FRANCES BENTON. I AM NAMED AFTER HER. SHE HAS BEEN GONE FOR QUITE A WHILE NOW, BUT HER CAKE AND MEMORIES OF OUR TIMES TOGETHER WILL ALWAYS BE HERE. SHE WAS FROM MACON, GEORGIA.

> Fran

INGREDIENTS FOR CAKE LAYERS

2 cups of sugar
1 cup (8 ounces/2 sticks) butter, at room temperature
3 cups flour (all purpose)
1 tablespoon baking powder
1/4 teaspoon salt
4 large eggs
1 cup whole milk
1 teaspoon vanilla extract

INGREDIENTS FOR FROSTING

3 cups sugar
3/4 cup whole milk
1/2 cup cocoa powder
1/2 cup (4 ounces/1 stick) butter, at room temperature
Pinch of salt
1 teaspoon vanilla extract
Pecan halve for garnish

PREPARATION FOR CAKE LAYERS

Preheat the oven to 350°F. Grease and flour two 9-inch cake pans, 3 inches deep. In a large mixing bowl, beat the sugar and butter with a portable mixer on medium until creamy. Into a second bowl, sift the flour, baking powder, and salt. Beat the eggs, 1 at a time, into the butter mixture until well blended. Stir the flour mixture and milk alternately into the batter until completely blended. Stir in the vanilla. Divide the batter between the pans.

Bake for 25 minutes, or until a toothpick inserted in the center comes out clean. Completely cool cake layers before frosting.

PREPARATION FOR FROSTING

To make the frosting, combine all the ingredients in a saucepan, and heat over medium heat until it boils, stirring constantly. Cook for 4 minutes. Remove from the heat, and beat until it is spreadable. Decorate the top of the cake with pecan halves placed around the perimeter.

grandmother's walnut cake

Judy Pender > *Greenville, South Carolina*

Serves 12

INGREDIENTS

1 cup (8 ounces/2 sticks) butter, at room temperature
2 cups sugar
4 eggs, separated
3 cups all-purpose flour
3/4 cup chopped walnuts, toasted
1 tablespoon baking powder
1 1/2 teaspoons ground mace
1/2 teaspoon salt
1 cup whole milk
1 tablespoon vanilla extract

PREPARATION

Preheat the oven to 350°F. Butter and flour a 10-inch tube pan. In a large mixing bowl, cream the butter and sugar with a portable mixer until fluffy. Beat in the egg yolks, 1 at a time, until well combined; set aside. In a large bowl, stir together the flour, walnuts, baking powder, mace, and salt; set aside. Add the milk and vanilla to the butter mixture; beat until smooth. Add half the flour mixture, beating just until combined. Add the remaining flour mixture.

In a small bowl, beat the egg whites until soft peaks form. Fold the whites into the cake batter. Pour the batter into the prepared pan. Bake for 1 hour and 15 to 20 minutes, or until light brown. Cool before removing from the pan.

APPETIZERS

BREADS

BREAKFAST & BRUNCH

ENTRÉES

VEGETABLES & SIDE DISHES

SALADS

SOUPS

hawaiian pineapple cake

Alan Durham > *Chicago, Illinois*

Serves 12

INGREDIENTS FOR CAKE

2 cups sugar
2 beaten eggs
2 cups flour
2 teaspoons baking soda
1 teaspoon vanilla
1 (20 ounce) **can crushed pineapple with juice**

INGREDIENTS FOR FROSTING

1 (8 ounce) **package cream cheese**
1/2 cup (4 ounces/1 stick) **margarine**
1 3/4 cup powdered sugar
1 teaspoon vanilla
1/2 cups chopped pecans

PREPARATION FOR CAKE

Mix all the ingredients in mixing bowl. Place in well-greased 9 by 11-inch cake pan. Bake at 350°F for 40 to 45 minutes.

PREPARATION FOR FROSTING

Mix all the ingredients until fluffy. Spread on warm cake.

holiday elderberry pie

Mary Kuhns > *Greensburg, Pennsylvania*

Yields one 9-inch pie

INGREDIENTS FOR PIE FILLING

3 1/2 cups elderberries
1 1/2 cups sugar (if berries are very tart, use 2 cups sugar)
1/4 cup tapioca or flour
1/4 cup orange juice concentrate (undiluted)
2 tablespoons lemon juice

INGREDIENTS FOR CRUST

1 1/2 cups flour
1/2 cup shortening (not butter flavor)
3 tablespoons ice water (more if needed)
1/2 teaspoon salt

PREPARATION FOR PIE FILLING

Preheat oven to 400°F. Combine all the ingredients, mixing well to combine. Set aside.

PREPARATION FOR CRUST

In a large mixing bowl, combine the flour, shortening, water, and salt. Stir together, and shape into a ball. Divide the ball in half. Roll out each half between wax paper to form a circle 1 inch larger than the pie pan.

Place one crust in a 9-inch pie pan. Pour in filling. Wet edges of bottom crust with water. Place top crust over filling, and flute the edges to seal. Cut a slit in the center of the top crust to allow steam to escape.

Bake for 30 minutes; decrease the heat to 375°F, and continue baking 45 minutes, or until crust is golden.

"THIS PIE WAS ALWAYS A THANKS-GIVING FAVORITE AT THE END OF THE BERRY SEASON."

> Mary

APPETIZERS

BREADS

BREAKFAST & BRUNCH

ENTRÉES

VEGETABLES & SIDE DISHES

SALADS

SOUPS

italian olive oil cake

Penny Fischetti > *Allison Park, Pennsylvania*

Serves 12

INGREDIENTS FOR CAKE

3 eggs
2 1/2 cups sugar
1 1/2 cups mild olive oil
1 1/2 cups whole milk
Zest of 3 oranges
2 cups sifted all-purpose flour
1/2 teaspoon baking powder
1/2 teaspoon baking soda
1/4 teaspoon salt
2 teaspoons allspice
Whipped cream for serving

INGREDIENTS FOR GLAZE

12 ounces orange marmalade
6 ounces orange liquor

PREPARATION FOR CAKE

Preheat the oven to 350°F. Grease and flour a Bundt pan. In a large mixing bowl, whisk together the eggs and sugar by hand until light, about 1 minute. Mix together the olive oil and milk, and stir it into the egg mixture. Stir in the zest.

Into a separate mixing bowl, sift the flour, baking powder, baking soda, salt, and allspice, and fold the dry ingredients into the egg mixture. Do not over mix. Pour into the prepared pan. Bake about 50 minutes, or until a toothpick inserted in the center comes out clean. Cool on a rack for about 15 minutes.

PREPARATION FOR GLAZE

For the glaze, blend the orange marmalade and the liqueur. Adjust the amount of liqueur to make a smooth glaze that pours off a spoon. Set aside.

When cool, turn the cake onto a serving plate, and spoon the glaze over the cake. Serve at room temperature with whipped cream.

john's carrot cake

John W. Kennedy > *Fishers, Indiana*

Serves 10

INGREDIENTS FOR CAKE

1 pound fresh carrots, grated
2 cups all-purpose flour
2 cups sugar
2 teaspoons baking soda
1/2 teaspoon salt
3 teaspoons cinnamon
1/2 teaspoon nutmeg
1/2 cup applesauce
1/2 cup vegetable oil
3 eggs
1/4 cup Amaretto liqueur (optional)
1/2 cup chopped walnuts (optional)
1 small can pineapple tidbits, drained (optional)
1/2 cup raisins (optional)

INGREDIENTS FOR FROSTING

8 ounces cream cheese, at room temperature
2/3 stick butter or margarine
1-pound box powdered sugar
1 teaspoon vanilla extract

PREPARATION FOR CAKE

Mix all ingredients thoroughly in a large bowl. Bake at 350°F (325°F if using glass pans) in two 9-inch round or one 13 by 9-inch greased and floured cake pan for about 45 to 50 minutes (oven times vary). Let round pans cool for 10 to 15 minutes before removing.

PREPARATION FOR FROSTING

Mix all ingredients together thoroughly. Frost cake when cool.

"I ENTERED THIS CAKE IN THE INDIANA STATE FAIR. I DIDN'T WIN BUT EVERYONE LOVES THIS CAKE!"

> John

APPETIZERS

BREADS

BREAKFAST & BRUNCH

ENTRÉES

VEGETABLES & SIDE DISHES

SALADS

SOUPS

kelley's zucchini bread

Thomas Dunlop > *Geneva, Illinois*

Yields 2 loaves

INGREDIENTS

3 eggs
2 cups sugar
1 cup canola oil
1 teaspoon vanilla extract
2 1/2 cups peeled and grated zucchini
1 1/2 cups all-purpose flour
1 1/2 cups whole wheat flour
1 tablespoon ground cinnamon
1 teaspoon salt
1 teaspoon baking soda
1/2 teaspoon baking powder

PREPARATION

Preheat the oven to 350°F. Grease two 9-inch loaf pans. In a large mixing bowl, beat the eggs until foamy with a portable mixer. Fold in the sugar, oil, vanilla, and zucchini. In a separate bowl, sift together the flours with the cinnamon, salt, baking soda, and baking powder. Stir into the egg mixture. Bake for 60 minutes.

super moist chocolate chip cake

Charles Aboyoun > *Columbia, Maryland*

Serves 6

INGREDIENTS FOR SMALL BOWL

1 teaspoon cinnamon
1 teaspoon cocoa powder
1/2 cup sugar
6 ounces chocolate chips

INGREDIENTS FOR LARGE BOWL

4 eggs (may substitute egg beaters)
1 package yellow cake mix
1 package instant vanilla pudding
8 ounces plain yogurt
1/2 cup canola oil

PREPARATION

Preheat oven to 350°F. Spray a 10-inch tube pan with pan spray. Mix together the Small Bowl items. Beat the Large Bowl items with a portable mixer for 5 minutes. Sprinkle one-third of the Small Bowl mixture to cover the bottom of the pan. Add one-half of the Large Bowl mixture. Sprinkle on one-third of the Small Bowl mixture. Add the last one-half of the Large Bowl mixture. Sprinkle on the last one-third of the Small Bowl mixture. Bake for 50 to 60 minutes.

APPETIZERS

BREADS

BREAKFAST & BRUNCH

ENTRÉES

VEGETABLES & SIDE DISHES

SALADS

SOUPS

"MY WIFE'S AUNT MARSHA MADE THIS DESSERT FOR MY WIFE AND HER BRIDESMAIDS TO SNACK ON WHILE PREPARING FOR OUR WEDDING. I'M NOT SURE IF IT WAS THE HAPPINESS OF MARRYING ME OR EATING CAKE, BUT MY WIFE LOOKED BEAUTIFUL AND WAS HAPPY THROUGH THE EVENING."

> Charles

magic bars

Mick & Lisa Rhyne > *Jefferson City, Missouri*

Yields 2 to 3 dozen

INGREDIENTS

1 1/2 cups graham cracker crumbs
1/2 cup (4 ounces/1 stick) **margarine, melted**
1 (14-ounce) **can sweetened condensed milk**
2 cups semisweet chocolate chips
1 1/3 cups flaked coconut
1 cup chopped pecans

PREPARATION

Preheat the oven to 350°F. In a large bowl, combine the crumbs and margarine, and mix well with a sturdy wooden spoon. Press the crumb mixture firmly onto the bottom of a 13 by 9-inch baking pan. Pour the milk over the crumbs. Layer the remaining ingredients evenly. Press down firmly with fork. Bake 25 minutes or until lightly brown. Cool, chill, and cut into bars. Store covered at room temperature.

Variations: You can substitute butterscotch or peanut butter chips for 1 cup of chocolate chips.

microwave fudge

Rich Friedman > *Longmont, Colorado*

Serves 10

INGREDIENTS

3 1/4 cup confectioners' sugar (1-pound package)
1 cup unsweetened Hershey's cocoa powder (comes in a brown wrapper tin)
1 cup (8 ounces/2 sticks) **butter, cut into 8 pieces**
1 cup milk, skim works just fine
1 tablespoon vanilla
1 cup chopped pecans or walnuts

PREPARATION

Measure the sugar and put in an 8 by 8 or 6 by 10-inch glass baking dish. Measure the cocoa powder and put in the dish. Stir to mix. Top with the pats of butter. Pour milk over mixture. Do not stir. Microwave on high for 2 minutes. Stir in vanilla and nuts. Cover and refrigerate for 2 hours or until set. Freezes well.

> "THIS IS REALLY FOOLPROOF AND ONLY TAKES ABOUT 10 MINUTES TO MAKE. IT FREEZES WELL AND CAN BE MADE WAY AHEAD OF THE REST OF THE COOKIE BAKING DURING THE HOLIDAYS."
>
> > Rich

marco island cookies

Kimberly Lauber > *Buffalo, New York*

Serves 20

INGREDIENTS

1 box Club crackers
1/2 cup (4 ounces/1 stick) butter
3/4 cup firmly packed brown sugar
1/2 cup granulated sugar
1 cup graham cracker crumbs
1/3 cup whole milk
2/3 cup chocolate chips
2/3 cup creamy peanut butter

PREPARATION

Lightly grease a 9 by 12-inch baking pan and line it with Club crackers. In a large saucepan, combine the butter, brown sugar, granulated sugar, graham cracker crumbs, and milk. Heat over medium heat, and bring to a boil; cook for 5 minutes. Pour the milk mixture over the crackers, and add another layer of Club crackers. In a small saucepan, melt the chocolate chips and the peanut butter over medium-low heat. Frost the cookies. Chill, and cut the cookies out, following the cracker lines.

> "THIS RECIPE WAS ONE OF MY HUSBAND'S AUNT BETTY'S FAVORITES. THIS RECIPE WAS FROM A COOKBOOK THAT WAS CREATED IN HER MEMORY. SHE PASSED AWAY FROM CANCER IN 2003."
>
> > Kimberly

APPETIZERS

BREADS

BREAKFAST & BRUNCH

ENTRÉES

VEGETABLES & SIDE DISHES

SALADS

SOUPS

DESSERTS

missma's pear preserves

Angie Boykin > *Zebulon, North Carolina*

INGREDIENTS

Pears
Sugar
1/2 cup lemon juice
Canning jars

PREPARATION

Peel and core the pears, cut into bite-sized pieces, and put the pieces into a stockpot. You will need 2 parts fruit to 1 part sugar, depending on how many pints you plan to can. Heat the pear-sugar mixture over medium heat, and bring to a rolling boil. Decrease the heat to medium-low, and cook until the pears are translucent. Stir in the lemon juice, and cook about 10 more minutes. To preserve, process jars in a boiling water bath about 25 minutes according to manufacturer's directions.

nut roll

Denise Lawson > *Chester, South Carolina*

Serves 12

INGREDIENTS

1 box vanilla wafers, crushed
1 pound candied mixed fruit
2 cups pecans, chopped
1 can sweetened condensed milk
1 (16-ounce) **box confectioners' sugar**

PREPARATION

In a large mixing bowl, combine the wafers, mixed fruit, pecans, and milk, and stir to combine well. Roll the mixture into multiple logs; sprinkle a work surface with confectioners' sugar. Roll each log in the sugar, coating it well. Wrap it in wax paper, and overwrap in aluminum foil. Chill for several hours before slicing.

monkey pull apart

Annette Gubish > *Allentown, Pennsylvania*

Serves 6

INGREDIENTS

4 cans buttermilk biscuits
1/2 cup granulated sugar
3 tablespoons cinnamon
1 cup firmly packed light brown sugar
1/2 cup (4 ounces/1 stick) **butter, melted**

PREPARATION

Preheat the oven according to directions on the biscuit package. Mix granulated sugar and cinnamon in a small bowl. Set aside. Take 2 cans of the biscuits and pull each biscuit in half and roll into balls. Roll balls in sugar and cinnamon. Place the balls in a Bundt pan. Mix brown sugar and melted butter together. Whisk to get a medium to thin paste. (You can add more butter if it is too thick and add more sugar if it's too runny). Pour 1/2 the mixture over the biscuits. Take the other 2 cans of biscuits, pull each biscuit in half, roll into balls, and roll balls into sugar and cinnamon. Place the balls in the Bundt pan. Pour the rest of the brown sugar and butter mixture over the biscuits. Bake according to directions on the biscuit can. Take out of oven and flip over onto a cookie sheet.

> "MY KIDS DEVOUR THIS WITHIN 10 MINUTES. IT MUST BE SERVED WITH A TALL COLD GLASS OF MILK."
>
> > Annette

APPETIZERS

BREADS

BREAKFAST & BRUNCH

ENTRÉES

VEGETABLES & SIDE DISHES

SALADS

SOUPS

279

DESSERTS

no-bake banana/graham cracker cake

Cindy Faulisi > *Greensburg, Pennsylvania*

Serves 12

INGREDIENTS

1 box of graham crackers
Very ripe bananas (approximately 6 or 7)
1 box of your favorite chocolate icing mix

PREPARATION

Using a 9 by 11-inch cookie sheet, lay down one layer of graham crackers covering the bottom of the pan. Cut bananas (about 1/2 inch thick) crosswise and put a single layer on top of the graham crackers (covering graham crackers completely). Top with another layer of graham crackers and another layer of bananas. Finish off the top layer with graham crackers. You can make this as many layers as you would like to use up your bananas and/or graham crackers. Mix together your favorite box of chocolate icing according to the directions on the box and cover the top. Allow to sit overnight. The next morning the crackers will have softened. Slice and enjoy!

no-bake chocolate oatmeal cookies

Teresa Laskey > *Casa Grande, Arizona*

Yields at least 2 dozen cookies

INGREDIENTS

2 cups sugar
1 cup (8 ounces/2 sticks) **butter or margarine**
1/2 cup whole milk
1/4 cup smooth or chunky peanut butter
4 tablespoons cocoa powder
3 cups quick-cooking rolled oats

PREPARATION

In a 5-quart saucepan, combine the sugar, butter, and milk, and heat over medium heat. Boil, stirring, for 1 minute. Remove from heat. Add the peanut butter and cocoa powder, and stir until smooth. Stir in the oats until these are evenly coated. Drop the dough by tablespoonfuls onto wax paper or spread into a greased 9 by 13-inch pan for bars. Let cool, slice, and enjoy.

DESSERTS

oatmeal cake with toasted coconut frosting

David Ficarra > *Rosemont, Illinois*

Serves 6 to 12

INGREDIENTS FOR CAKE

1 1/4 cups boiling water
1 cup quick-cooking rolled oats
1/2 cup (4 ounces/1 stick) margarine
2 eggs, lightly beaten
1 1/3 cups flour
1 cup firmly packed brown sugar
1 cup granulated sugar
1 teaspoon salt
1 teaspoon baking soda
1 teaspoon vanilla extract
1 teaspoon ground cinnamon
1 teaspoon ground nutmeg

INGREDIENTS FOR TOPPING

2 cups shredded coconut
1 cup sugar
1/2 cup evaporated milk
1 teaspoon vanilla extract
1 cup nuts (optional)

PREPARATION FOR CAKE

Preheat the oven to 350°F. Grease a 9 by 13-inch baking pan. In a large bowl, pour the boiling water over the oats and margarine. Cover and let stand for 20 minutes. Stir in the eggs, flour, sugars, salt, baking soda, vanilla, cinnamon, and nutmeg with a sturdy wooden spoon, mixing very well. Spread into the prepared pan. Bake for 30 to 35 minutes, or until a toothpick inserted in the center comes out clean. Cool slightly before putting on the topping.

PREPARATION FOR TOPPING

In a large bowl, stir all the ingredients together, and put on the cake while the cake is still warm (not hot). Put the under the broiler for about 5 minutes checking it often. Watch carefully; it burns easily.

"THIS IS AN OLD FAMILY RECIPE PASSED ON FROM MY WIFE MELINDA'S GREAT AUNT. IT'S A HEARTY FAMILY FAVORITE, AND A CROWD PLEASER."

> David

APPETIZERS

BREADS

BREAKFAST & BRUNCH

ENTRÉES

VEGETABLES & SIDE DISHES

SALADS

SOUPS

DESSERTS

281

oatmeal squares

Dan Salem > *Plymouth, Minnesota*

Serves 24

INGREDIENTS

3 cups regular rolled oats
2 1/2 cups all-purpose flour
2 cups firmly packed brown sugar
1 1/2 cups (12 ounces/3 sticks) butter, melted
1 teaspoon baking powder
1/2 teaspoon salt
6 ounces chocolate chips
1 (12-ounce) jar caramel ice cream topping

PREPARATION

Preheat the oven to 350°F. Grease a 9 by 11-inch baking pan. In a large mixing bowl, stir together the oats, flour, brown sugar, butter, baking powder, and salt with a sturdy wooden spoon. Press half the mixture into the prepared pan. Bake 12 minutes. Remove from the oven, and layer the chocolate chips and caramel topping over top. Press the remaining oatmeal mixture on top. Bake 20 to 24 minutes more, or until the top is slightly brown and bubbly.

old-time bread pudding

Judi Seyez > *Charlotte, North Carolina*

Serves 20

INGREDIENTS

16 slices buttered toast, cut into 1-inch squares
6 eggs, lightly beaten
3 cups evaporated milk
2 1/2 cups plus 1 cup sugar
1 to 1 1/2 cups raisins (optional)
1 tablespoon vanilla extract
1 tablespoon rum extract (or use 6 teaspoons of vanilla extract)
3 cups of boiling water
1 1/2 tablespoons ground cinnamon

PREPARATION

Preheat the oven to 350°F. Butter a 9 by 13-inch baking dish. Line the baking dish with the bread squares. In a large bowl, combine the eggs, milk, 2 1/2 cups sugar, raisins if using, and vanilla or rum extracts, stirring well. Stir in the boiling water slowly. Pour the mixture over the toast, and let stand for 15 to 20 minutes, or until the toast has soaked up most of the mixture. Combine the remaining 1 cup sugar with the cinnamon, and sprinkle over top. Bake for 50 to 60 minutes.

Optional: Once cooled, you may cut the pudding into squares, and top with whipped cream and a cherry.

APPETIZERS

BREADS

BREAKFAST & BRUNCH

ENTRÉES

VEGETABLES & SIDE DISHES

SALADS

SOUPS

DESSERTS

ooey gooey cake

Bobbie Hughes > *Deatsville, Alabama*

Serves 10

INGREDIENTS FOR CAKE

1 box of yellow cake mix
1/2 cup (4 ounces/1 stick) of margarine, melted
1 egg

INGREDIENTS FOR ICING

1 (8 ounce) stick of cream cheese, softened
1 box of confectioner or powdered sugar
2 eggs

PREPARATION FOR CAKE

Mix the cake mix, margarine, and egg in a bowl. Make sure it is mixed well because these are the only three ingredients used for the cake. Batter will be kind of stiff when finished. Pour the batter in an ungreased 8 by 11-inch oblong pan or casserole dish. Take a large spoon and spread the mix evenly in the pan. Set aside and make the icing.

PREPARATION FOR ICING

Mix the cream cheese, powdered sugar, and eggs. After it is well mixed, pour it on top of the cake mixture. Bake the cake at 350°F for 45 minutes. After the first 30 minutes check it to make sure it is not baking too fast. Let it cook until it is brown on the top. Take it out of the oven and let it cool. Cut into squares and serve. It is so good.

> "APPROXIMATELY 18 YEARS AGO, JULIE WILSON (WHO STILL WORKS FOR U.S. FOODSERVICE) WAS PREGNANT. WE WERE CELEBRATING SOMETHING IN THE OFFICE (I DON'T RECALL WHAT). I BROUGHT THIS CAKE, WHICH WAS CALLED *I CAN'T BELIEVE IT IS A CAKE*. JULIE TOOK A BITE AND STOOD UP AND SAID, 'UM UM, THIS IS A OOEY GOOEY CAKE.' IT'S BEEN CALLED THAT EVER SINCE."
>
> > Bobbie

papa's chocolate pie and german chocolate pie

Bob Snavely > *Midwest City, Oklahoma*

Serves 8

INGREDIENTS

1 1/4 cup sugar
1/3 cup all-purpose flour
4 heaping tablespoons cocoa powder
1 egg
2 cups milk
1/3 cup margarine
1 teaspoon vanilla extract
1 (9-inch) piecrust, baked
1 cup pecans, chopped (optional)
1 cup coconut, shredded

PREPARATION

Mix the sugar, flour, and cocoa powder together in a saucepan. Add the egg and gather as much of dry ingredients as possible with egg (this is very important), and then add only enough milk to moisten all of the above ingredients. Mix well and then add remaining milk. Cook over medium heat, stirring constantly to prevent lumping and burning. Bring to a full rolling boil and cook until the mixture thickens. Remove from heat and add the vanilla and margarine. Combine well. (Note: mixture may not come to a boil before is starts thickening. That is fine as long as it thickens.)

Pour mixture into 9-inch baked piecrust and cover with wax paper. Keep refrigerated. To turn this into German Chocolate pie (my favorite), mix in one cup chopped pecans before pouring into the piecrust. Cover with enough coconut to cover pie.

> "I ALWAYS DOUBLE THE RECIPE AND MAKE TWO, BECAUSE THE FIRST ONE DOESN'T LAST LONG."
>
> > Bob

APPETIZERS

BREADS

BREAKFAST & BRUNCH

ENTRÉES

VEGETABLES & SIDE DISHES

SALADS

SOUPS

peanut brittle

Kathy Miller > *Gladstone, North Dakota*

Yields 2 pans of peanut brittle

INGREDIENTS

1 cup sugar
1 cup light corn syrup
1 cup water
2 cups raw Spanish peanuts
1/2 teaspoon salt
1 tablespoon butter (not margarine)
1 teaspoon baking soda

PREPARATION

Grease 2 large baking pans. In a 3-quart saucepan, heat the sugar, corn syrup, and water over medium heat, and cook, stirring, until the sugar dissolves. Continue to cook over medium heat to the soft ball stage (234°F). Stir in the peanuts and salt carefully to avoid splattering. Cook to the hard crack stage (305°F), stirring often. Remove from the heat. Quickly add the butter and baking soda. Pour at once into the prepared pans, spreading with a spatula. Cool slightly, and stretch with a form to make it thin. Cool completely before breaking into pieces.

peanut butter bars

Randy Bergey > *Mohrsville, Pennsylvania*

Yields 20 bars

INGREDIENTS

1/2 cup (4 ounces/1 stick) butter, at room temperature
1/2 cup granulated sugar
1/2 cup firmly packed brown sugar
1/2 cup creamy peanut butter
1 egg, beaten
1 teaspoon vanilla extract
1 cup all-purpose flour
1/2 cup quick-cooking rolled oats
1 teaspoon baking soda
1/4 teaspoon salt
1 cup chocolate chips

PREPARATION

Preheat the oven to 350°F. Grease a 9 by 13-inch baking pan.

In a large mixing bowl, cream the butter, sugars, and peanut butter with a portable mixer. Add the egg and vanilla, and mix well. Stir in the flour, oats, baking soda, and salt. Spread into the prepared pan, and sprinkle with chocolate chips.

Bake for 20 to 25 minutes, or until lightly browned.

"THESE BARS ARE QUICK AND EASY TO MAKE. EVERYONE LOVES THEM."

> Randy

APPETIZERS

BREADS

BREAKFAST & BRUNCH

ENTRÉES

VEGETABLES & SIDE DISHES

SALADS

SOUPS

DESSERTS

peanut butter fudge

Susan Clark > *Columbia, South Carolina*

Yields 100 1-inch squares

INGREDIENTS

1 tablespoon butter for greasing pan
4 cups sugar
1 cup evaporated milk
18 ounces peanut butter, creamy or crunchy
1 jar marshmallow cream
2 teaspoons vanilla extract

PREPARATION

Grease a 9 by 13-inch pan with the 1 tablespoon of butter. Set aside. In a heavy 4-quart saucepan, combine the sugar and evaporated milk, mixing well. Heat over medium heat, stirring, until the mixture comes to a full rolling boil. Cook, stirring constantly, for 2 minutes. Remove from the heat and, working quickly, add the remaining ingredients, stirring until smooth. Pour the mixture into the prepared pan. Cool at room temperature until firm. Store in an airtight container at room temperature. Cut into squares as needed.

peanut butter pie

Valerie Worthington > *Richmond, Virginia*

Serves 8

INGREDIENTS

8 ounces cream cheese, at room temperature
1 cup chunky peanut butter
1 1/2 cups confectioners' sugar
1 tablespoon vanilla extract
1 (16-ounce) container frozen whipped topping, thawed
1 (9-inch) chocolate pie crust, baked
Whipped cream for garnish, if desired
Chocolate-covered peanuts for garnish, if desired

PREPARATION

In a large mixing bowl beat the cream cheese and peanut butter together with a portable mixer. Gradually add the confectioners' sugar and vanilla. Fold in the whipped topping until well blended. Pour into the prepared crust, and freeze. Before serving, top with whipped cream and chocolate-covered peanuts, if desired.

> "I USED TO MAKE AND SELL THIS PIE TO AREA RESTAURANTS WHEN I WAS IN COLLEGE AT EAST CAROLINA UNIVERSITY. AT THAT TIME, I HAD NO IDEA THAT I WOULD LATER GRADUATE FROM JOHNSON & WALES UNIVERSITY IN CHARLESTON, SOUTH CAROLINA, WITH A CULINARY ARTS DEGREE."
>
> > Valerie

peanut clusters

Sandra Olberding > *Topeka, Kansas*

Serves 24

INGREDIENTS

1 pound almond bark
18 ounces chocolate chips
1 pound Spanish peanuts

PREPARATION

Line a cookie sheet with waxed paper. Melt the almond bark in a double boiler. Add the chocolate chips and stir until melted. Add peanuts. Drop onto the wax paper-lined cookie sheet. Place in refrigerator until hardened. Yummy!

pecan praline grahams

Cathy Wofford > *Fayetteville, Georgia*

Yields 3 dozen

INGREDIENTS

1 package graham crackers
3/4 cup (1 1/2 sticks) margarine
1/2 cup sugar
1 cup chopped pecans

PREPARATION

Preheat the oven to 300°F. Line a baking sheet with parchment paper or non-stick sheets. Break the crackers into quarters and lay with sides touching on the prepared baking sheet. In a small saucepan, heat the margarine over medium-high heat. Add the sugar, stirring until it dissolves. Stir in the pecans. Continue stirring until mixture comes to a boil. Decrease the heat to medium, and cook for 3 minutes, stirring constantly. Spread mixture quickly and evenly over the graham crackers. Bake for 10 to 12 minutes. Remove from the pan, and cool on a wire rack or waxed paper.

APPETIZERS

BREADS

BREAKFAST & BRUNCH

ENTRÉES

VEGETABLES & SIDE DISHES

SALADS

SOUPS

peppernuts

Dallon E. Nye > *Ogden, Utah*

Yields 5 dozen

These are great dunked briefly in hot chocolate! They make great gifts!

INGREDIENTS

3 large or 4 small eggs, lightly beaten
1/4 cup (2 ounces/1/2 stick) butter, melted
1 cup granulated sugar
1 cup brown sugar
4 to 4 1/2 cups all-purpose flour
1 teaspoon cinnamon
1/2 teaspoon ginger
1/4 teaspoon allspice or cloves
1/4 teaspoon salt
1/2 teaspoon cardamom
1/2 to 1 teaspoon white pepper

PREPARATION

In a large mixing bowl. Combine all the ingredients, mixing well with a portable mixer. Chill the dough. Preheat the oven to 350°F. Spray a large baking sheet with nonstick spray, if desired. Roll out pieces of dough into the circumference of a finger. Cut with a table knife into pieces about 1/3 to 1/2-inch long. Place the pieces on the baking sheet. Bake for 15 to 20 minutes.

pig-lickin' cake

Darra VanAlstyne > *Port Orange, Florida*

Serves 8 to 10

INGREDIENTS FOR CAKE

1 box butter recipe cake mix
4 eggs
3/4 cup vegetable oil
1 (11 ounce) can mandarin oranges, do not drain

INGREDIENTS FOR ICING

1 container Cool Whip Extra Creamy
1 large box Jell-O Instant Vanilla Pudding
1 (20-ounce) can crushed pineapple, do not drain

PREPARATION FOR CAKE

Beat together all the cake ingredients. Pour into 2 greased and floured round cake pans. Bake at 350°F for 25 to 30 minutes until set.

PREPARATION FOR ICING

Blend together all Icing ingredients. Refrigerate until firm (1 to 2 hours).

> "THIS IS MY HUSBAND'S FAVORITE CAKE. I LIKE IT TOO BECAUSE IT'S SO EASY TO MAKE! IT IS UNBELIEVABLY MOIST, AND THE ICING IS REFRESHING—NOT SWEET LIKE SOME ICINGS. I HAVE NO IDEA WHERE THE NAME 'PIG-LICKIN' CAKE' COMES FROM, BUT ONCE YOU TRY THIS CAKE YOU WON'T FORGET THE NAME!"
>
> > Darra

pink velvet pie

Marge Arndt > *Blaine, Minnesota*

Serves 8

INGREDIENTS

16 graham crackers, crushed
4 tablespoons butter, melted
1 small package strawberry Jell-O
1/2 cup hot water
1/4 cup lemon juice
1/4 cup sugar
1 can Carnation milk, chilled ice crystal cold

PREPARATION

In a large bowl, combine the crackers and butter well. Pat the mixture into a 9-inch pie plate, reserving 1/4 cup to sprinkle on the top. In a small bowl, dissolve the Jell-O in the hot water. Add the lemon juice and sugar. Let stand while whipping the milk until stiff with a portable mixer on high. Stir in the Jell-O mixture, and continue beating until stiff peaks form. Pour into the piecrust, and sprinkle the remaining cracker crumbs on top. Chill about 4 hours.

> "MY GRANDMA MADE THIS PIE EVERY CHRISTMAS. IT WAS A FAVORITE WITH ALL OF US KIDS. IT'S A VERY LIGHT DESSERT AFTER A BIG MEAL."
>
> > Marge

pound cake

Judith Miller > *Raleigh, North Carolina*

Serves 12

INGREDIENTS

3 cups sifted all-purpose flour
1/2 teaspoon baking powder
1/4 teaspoon salt
3 cups sugar
1 cup (8 ounces/2 sticks) butter, at room temperature
1/2 cup vegetable shortening
5 eggs, at room temperature
1 cup evaporated milk
2 teaspoons vanilla extract

PREPARATION

Into a large mixing bowl, sift the flour, baking powder, and salt together. Beat the sugar, butter, and vegetable shortening with a portable mixer, until the mixture is almost white and very light. Add the unbeaten eggs one at a time. Add the flour mixture alternately with the evaporated milk. Stir in the vanilla. Pour in a tube pan. Put it into a *cold* oven.

Bake at 300°F. Do not open the oven door for 1 hour, 45 minutes. The cake is done when it leaves the sides of the pan. Delicious.

pumpkin bread

Jim Guthrie > *Roanoke, Virginia*

Yields 2 loaves

Top these loaves with a cream cheese frosting and you have an instant dessert. Delicious!

INGREDIENTS

3 cups all-purpose flour
1 1/2 cups sugar
1 1/2 teaspoons ground cinnamon
1 teaspoon baking soda
1 teaspoon salt
3/4 teaspoon ground nutmeg
3/4 teaspoon ground cloves
1/2 teaspoon baking powder
3 eggs
1 (16-ounce) **can pumpkin purée**
1 cup vegetable oil

PREPARATION

Preheat the oven to 350°F. Grease two 8 1/2 by 4 1/2-inch loaf pans. In a large bowl, mix the flour, sugar, cinnamon, baking soda, salt, nutmeg, cloves, and baking powder with a fork. In a medium bowl, beat the eggs, pumpkin purée, and oil with a fork until blended. Stir into flour mixture just until flour is moistened. Spoon evenly into loaf pans. Bake 55 to 60 minutes, or until a toothpick inserted in the center comes out clean. Cool in pans on a rack for 10 minutes. Remove from the pans, and cool completely on a rack.

APPETIZERS

BREADS

BREAKFAST &
BRUNCH

ENTRÉES

VEGETABLES &
SIDE DISHES

SALADS

SOUPS

293

DESSERTS

pumpkin cake

Gary Hinson > *North Augusta, South Carolina*

Serves 6 to 8

INGREDIENTS FOR CAKE

1 box yellow cake mix
4 eggs, beaten
3/4 cup sugar
1/2 cup oil
1 cup pumpkin pie mix
1/4 cup water
1 teaspoon ground cinnamon
1 teaspoon ground nutmeg

INGREDIENTS FOR ICING

1/2 cup (1 stick) margarine, melted
1 box confectioners' sugar
3 ounces cream cheese, at room temperature
1 teaspoon vanilla extract
1 cup pecans, toasted

PREPARATION FOR CAKE

Preheat oven to 350°F. Grease and flour a Bundt pan. In a large mixing bowl, combine the cake mix, eggs, sugar, oil, pumpkin pie mix, water, cinnamon, and nutmeg, and beat with a portable mixer. Pour the batter into the prepared pan. Bake for 35 minutes, or until a toothpick inserted in the center comes out clean.

PREPARATION FOR ICING

Meanwhile, in a large bowl, combine the margarine, sugar, cream cheese, and vanilla, beating well with a portable mixer. When the cake is cool, spread on the icing, and garnish the cake with the pecans,

pumpkin cheesecake bars

Linda Pacione > *West Bloomfield, Michigan*

Yields 48 bars

INGREDIENTS

1 (16-ounce) package pound cake mix
3 eggs
2 tablespoons margarine or butter, melted
4 teaspoons pumpkin pie spice
1 (8-ounce) package cream cheese, at room temperature
1 (14-ounce) can sweetened condensed milk (NOT evaporated milk)
1 (16-ounce) can pumpkin purée (about 2 cups)
1/2 teaspoon salt
1 cup chopped nuts

PREPARATION

Preheat oven to 350°F. Grease a 10 by 15-inch jellyroll pan. In large mixing bowl, combine the cake mix, 1 egg, margarine, and 2 teaspoons pumpkin pie spice. Beat with a portable mixer on low speed until crumbly. Press the mixture into the bottom of the prepared pan.

In a large mixing bowl, beat the cream cheese with a portable mixer until fluffy. Gradually beat in the condensed milk, the remaining 2 eggs, pumpkin puree, remaining 2 teaspoons pumpkin pie spice, and the salt; mix well. Pour the mixture over the crust and sprinkle with nuts.

Bake 30 to 35 minutes or until set. Cool. Chill, and cut into bars. Store the bars covered in the refrigerator.

APPETIZERS

BREADS

BREAKFAST & BRUNCH

ENTRÉES

VEGETABLES & SIDE DISHES

SALADS

SOUPS

pumpkin crunch

Melissa Moon > *Lenexa, Kansas*

Serves 20

INGREDIENTS

1 (15-ounce) can pumpkin puree
1 (12-ounce) can evaporated milk
3 eggs
1 1/2 cups sugar
1 teaspoon ground cinnamon
1/2 teaspoon salt
1 package yellow cake mix
1/2 cup chopped pecans
1 cup butter, melted

PREPARATION

Preheat the oven to 350°F. Grease a 9 by 13-inch pan. In a large mixing bowl, combine the pumpkin purée, milk, eggs, sugar, cinnamon, and salt. Pour into the prepared pan. Sprinkle the cake mix evenly over the mixture. Top with pecans. Drizzle the melted butter over pecans. Bake for 50 to 55 minutes, or until golden brown. Let cool, and serve chilled.

pumpkin pecan pie

Brenda Turner > *North Newton, Kansas*

Serves 8 to 10

INGREDIENTS

3 eggs, lightly beaten
1 can pumpkin purée
1 cup sugar
1/2 cup dark corn syrup
1 teaspoon vanilla extract
1/2 teaspoon ground cinnamon
1/4 teaspoon salt
1 (9-inch) piecrust, unbaked
1 cup chopped pecans
Whipped cream for topping

PREPARATION

Preheat the oven to 350°F. In a large mixing bowl, beat the eggs, pumpkin purée, sugar, corn syrup, vanilla, cinnamon, and salt with a portable mixer on medium speed. Pour the mixture into the piecrust, and top it with the pecans. Bake for about 40 minutes, or until a knife inserted halfway between center and edge comes out clean. Serve topped with whipped cream.

> "MY MOM FOUND THIS RECIPE IN 1966 IN A MENNONITE COOKBOOK FROM MY DAD'S HOME CHURCH IN MT. LAKE, MINNESOTA. IT IS A DELICIOUS COMBINATION BETWEEN A PUMPKIN PIE AND A PECAN PIE, AND THE ONLY KIND OF PIE I EVER REMEMBER HAVING AT THANKSGIVING AND CHRISTMAS. NOW THAT I HAVE MY OWN FAMILY, IT IS STILL THE MOST POPULAR PIE IN OUR HOUSE, WHICH BOTH KIDS INSIST ON HAVING. EVEN MY HUSBAND'S FAMILY REALLY ENJOYS IT AT THE HOLIDAYS AND WE "CAN'T COME OVER UNLESS WE BRING THIS PIE."
>
> > Brenda

quick cobbler

Teresa Laskey > *Casa Grande, Arizona*

Serves 20

INGREDIENTS FOR COBBLER

1 (15-ounce) can of fruit, drained
1 cup sugar
1 cup flour
1 teaspoon baking powder
1 cup milk
1 egg

INGREDIENTS FOR TOPPING

1/4 cup butter
1 teaspoon sugar
1 teaspoon cinnamon

PREPARATION

Heat the fruit in a saucepan. Pour the fruit into 9 by 13-inch baking dish. Mix the sugar, flour, baking powder, milk, and egg and stir until smooth. Pour over fruit. Dot with the butter and sprinkle the sugar and cinnamon on top. Bake at 350°F 15 to 20 minutes until brown. Best if served when warm.

"THIS RECIPE WAS GIVEN TO ME BY MY AUNT. SHE WOULD ALWAYS MAKE ME PEACH COBBLER BECAUSE IT WAS MY FAVORITE."

> Teresa

APPETIZERS

BREADS

BREAKFAST & BRUNCH

ENTRÉES

VEGETABLES & SIDE DISHES

SALADS

SOUPS

DESSERTS

rhubarb crunch coffee cake

Marilyn Cuber > *Darien, Illinois*

Serves 20

INGREDIENTS

2 cups sugar
3/4 cup (1 1/4 sticks) margarine
1 egg, beaten
2 cups flour
1 teaspoon baking soda
1 teaspoon salt (scant)
1 cup buttermilk
2 cups finely diced rhubarb
1 teaspoon vanilla extract
1 teaspoon ground cinnamon

PREPARATION

Preheat the oven to 350°F. Spray one 9 by 13-inch baking pan with nonstick spray. In a large bowl, beat together 1 1/2 cups sugar and 1/2 cup margarine with a portable mixer. Add egg, mixing well. Into a large bowl, sift the flour, baking soda, and salt together. Beat the flour mixture into the margarine mixture alternately with the buttermilk. Fold in the rhubarb and vanilla. Pour the mixture into the prepared pan. Mix the remaining 1/2 cup sugar, 1/4 cup margarine, and cinnamon until crumbly, and sprinkle over the batter. Bake for 35 to 45 minutes.

> " THERE WERE EIGHT CHILDREN IN MY FATHER'S FAMILY, WITH LOTS OF COUSINS. A FEW YEARS BACK, AS A 'FAMILY,' WE DECIDED TO PUBLISH A COOKBOOK, *SHOVER FAMILY FAVORITES*. THIS IS ONE OF OUR FAVORITE RECIPES. AS A MATTER OF FACT, IT IS SO GOOD, BOTH MY SON AND HUSBAND ENJOY IT WITHOUT KNOWING THEY ARE EATING RHUBARB! MUCH GOOD EATING. "
>
> > Marilyn

ricotta cheese cookies

Marlene Groh > *Charlotte, North Carolina*

Yields 5 dozen

INGREDIENTS FOR COOKIE DOUGH

3 eggs
2 cups sugar
1 pound ricotta
1 cup (8 ounces/2 sticks) butter, at room temperature
2 teaspoons vanilla extract
1 teaspoon baking soda
1 teaspoon salt
4 cups all-purpose flour

INGREDIENTS FOR COOKIE ICING

1 box of confectioners' sugar
3 ounces cream cheese, at room temperature
2 tablespoons butter, at room temperature
A little milk

PREPARATION FOR COOKIE DOUGH

Preheat the oven to 350°F. In a large mixing bowl, beat together the eggs, sugar, ricotta, butter, vanilla, baking soda, and salt with a portable mixer. Gradually beat in the flour. Drop by teaspoons onto cookie sheet. Bake for about 15 minutes. Cool cookies before icing.

PREPARATION FOR ICING

Beat together all ingredients except milk. Add milk to give correct texture. When icing cookies, you can add sprinkles to decorate or put a little food coloring in the icing mixture.

> "THIS IS ONE OF OUR FAMILY'S FAVORITE CHRISTMAS COOKIES. THE SEASON IS NOT COMPLETE UNTIL SOMEONE PULLS OUT THESE COOKIES AND MILK."
>
> > Marlene

APPETIZERS

BREADS

BREAKFAST & BRUNCH

ENTRÉES

VEGETABLES & SIDE DISHES

SALADS

SOUPS

DESSERTS

rose's zucchini bread

Jack Collins > *Grass Valley, California*

Yields 2 loaves

INGREDIENTS

3 cups all-purpose flour
1 tablespoon cinnamon
1 teaspoon salt
1 teaspoon baking soda
1 teaspoon baking powder
1 teaspoon allspice
3 eggs
1 cup vegetable oil
2 1/4 cups sugar
2 cups grated zucchini
1 cup grated carrots
1 cup chopped nuts (optional)
1 cup chopped walnuts (optional)
1 tablespoon vanilla extract

PREPARATION

Preheat oven to 325°F. Grease and flour two 8 by 4-inch loaf pans. Into a large bowl, sift the flour, cinnamon, salt, baking soda, baking powder, and allspice together. In a separate bowl, beat the eggs, oil, and sugar together with a hand-held beater on high until it looks like lemon pie filling (at least 2 minutes on high). Slowly add the flour mixture to the creamed mixture, beating well. Stir in the zucchini, carrots, and nuts, if using, and the vanilla. Pour into prepared pans. Bake for 40 to 60 minutes, or until a toothpick inserted in the center comes out clean. Cool in pan for 20 minutes to overnight. Turn upside down, tap the corners lightly, and remove the bread to completely cool.

"THIS RECIPE IS FROM ONE OF MY FAVORITE PEOPLE. ROSE WAS A PREP COOK AT THE RUSTY SCUPPER IN LIVINGSTON, NEW JERSEY, WAY BACK IN THE MID-1980s. SHE WAS ITALIAN AND BROUGHT HER HERITAGE WITH HER TO THE RESTAURANT. SHE LOVED FEEDING LARGE GROUPS OF PEOPLE AND THAT'S EXACTLY WHAT SHE DID, ONLY IF YOU CAN IMAGINE, IT WAS ON A 5-DAY-A-WEEK BASIS. MONDAY THROUGH FRIDAY, ROSE WAS IN THE KITCHEN, BAKING AND COOKING FROM HER FAMILY HERITAGE TO GIVE A SLICE OF HER HOME TO THE LUCKY ONES WHO FREQUENTED THAT PARTICULAR PLACE. HOW FORTUNATE LESLIE AND I WERE TO HAVE KNOWN ROSE SALVATORE."

> Jack

ruby's refrigerator fruitcake

Barbara Hankins > *Charlotte, North Carolina*

Yields 2 loaves

These make great Christmas gifts. Note that the smaller aluminum loaf pans work great when you need several for gifts. This recipe freezes very well for later use.

INGREDIENTS

1 pound vanilla wafers, crushed
1 pound walnuts, chopped
1 pound pecans, chopped
1 pound golden raisins
8 ounces green candied cherries, coarsely chopped
8 ounces red candied cherries, coarsely chopped
1 (14-ounce) **bag flaked coconut**
1 pound mini marshmallows
2 cups evaporated milk

PREPARATION

Line 2 large loaf pans with waxed paper. In a large mixing bowl, combine the wafers, walnuts, pecans, raisins, candied cherries, and coconut. In a large saucepan, melt the marshmallows in the evaporated milk over low heat, while stirring constantly until smooth. Mix the mixture with the dry ingredients. Pack the mixture into the prepared loaf pans. Chill overnight.

Remove from the pans, and slice as needed.

"RUBY WAS MY MOM. EACH YEAR EVERYONE LOOKED FORWARD TO RECEIVING HER FRUITCAKES AS GIFTS, BECAUSE OF ITS RICH, SWEET TASTE. WHEN HER HEALTH STARTED FAILING, I TOOK OVER. MY CHILDREN ARE NOW LEARNING HOW TO MAKE THIS FRUITCAKE SO WE CAN CONTINUE THIS FAMILY TRADITION. WE HOPE YOU WILL ENJOY IT AS MUCH AS WE HAVE."

> Barbara

APPETIZERS

BREADS

BREAKFAST & BRUNCH

ENTRÉES

VEGETABLES & SIDE DISHES

SALADS

SOUPS

ruth's banana bread

Ruth Clevenger > *Lexington, South Carolina*

Yields 1 loaf

INGREDIENTS

1 1/4 cup all-purpose flour
1/2 cup whole wheat flour
1 tablespoon wheat germ
1 teaspoon baking soda
1/4 teaspoon salt
1/2 cup pecans or walnuts chopped
1/2 cup sugar
1/4 cup canola oil or vegetable oil
1 teaspoon water
1 large egg
1 cup mashed ripe bananas (about 2 medium)
1 teaspoon vanilla extract

PREPARATION

Preheat oven to 350°F. Lightly grease an 8 by 4 by 2-inch loaf pan. Combine the flours, wheat germ, baking soda, and salt in a small bowl. Mix well, stir in nuts and set aside. In medium mixing bowl combine sugar and oil. Beat at medium speed 2 minutes or until well blended. Add water and egg; beat until light and lemon colored. Mixing at low speed, add flour mixture alternately with bananas, beginning and ending with flour mixture. Blend well after each addition. Stir in vanilla. Pour batter into the prepared loaf pan. Bake 45 to 50 minutes or until toothpick inserted in center comes out clean. Cool 15 minutes in pan. Remove from pan and let cool completely on wire rack.

"YOU CAN USE FEWER EGGS, OIL, AND SUGAR AND STILL MAKE GOOD BREAD. YOU CAN EASILY DOUBLE THIS RECIPE AND FREEZE SOME. EVERYONE AT WORK ENJOYED IT AND ASKED FOR MORE."

> Ruth

santa's snickers surprises

Mary Kuhns > *Greensburg, Pennsylvania*

Yields about 6 dozen cookies

INGREDIENTS

1 cup (8 ounces/2 sticks) **butter, at room temperature**
1 cup creamy peanut butter
1 cup firmly packed brown sugar
1 cup granulated sugar
2 eggs
1 teaspoon vanilla extract
3 1/2 cups all-purpose flour, sifted
1 teaspoon baking soda
1/2 teaspoon salt
2 13-ounce bags of mini Snickers

PREPARATION

Preheat the oven to 325°F. Grease a baking sheet.

In a large bowl, beat together the butter, peanut butter, and both sugars with a portable mixer on medium speed until light and fluffy. Beat in eggs, one at a time. Beat in the vanilla until well mixed. Stir in the flour, baking soda, and salt. Cover and chill dough for 2 to 3 hours.

Meanwhile, unwrap all the Snickers. Remove the dough from the refrigerator, and spoon out a 1-tablespoon-sized piece. Roll it around a Snicker to form a ball. Place on the prepared sheet. Repeat with the remaining ingredients.

Bake for 10 to 12 minutes. Cool on a rack.

APPETIZERS

BREADS

BREAKFAST & BRUNCH

ENTRÉES

VEGETABLES & SIDE DISHES

SALADS

SOUPS

sharon's banana nut bread

Sharon K. Parker > *Daytona Beach, Florida*

Yields 1 loaf

INGREDIENTS

1 cup sugar
2 cups all purpose flour
3 ripe bananas, mashed
1/2 cup salad oil
1 teaspoon soda
1 teaspoon baking powder
1/2 teaspoon salt
1 teaspoon vanilla
1 cup black walnuts

PREPARATION

Combine the sugar and flour. In a large mixing bowl, mix the remaining ingredients. Add wet ingredients to dry ingredients. Bake in a small bread loaf pan at 350°F for about 50 minutes. Don't bake too long or it will be dry (check with a toothpick).

sunflower seed cookies

Waynetta Parker > *St. Louis, Missouri*

Yields approximately 5 dozen

INGREDIENTS

1 cup (8 ounces/2 sticks) **butter**
1 cup firmly packed brown sugar
1 cup granulated sugar
2 eggs
1 teaspoon vanilla extract
3 cups quick-cooking rolled oats
1 1/2 cups all-purpose flour
1 teaspoon salt
3/4 teaspoon baking soda
1 cup sunflower seed kernels, roasted and salted

PREPARATION

Preheat the oven to 350°F. Lightly grease 2 baking sheets. In a mixing bowl, beat together the butter and sugars with a portable mixer until creamy. Add the eggs and vanilla, and beat to blend well. Fold in the oats, flour, salt, and baking soda with a sturdy wooden spoon. Mix thoroughly. Gently blend in the sunflower seeds. Form the dough into long rolls, about 1 1/2 inches in diameter. Wrap the rolls in plastic wrap and chill thoroughly. When firm, slice each roll into pieces 1/4-inch thick. Bake for 10 minutes, or until lightly browned.

> "I DISCOVERED THIS RECIPE IN 2003. IT SOON BECAME MY DAUGHTER'S FAVORITE!"
>
> > Waynetta

APPETIZERS

BREADS

BREAKFAST & BRUNCH

ENTRÉES

VEGETABLES & SIDE DISHES

SALADS

SOUPS

DESSERTS

swedish tea ring

Jody Hollister > *Rosemont, Illinois*

Serves 12

INGREDIENTS

2 packages active dry yeast
1 1/2 cups warm water
1 cup sugar
1 3/4 teaspoon salt
1/4 cup shortening, melted
1 egg, well beaten
5 to 5 1/4 cups sifted all-purpose flour
2 to 5 teaspoons melted butter, or more as needed
6 tablespoons sugar
1 tablespoon ground cinnamon, or more as needed

PREPARATION

In a small mixing bowl, dissolve the yeast in the warm water. Stir in the sugar, salt, shortening, and egg. Add the flour, slowing beating lightly with a sturdy wooden spoon until the dough is ready to knead (it will not be tacky or sticky). Lightly flour a work surface, and turn the dough onto the flour. Knead until smooth and elastic. (This dough should be slightly softer than bread dough.) Place in a bowl, and cover with a warm, damp cloth. Set in a warm place away from drafts. Allow the dough to double in bulk. Work the dough down lightly, and cover with a warm, damp cloth, and allow the dough to double in bulk again. Preheat the oven 425°F. Spray a baking sheet with nonstick spray.

Turn the dough onto the lightly floured surface, and roll the dough with a rolling pin into a rectangular sheet about 1 1/2 inches thick. Spread the melted butter on the dough, and liberally sprinkle sugar and cinnamon on the butter. Let mixture absorb into butter, and roll one long side toward the other long side to form a log. Pinch the seams together and join the two ends to form a ring. Pinch the two ends together to seal. Carefully move to the prepared sheet. Cut the dough on top with kitchen scissors or a knife to form 3-inch sections, each 1/2-inch deep. Slightly pull down each section so that it lies flat on the baking sheet. Sprinkle with more sugar and cinnamon. Cover with a warm, damp cloth until the ring triples in size. Bake for 30 minutes. You can make individual rolls by slicing the log before joining the two ends. Place flat on baking sheet, sprinkle with sugar and cinnamon and bake 12 to 15 minutes.

> "THE FIRST TIME I REMEMBER HAVING MY GRANDMA ALICE'S SWEDISH TEA RING WAS DURING THE 1967 CHICAGO BLIZZARD. I WAS 12, MY SISTER WAS 10, AND MY BROTHER WAS 8. WE TRUDGED THROUGH THE SNOW TO BRING THEM SUPPLIES FROM THE GROCERY STORE. MY FATHER LED THE WAY BECAUSE THE POWDERED SNOW WAS UP TO OUR WAISTS IN SPOTS. ONE OF THE ITEMS ON GRANDMA'S LIST WAS YEAST. WE THREE CHILDREN WONDERED WHAT THIS TINY PACKET WAS FOR.
>
> AFTER GRANDMA HELPED US UNWRAP OUR LAYERS OF CLOTHING, SHE PLACED PAPER NAPKINS WITH WARM, CINNAMON SLICES OF HER TEA RING INTO OUR CHILLED HANDS. WE LICKED OUR FINGERS CLEAN. GRANDMA MADE SURE WE HAD PLENTY OF SWEDISH TEA RING TO TAKE HOME WITH US THAT DAY. THAT'S WHEN WE REALIZED WHAT THE LITTLE PACKETS WERE FOR.
>
> THE TRIP HOME DIDN'T SEEM NEARLY AS LONG; THE SNOW WASN'T AS DEEP, AND THE COLD WASN'T AS BITTER. WITH WARM HEARTS AND SMILES, WE ARRIVED HOME SAFE AND SOUND TO SHARE THE GOODIES WITH OUR MOTHER AND BABY SISTER."
>
> > Jody

tater candy

Jeanene Bishop > *Douglasville, Georgia*

Serves 12

INGREDIENTS

1 small white potato
2 pounds confectioners' sugar
1 (28-ounce) jar creamy or crunchy peanut butter

PREPARATION

The size of your potato will dictate your yield. I strongly suggest you make it a small one. Boil, peel, and mash the potato. Add the sugar until you get a dough-like consistency (it will get soupy before it gets doughy). Roll the dough out on wax paper and use the confectioners' sugar as a flouring agent.

Roll the mixture to about 3/16-inch thick. Spread it evenly with peanut butter to about 1/8-inch thick. Using the confectioners' sugar to dust the work surface, roll the mixture into a log, and slice it into 1/2-inch-thick pieces. Enjoy immediately. Place extras in an airtight container to keep fresh.

simple cobbler

Paula Jackson > *Bartlett, Illinois*

Serves 8

INGREDIENTS

1 cup all-purpose flour
1 cup sugar
1 1/2 teaspoon baking powder
1/2 cup milk
Pinch of salt
1/2 cup (4 ounces/1 stick) butter
1 large can of fruit

PREPARATION

Preheat the oven to 350°F. In a large bowl, combine the flour, sugar, baking powder, milk, and salt, and stir into a batter. Cut the butter into thin slices, and place in the bottom of a 9-inch cake pan. Drain the fruit, and reserve the juice. Pour the batter over the butter, evening it out with a spoon to cover the bottom of the pan. Pour in the fruit, and add the juice. If desired, you may add a small amount of water. Bake at for 50 to 60 minutes.

> "MY PAPA HOYT MADE THIS CANDY OFTEN WHEN I WAS A KID. IN MY FAMILY IT WAS ALWAYS CALLED 'TATER CANDY,' AND I WOULDN'T EAT IT BECAUSE I THOUGHT IT WAS MADE OF SWEET POTATOES. IT WASN'T UNTIL LATER, THAT I REALIZED IT WAS PEANUT BUTTER, NOT SWEET POTATOES THAT GAVE IT THE COLOR. I NOW PREFER THE CRUNCHY OVER THE CREAMY."
>
> > Jeanene

> "THIS WAS MY GRANDMOTHER IMOGENE KINNEY'S RECIPE. I ASKED HER WHERE SHE GOT IT, AND SHE TOLD ME SHE MADE IT UP. I'VE USED PEACHES, CHERRIES, AND BLACKBERRIES TO MAKE DIFFERENT COBBLERS. THE RECIPE IS QUICK, EASY, AND DELICIOUS."
>
> > Paula

APPETIZERS

BREADS

BREAKFAST & BRUNCH

ENTRÉES

VEGETABLES & SIDE DISHES

SALADS

SOUPS

thumbprint cookies

Patricia Stephens > *Kyle, Texas*

Yields 3 dozen

INGREDIENTS FOR COOKIES

1/2 cup butter, at room temperature
1/2 cup confectioners' sugar
1/4 teaspoon salt
1 teaspoon vanilla extract
1 to 1 1/4 cups all-purpose flour

INGREDIENTS FOR FILLING

1 (3-ounce) package cream cheese, at room temperature
1 cup sifted confectioners' sugar
2 tablespoons all-purpose flour
1 teaspoon vanilla extract
1/2 cup chopped pecans
1/2 cup flaked coconut

INGREDIENTS FOR FROSTING

1/2 cup semisweet chocolate chips
2 tablespoons butter
2 tablespoons water
1/2 cup sifted confectioners' sugar

PREPARATION FOR COOKIES

Heat oven to 350°F. In a large bowl, cream the butter with a portable mixer on high. Beat in the sugar, salt, and vanilla, and beat until smooth. Gradually add the flour, beating until well incorporated. Shape by teaspoonfuls into balls. Place on a cookie sheet. Press a thumb into the center of each ball.

Bake for 12 to 15 minutes, or until delicately browned. Fill the cookies while warm. Cool, and frost.

PREPARATION FOR FILLING

In a large mixing bowl, beat together the cream cheese, sugar, flour, and vanilla. Mix well. Stir in the pecans and coconut. Place a teaspoon of filling into the thumbprint of each warm cookie.

PREPARATION FOR FROSTING

Into a small saucepan, put the chocolate chips, butter, and water, and heat over low heat, stirring constantly. Beat in the confectioners' sugar until smooth. Pour a teaspoonful of frosting over top of each filled cookie.

THESE COOKIES WERE THE OBJECT OF A GREAT COOKIE RAID. THIS RECIPE HAS BEEN A FAMILY FAVORITE FOR OVER 40 YEARS. DURING A FAMILY REUNION A FEW YEARS AGO, SOME OF THE LADIES DECIDED ABOUT MIDNIGHT THAT THEY NEEDED A MIDNIGHT SNACK. EIGHT LADIES, ALL OVER 50 YEARS OLD, WENT QUIETLY SEARCHING THROUGH HOTEL ROOMS OF SEVERAL FAMILY MEMBERS FOR THESE COOKIES. THERE WAS A LOT OF LAUGHTER, A SHORT CHASE AROUND THE HOTEL PARKING LOT, AND THE PRIZE WAS THUMBPRINT COOKIES.

> Patricia

to-die-for lemon bars

Carol Wenker > *Champlin, Minnesota*

Serves 20

INGREDIENTS FOR CRUST

1 cup all-purpose flour
1/2 cup (4 ounces/1 stick) butter, melted
1/4 cup confectioners' sugar

INGREDIENTS FOR FILLING

1 cup sugar
3 tablespoons all-purpose flour
1/2 teaspoon baking powder
Pinch of shredded coconut
2 eggs
4 tablespoons freshly squeezed lemon juice

INGREDIENTS FOR FROSTING

1/2 (4 ounces/1 stick) cup butter, melted
1 cup confectioners' sugar plus extra as desired
Lemon juice, as desired

PREPARATION FOR CRUST

Preheat the oven to 350°F. In a large mixing bowl, mix together the flour, butter, and sugar, and press the mixture into an ungreased 9 by 13-inch baking pan. Bake until light brown, about 10 minutes.

PREPARATION FOR FILLING

Meanwhile, in a large mixing bowl, combine the sugar, flour, baking powder, and coconut, mixing well. Set aside. In a separate bowl, beat the eggs with a portable mixer until foamy. Add the lemon juice, then stir the egg mixture into the sugar mixture, mixing well. Pour this over the crust. Bake for 20 to 25 minutes.

PREPARATION FOR FROSTING

Meanwhile, in a large mixing bowl, beat together the butter and sugar with a portable mixer. Beat for 10 minutes. For additional lemon flavoring, add 2 tablespoons lemon juice to the frosting ingredients and increase the sugar to 1 1/4 cups. When bars are cool, spread the frosting on top.

APPETIZERS

BREADS

BREAKFAST & BRUNCH

ENTRÉES

VEGETABLES & SIDE DISHES

SALADS

SOUPS

DESSERTS

warren's christmas fudge

Judy Hedrick > *Remington, Virginia*

Serves 20

INGREDIENTS

3/4 cups (6 ounces/1 1/2 sticks) **butter**
3 cups sugar
3/4 cup evaporated milk
1 12-ounce bag of either chocolate or peanut butter chips
8 ounce jar marshmallow cream
1 teaspoon vanilla
Walnuts (optional)

PREPARATION

Melt the butter, sugar, and evaporated milk together. Bring to a rolling boil. Continue boiling for 5 minutes stirring continually. Add either chocolate or peanut butter chips. Stir until melted. Remove from heat. Add remaining ingredients and stir until smooth. Pour into a 9 by 13-inch pan. Chill for 4 hours or overnight. Cut into squares and enjoy.

yum yum cake

Robert Campbell > *Altoona, Pennsylvania*

Serves 20

INGREDIENTS

1 box yellow cake mix
1 box vanilla instant pudding
1 cup milk
1 8-ounce package Cool Whip
1 8-ounce package softened cream cheese
1 20-ounce can crushed pineapple
Coconut
Walnuts

PREPARATION

Grease and flour a 9 by 13-inch cake pan. Mix cake as directed on package. Pour batter into prepared pan and bake as directed on package. Cool. Mix together the pudding mix and milk. Set aside. Mix together the cream cheese and Cool Whip. Blend well into pudding mixture. Spread on cool cake. Top with pineapple after draining juice completely. Sprinkle coconut and chopped walnuts on top of the pineapple.

willie's banana nut bread

Brenda Jederlinic > *Albuquerque, New Mexico*

Yields 1 loaf

INGREDIENTS

2 cups all-purpose flour
2 cups sugar
Pinch of salt
1 1/2 teaspoons baking soda
4 eggs
2 teaspoons vanilla
1/2 cup oil
6 ripe bananas
1 cup chopped pecans or walnuts

PREPARATION

Preheat oven to 350°F. Grease and flour a loaf or Bundt pan. Sift the flour, sugar, salt, and baking soda together in a medium-sized bowl. Set aside. In a large-sized bowl, beat the eggs, vanilla, oil, and mashed bananas. Add the flour mixture to the egg mixture and blend. Stir in the nuts. Pour mixture into the prepared pan and bake for 1 hour, or until toothpick inserted comes out clean. Remove from oven, turn upside down to cool for 15 minutes. Place on serving plate. Slice and serve.

> "THIS RECIPE CAME FROM MY SISTER, TERESA. IT IS CALLED 'WILLIE'S BANANA NUT BREAD' BECAUSE MY SISTER'S MOTHER-IN-LAW, WILLIE MULLICAN, WHO PASSED AWAY IN 1992, ALWAYS MADE THIS. IT WAS WONDERFUL. I DO NOT KNOW WHERE WILLIE ACTUALLY GOT THIS RECIPE OR IF SHE CREATED IT HERSELF, BUT IT IS THE BEST BANANA NUT BREAD YOU WILL EVER EAT!"
>
> > Brenda

APPETIZERS

BREADS

BREAKFAST & BRUNCH

ENTRÉES

VEGETABLES & SIDE DISHES

SALADS

SOUPS

DESSERTS

"MY MOM AND I BAKED THESE COOK-IES TOGETHER AT LEAST ONCE PER MONTH WHILE I WAS GROWING UP. AS A YOUNG CHILD, I WOULD STAND ON A STOOL NEXT TO HER AND MEASURE ALL OF THE INGREDIENTS WHILE SHE MIXED THEM. THEN I WOULD LICK THE BEATERS, OF COURSE. AS A TEENAGER, FRIENDS WOULD COME TO MY HOUSE AND HEAD STRAIGHT FOR THE FREEZER, WHERE WE KEPT THE COOKIES, TO GRAB A HANDFUL. EVERYONE LOVES THESE COOKIES. SHARING THE RECIPE WITH MY HOST-MOM IN SPAIN AND TWO FOREIGN EXCHANGE STUDENTS FROM GERMANY AND BRAZIL HAVE MADE THEM TRULY WORLD FAMOUS."

> Sarah

world-famous oatmeal chocolate chip cookies

Sarah Mellen > *Topeka, Kansas*

Serving size varies

INGREDIENTS

1 cup (2 sticks) margarine, at room temperature
3/4 cup granulated sugar
3/4 cup firmly packed dark brown sugar
2 eggs
1 teaspoon vanilla extract
1 cup all-purpose flour
3/4 cup whole wheat flour
1 teaspoon baking soda
3 heaping cups regular rolled oats
1 package semisweet chocolate chips

PREPARATION

Preheat the oven to 375°F. In a large mixing bowl, beat the margarine and sugars with a portable mixer until smooth. Add the eggs and vanilla, and beat until smooth. Stir in the flours and baking soda. Stir in the oats and chocolate chips until mixed. Using two regular spoons, drop the dough by tablespoonfuls onto a baking sheet. Bake until they look just done around the bottom edge; they will not look done on top. That is what makes them soft, chewy, and great!

THE HEART OF THE STORY

America's Second Harvest distributes more than 2 billion pounds of food each year through its network of more than 200 food banks and food-rescue organizations. These are some of the many thankful who've been helped.

GIVE AND YOU SHALL RECEIVE

County Line Food Pantry > *Agency of Mississippi Food Network*

Linda receives from and gives back to the County Line Food Pantry, an agency of the Mississippi Food Network. A single parent with an ill 11-year-old son at home, Linda's retirement doesn't provide enough for her to pay bills, purchase medicine for her son, and buy enough groceries for the month. Without the food from County Line, Linda and her son would not have enough food each month. She volunteers at County Line each week to give others the help she so gratefully receives.

Vernon, another recipient and volunteer, helps take care of his two brothers – one is intellectually challenged and the other suffers from heart problems. Vernon volunteers weekly at County Line because he knows how much the food they get from County Line means to his family.

HELPING SENIORS SURVIVE

Deliver Me Senior Support Services and County Line Food Pantry > *Agencies of Mississippi Food Network*

Eighty-eight-year-old Mrs. Donnie still lives in her own home. Although she worked for Norman Shirtmakers for many years, she now has to make do on her $641 in Social Security checks and $10 in food stamps each month. She depends on the County Line Food Pantry because after household expenses and purchase of medicine, there isn't enough remaining for sufficient food for the month.

Eighty-seven-year-old Mrs. Elvnia lives on a meager, fixed income of $625 a month from Social Security and Supplemental Security Income payments. From that, she pays her share of rent on her small duplex, utilities, medicine, gas, clothing and other daily expenses. Each month she receives a Commodity Supplemental Food Program Senior Food Box from Deliver Me Senior Support Services volunteers and seven additional bags of groceries every four months. "I am so thankful for the food I get. I don't know what I would do without it each month," she says, with tears in her eyes.

DO UNTO OTHERS...
Montgomery Area Food Bank

When Samantha moved to Alabama looking for a new beginning, she instead found a series of endings – prearranged housing plans that didn't work out, no vehicle, no money and no food. Eight months pregnant, with two teenagers to care for, and down to a single bag of rice and one can of beans, she made a call to Montgomery Area Food Bank (MAFB) and said, "I'm not complaining of my situation, I'm just in a difficult time right now and can use a little help." MAFB put her in touch with an agency that quickly made arrangements to get groceries and personal care products to her and her children. A deeply faithful young woman, she had worked previously with her local food bank to help the hunger needs of clients she served. Finding herself now on the receiving side of the goodness of others, Samantha was inspired to pass on the blessings. Filled with enthusiasm, she immediately encouraged her new church to become an agency of MAFB. After the birth of her child, Samantha will be instrumental in coordinating that agency.

TO HOMELESSNESS AND BACK
St. Mary's Center > *Agency of Alameda Community Food Bank*

Sixty-year-old Jeanette once lived in Silicon Valley with her husband and owned a home and a business. Never did they imagine ending up homeless. Unfortunately, Jeanette's husband became ill when they were uninsured and the unpaid bills began to pile up. When Jeanette's husband died, she lost her home. For awhile, she stayed with friends and family, but eventually was forced to seek assistance from St. Mary's Center, an agency of the Alameda County Community Food Bank. Jeanette was scared and ashamed but said that St. Mary's Center helped her feel more human. Now Jeanette attends school with the goal of becoming a psychologist and "helping others the way I have been helped." Jeanette's experience has shown her that hunger and homelessness can happen to anyone.

A HELPING HAND
Tyler Family Assistance > *Agency of East Texas Food Bank*

Cheryle, who is diabetic, feels that her 13-year-old son Zach's well-being is more important than her own. He has a very serious heart condition and needs a transplant. Cheryle was working full-time but had to take a leave of absence for medical reasons. While she's getting her GED and actively looking for a new job, she has no income other than food stamps, so it's a struggle to make ends meet. "My son and I are going to be okay, but right now we need help," she says. Fortunately, Cheryle found the help she needs at Tyler Family Assistance, an agency of the East Texas Food Bank. "You help so much!" she says. "It is so appreciated. You give us inspiration and a chance to get back on our feet. Thank you is not enough!"

INDIANA FOOD BANK RECIPIENTS SEND THANKS
Second Harvest Food Bank of East Central Indiana

"I have health issues and can't always afford fresh vegetables and fruit on my Social Security after rent, lights, gas, and things. Thanks so much for your help." **Mary**, age 63

"I was injured in a wreck and can't work. I live with my sister and her baby grandson and her two older boys. Hard to stretch food stamps for a whole month." **Laura**, age 45

"I am a full-time student and do work-study. We rely on my small paycheck and government assistance to pay bills. It sometimes gets tough the weeks before we get our food stamps. We will take $40 and try to stretch it for 2 weeks. We eat last and make sure the kids eat first." **Amber,** age 29

"My husband is on disability, I am bi-polar. We live on a fixed income and get a few food stamps, but not enough to get us through the month. There are times when we don't have anything to eat if I can't go to the food pantry. The food pantry helps us a lot." **Dorothy,** age 50

"While raising my children, there were times I didn't know what I was going to feed them. But we survived. I'm thankful for food stamps and pantries." **Kathryn,** volunteer

"I sure don't like to be hungry, and I don't like to see anyone else hungry. Thanks to the food bank network. It helps so much." **Mable,** age 65

"Sometimes I don't have enough money to feed and provide for my family. This food pantry makes it a little easier." **Lindsay,** age 23

HOW YOU CAN HELP MAKE A DIFFERENCE

- **Buy extra copies of this cookbook** as gifts for family, friends, and neighbors. Be sure to tell them that the net sale proceeds go to America's Second Harvest to help feed the hungry. Ask them to buy copies for their friends and families.

- **Volunteer!** Tutor kids at your local Kids Cafe, repackage donated food for use at food pantries, transport food to charitable agencies, help with disaster response by getting donated food to where it's needed most, do clerical work at member agencies or America's Second Harvest national office. Get involved today and get your friends and family involved too. Find your local food bank at www.secondharvest.org, and start finding volunteer opportunities in your community.

- **Make a monetary donation** to America's Second Harvest:
America's Second Harvest
Individual Giving Assistant
35 East Wacker Drive, Suite 2000
Chicago, IL 60601

Or donate online at www.secondharvest.org

- **Make a product donation** to your local food bank or food-rescue organization. Find your local food bank at www.secondharvest.org, and contact them to find out what items they currently need.

- **Donate in someone's honor** or in memory of a loved one. Every day more and more people are choosing alternative gift options for birthdays, holidays, memorials and many other occasions. Visit www.secondharvest.org to make an honor or memorial gift.

- **Find out if your company has a matching gift program**. If America's Second Harvest meets your company's requirements, contact:
America's Second Harvest
Matching Gifts
35 East Wacker Drive, Suite 2000
Chicago, IL 60601

- **Consider a legacy gift** to America's Second Harvest. A legacy gift results from the donor's careful consideration of a number of important factors, including the purpose of the gift, the assets to be used to fund the gift, the gift's timing, its effect on income tax and estate tax planning, and its impact on the donor's family members and friends. A legacy gift is best made with the counsel of your legal, tax or financial advisor.

- **Join the Harvesters** monthly giving program. Funds are automatically transferred once each month from your checking account or credit card to America's Second Harvest.

- **Donate stock or mutual fund shares** to America's Second Harvest. If you own appreciated securities (stocks, bonds or mutual funds held by you for more than one year), donating them to America's Second Harvest may allow you to reduce or avoid more capital gains taxes and receive a federal income tax charitable deduction.

- **Hold a food drive.** Food drives provide nearly one-third of the food distributed annually by America's Second Harvest. By hosting a food drive you help meet the needs of so many people in your community. Contact your local food bank for more details or go to www.secondharvest.org to find a food bank near you.

FOOD BANKS

Food Bank of Alaska, Inc.
Anchorage, AK • 907-272-3663
www.foodbankofalaska.org

Bay Area Food Bank
Theodore, AL • 251-653-1617
www.bayareafoodbank.org

Food Bank of North Alabama
Huntsville, AL • 256-539-2256

Montgomery Area Food Bank, Inc.
Montgomery, AL • 334-263-3784
www.montgomeryareafoodbank.org

The United Way Community
Food Bank, Inc.
Birmingham, AL • 205-942-8911
www.alfoodbanks.org

Arkansas Foodbank Network, Inc
Little Rock, AR • 501-565-8121
www.arkansasfoodbank.org

Food Bank of Northeast Arkansas
Jonesboro, AR • 870-932-3663

Ozark Food Bank
Bethel Heights, AR • 479-872-8774
www.ozarkfoodbank.org

River Valley Regional Food Bank
Ft. Smith, AR • 479-785-0582

Community Food Bank of Tucson
Tucson, AZ • 520-622-0525
www.communityfoodbank.org

St. Mary's Food Bank Alliance
Phoenix, AZ • 602-352-3640
www.firstfoodbank.org

United Food Bank
Mesa, AZ • 480-926-4897
www.unitedfoodbank.org

Yuma Community Food Bank
Yuma, AZ • 928-343-1243
www.yumafoodbank.org

Alameda County Community Food Bank
Oakland, CA • 510-635-3663
www.accfb.org

Community Food Bank
Fresno, CA • 559.237.3663
www.communityfoodbank.net

Community Resources Council, Inc.
Roseville, CA • 916-783-0481

FIND, Inc.
Cathedral City, CA • 760-328-3663
www.FINDfoodbank.org

Food Bank for Monterey County
Salinas, CA • 831-758-1523
www.food4hungry.org

Food Bank of Contra Costa and Solano
Concord, CA • 925-676-7543
www.foodbankccs.org

Food Share, Inc.
Oxnard, CA • 805-983-7100
www.foodshare.com

Foodbank of Santa Barbara County
Santa Barbara, CA • 805-967-5741 ext 100
www.foodbanksbc.org

FoodLink for Tulare County
Visalia, CA • 559-651-3663
www.foodlinktc.org

Los Angeles Regional Foodbank
Los Angeles, CA • 323-234-3030
www.lafoodbank.org

Redwood Empire Food Bank
Santa Rosa, CA • 707-523-7900
www.refb.org

San Francisco Food Bank
San Francisco, CA • 415-282-1900
www.sffoodbank.org

Second Harvest Food Bank
of Orange County
Irvine, CA • 949-653-2900
www.FeedOC.org

Second Harvest Food Bank of San Diego
San Diego, CA • 858-653-3663

Second Harvest Food Bank of San
Joaquin and Stanislaus Counties
Manteca, CA • 209-239-2091
www.localfoodbank.org

Second Harvest Food Bank of Santa
Clara & San Mateo Counties
San Jose, CA • 408-266-8866
www.2ndharvest.net

Second Harvest Food Bank of Santa Cruz
and San Benito Cos.
Watsonville, CA • 831-722-7110 ext 228
www.thefoodbank.org

Second Harvest Food Bank Serving
Riverside and San Bernardino Cos.
Riverside, CA • 951-359-4757

Care and Share Food Bank
Colorado Springs, CO • 719-528-1247
www.careandshare.org

Community Food Share
Longmont, CO • 303-652-3663
www.communityfoodshare.org

Food Bank for Larimer County
Ft. Collins, CO • 970-493-4477
www.foodbanklarimer.org

Food Bank of the Rockies
Denver, CO • 303-371-9250
www.foodbankrockies.org

Weld Food Bank
Greeley, CO • 970-356-2199
www.weldfoodbank.org

Connecticut Food Bank
New Haven, CT • 203-469-5000
www.ctfoodbank.org

Foodshare
Bloomfield, CT • 860-286-9999
www.foodshare.org

FOOD BANKS

Capital Area Food Bank
Washington, DC • 202-526-5344
www.capitalareafoodbank.org

Food Bank of Delaware
Newark, DE • 302-292-1305
www.fbd.org

All Faiths Food Bank
Sarasota, FL • 941-379-6333
www.allfaithsfoodbank.org

America's Second Harvest of Tampa Bay
Tampa, FL • 813-254-1190
www.a2htampabay.org

America's Second Harvest of
the Big Bend, Inc.
Tallahassee, FL • 850-562-3033
www.fightinghunger.org

Daily Bread Food Bank
Miami, FL • 305-633-9861
www.dailybread.org

Harry Chapin Food Bank of
Southwest Florida
Ft. Myers, FL • 239-334-7007
www.harrychapinfoodbank.org

LSS Second Harvest Food Bank
of Northeast Florida
Jacksonville, FL • 904-353-3663
www.lssjax.org/aboutthefoodbank.html

Second Harvest Food Bank of
Central Florida
Orlando, FL • 407-295-1066
www.foodbankcentralflorida.org

America's Second Harvest of
Coastal Georgia, Inc.
Savannah, GA • 912-236-6750
www.helpendhunger.org

America's Second Harvest of
South Georgia, Inc.
Valdosta, GA • 229-244-2678
www.valdostafoodbank.org

Atlanta Community Food Bank
Atlanta, GA • 678-553-5998
www.acfb.org

Food Bank of Northeast Georgia
Athens, GA • 706-354-8191
www.foodbanknega.org

Golden Harvest Food Bank
Augusta, GA • 706-736-1199
www.goldenharvest.org

Middle Georgia Community Food Bank
Macon, GA • 478-742-3958
www.mgcfb.org

Second Harvest Food Bank of the
Chattahoochee Valley
Columbus, GA • 706-561-4755
www.feedcolumbus.org

The Food Bank of Southwest Georgia
Albany, GA • 229-883-5959
www.foodbank-swga.org

Hawaii Foodbank, Inc.
Honolulu, HI • 808-836-3600
www.hawaiifoodbank.org

Food Bank of Iowa
Des Moines, IA • 515-564-0330

Food Bank of Southern Iowa, Inc.
Ottumwa, IA • 641-682-3403

HACAP Food Reservoir
Hiawatha, IA • 319-393-7811
www.hacap.org

Northeast Iowa Food Bank
Waterloo, IA • 319-235-0507
www.northeastiowafoodbank.org

The Idaho Foodbank
Boise, ID • 208-336-9643
www.idahofoodbank.org

Central Illinois Foodbank
Springfield, IL • 217-522-4022

Eastern Illinois Foodbank
Urbana, IL • 217-328-3663
www.eifoodbank.org

Greater Chicago Food Depository
Chicago, IL • 773-247-3663
www.chicagosfoodbank.org

Northern Illinois Food Bank
St. Charles, IL • 630-443-6910
www.northernilfoodbank.org

Peoria Area Food Bank
Peoria, IL • 309-671-3906
www.pcceo.org

River Bend Food Bank
Moline, IL • 309-764-7434

Community Harvest Food Bank
of Northeast Indiana, Inc.
Fort Wayne, IN • 260-447-3696
www.chfb.org

Food Bank of Northern Indiana
South Bend, IN • 574-232-9986
www.feedindiana.org

Food Bank of Northwest Indiana
Gary, IN • 219-980-1777
www.foodbanknwi.org

Food Finders Food Bank, Inc.
Lafayette, IN • 765-471-0062
www.food-finders.org

Gleaners Food Bank of Indiana, Inc.
Indianapolis, IN • 317-925-0191
www.gleaners.org

Hoosier Hills Food Bank
Bloomington, IN • 812-334-8374
www.hhfoodbank.org

Second Harvest Food Bank of
East Central Indiana
Anderson, IN • 765-287-8698
www.curehunger.org

FOOD BANKS

Terre Haute Catholic Charities
Terre Haute, IN • 812-232-1447

Tri-State Food Bank
Evansville, IN • 812-425-0775
www.tristatefoodbank.org

Kansas Foodbank Warehouse
Wichita, KS • 316-265-4421
www.ksfoodbank.org

America's Second Harvest of
Kentucky's Heartland
Elizabethtown, KY • 270-769-6997
www.secondharvestky.com

Dare to Care Food Bank
Louisville, KY • 502-966-3821
www.daretocare.org

God's Pantry Food Bank, Inc.
Lexington, KY • 859-255-6592
www.godspantry.org

Food Bank of Central Louisiana
Alexandria, LA • 318-445-2773
www.fbcenla.org

Food Bank of Northeast Louisiana
Monroe, LA • 318-322-3567
www.fbnela.org

Food Bank of Northwest Louisiana
Shreveport, LA • 318-675-2400
www.foodbanknla.org

Greater Baton Rouge Food Bank
Baton Rouge, LA • 225-359-9940
www.brfoodbank.org

Second Harvest Food Bank of Greater
New Orleans and Acadiana
New Orleans, LA • 504-734-1322
www.no-hunger.org

The Food Bank of Western
Massachusetts
Hatfield, MA • 413-247-9738
www.foodbankwma.org

The Greater Boston Food Bank
Boston, MA • 617-427-5200
www.gbfb.org

Worcester County Food Bank, Inc.
Shrewsbury, MA • 508-842-3663
www.foodbank.org

Maryland Food Bank
Baltimore, MD • 410-737-8282
www.mdfoodbank.org

Good Shepherd Food Bank
Auburn, ME • 207-782-3554
www.gsfb.org

American Red Cross Regional Food
Distribution Ctr.
Lansing, MI • 517-702-3355
www.midmichiganredcross.org

Food Bank of Eastern Michigan
Flint, MI • 810-239-4441
www.fbem.org

Food Bank of South Central Michigan
Battle Creek, MI • 269-964-3663
www.foodbankofscm.org

Food Gatherers
Ann Arbor, MI • 734-761-2796
www.foodgatherers.org

Forgotten Harvest
Oak Park, MI • 248-967-1500
www.forgottenharvest.org

Gleaners Community Food Bank of
Southeastern Michigan
Detroit, MI • 313-923-3535
www.gcfb.org

Second Harvest Gleaners Food Bank of
West Michigan, Inc.
Comstock Park, MI • 616-784-3250
www.wmgleaners.org

Channel One Food Bank
Rochester, MN • 507-424-1750
www.channel-one.org

North Country Food Bank, Inc.
Crookston, MN • 218-281-7356
www.northcountryfoodbank.org

Second Harvest Heartland
St. Paul, MN • 651-484-5117
www.2harvest.org

Second Harvest North Central Food Bank
Grand Rapids, MN • 218-326-4420
www.secondharvestncfb.com

Second Harvest Northern Lakes
Food Bank
Duluth, MN • 218-727-5653
www.northernlakesfoodbank.org

America's Second Harvest of
Greater St. Joseph
St. Joseph, MO • 816-364-3663
www.stjoefoodbank.org

Bootheel Food Bank
Sikeston, MO • 573-471-1818

Central Missouri Food Bank Network, Inc.
Columbia, MO • 573-474-1020
www.centralmofoodbank.org

Harvesters - The Community
Food Network
Kansas City, MO • 816-929-3000
www.harvesters.org

Ozarks Food Harvest
Springfield, MO • 417-865-3411
www.ozarksfoodharvest.org

St. Louis Area Foodbank
St. Louis, MO • 314-292-6262
www.stlfoodbank.org

Mississippi Food Network
Jackson, MS • 601-353-7286
www.msfoodnet.org

Missoula Food Bank
Missoula, MT • 406-549-0543
www.missoulafoodbank.org

FOOD BANKS

Montana Food Bank Network
Missoula, MT · 406-721-3825
www.montanafoodbanknetwork.org

Food Bank of Central & Eastern
North Carolina
Raleigh, NC · 919-875-0707
www.foodbankcenc.org

Food Bank of the Albemarle
Elizabeth City, NC · 252-335-4035
www.afoodbank.org

Inter-Faith Food Shuttle
Raleigh, NC · 919-250-0043
www.foodshuttle.org

MANNA FoodBank
Asheville, NC · 828-299-3663
www.mannafoodbank.org

Second Harvest Food Bank of Metrolina
Charlotte, NC · 704-376-1785
www.secondharvestmetrolina.org

Second Harvest Food Bank of
Northwest North Carolina
Winston-Salem, NC · 336-784-5770
www.hungernwnc.org

Second Harvest Food Bank of
Southeast North Carolina
Fayetteville, NC · 910-485-8809
www.ccap-inc.org

Great Plains Food Bank
Fargo, ND · 701-232-6219
www.lssnd.org/htmls/foodbank.asp

Food Bank of Lincoln, Inc.
Lincoln, NE · 402-466-8170
www.lincolnfoodbank.org

The Nebraska Food Bank Network, Inc.
Omaha, NE · 402-331-1213
www.omahafoodbank.org

New Hampshire Food Bank
Manchester, NH · 603-669-9725
www.nhfoodbank.org

Community Food Bank of New Jersey
Hillside, NJ · 908-355-3663
www.njfoodbank.org

Food Bank of South Jersey
Pennsauken, NJ · 856-662-4884
www.foodbanksj.org

The FoodBank of Monmouth and
Ocean Counties, Inc.
Neptune, NJ · 732-918-2600
www.foodbankmoc.org

Roadrunner Food Bank
Albuquerque, NM · 505-247-2052
www.rrfb.org

Food Bank of Northern Nevada
Sparks, NV · 775-331-3663
www.fbnn.org

City Harvest
New York, NY · 917-351-8700
www.cityharvest.org

Food Bank For New York City
New York, NY · 718-991-4300
www.foodbanknyc.org

Food Bank of Central New York
East Syracuse, NY · 315-437-1899
www.foodbankcny.org

Food Bank of the Southern Tier
Elmira, NY · 607-796-6061
www.foodbankst.org

Food Bank of Western New York
Buffalo, NY · 716-852-1305
www.foodbankwny.org

Foodlink, Inc.
Rochester, NY · 585-328-3380
www.foodlinkny.org

Island Harvest
Mineola, NY · 516-294-8528
www.islandharvest.org

Long Island Cares, Inc.
Hauppauge, NY · 631-582-FOOD ext 102
www.licares.org

Regional Food Bank Northeastern
New York
Latham, NY · 518-786-3691
www.regionalfoodbank.net

The Food Bank for Westchester, Inc.
Millwood, NY · 914-923-1100
www.foodbankforwestchester.org

Akron-Canton Regional Foodbank
Akron, OH · 330-777-7567
www.akroncantonfoodbank.org

Cleveland Foodbank, Inc.
Cleveland, OH · 216-738-2265
www.clevelandfoodbank.com

FreestoreFoodBank
Cincinnati, OH · 513-482-4500
www.freestorefoodbank.org

Mid-Ohio FoodBank
Columbus, OH · 614-274-7770
www.midohiofoodbank.org

Second Harvest Food Bank of
North Central Ohio
Lorain, OH · 440-960-2265
www.secondharvestfoodbank.org

Second Harvest Food Bank of
Southeastern Ohio
Logan, OH · 740-385-6813
www.hapcap.org

Second Harvest Food Bank of
the Mahoning Valley
Youngstown, OH · 330-792-5522
www.mahoningvalleysecondharvest.com

FOOD BANKS

Second Harvest Foodbank of Clark,
Champaign, & Logan Counties
Springfield, OH • 937-323-6507
www.springfieldcatholicsocialservices.org

Shared Harvest Foodbank
Fairfield, OH • 513-874-0114
www.sharedharvest.org

The Foodbank, Inc.
Dayton, OH • 937-461-0265
www.thefoodbankdayton.org

Toledo Northwestern Ohio Food Bank
Toledo, OH • 419-242-5000
www.toledofoodbank.org

West Ohio Food Bank
Lima, OH • 419-222-7946
www.westohiofoodbank.org

Community Food Bank of
Eastern Oklahoma
Tulsa, OK • 918-585-2800
www.cfbeo.org

Regional Food Bank of Oklahoma
Oklahoma City, OK • 405-972-1111
www.regionalfoodbank.org

FOOD for Lane County
Eugene, OR • 541-343-2822
www.foodforlanecounty.org

Oregon Food Bank
Portland, OR • 503-282-0555
www.oregonfoodbank.org

St. Vincent de Paul Food
Recovery Network
Portland, OR • 503-234-1114
www.svdppdx.org

Central Pennsylvania Food Bank
Harrisburg, PA • 717-564-1700
www.centralpafoodbank.org

Channels Food Rescue
Lemoyne, PA • 717-612-1300
www.channelsfoodrescue.com

Community Food Warehouse
Farrell, PA • 724-981-0353
www.foodwarehouse.org

Greater Berks Food Bank
Reading, PA • 610-926-5802
www.berksfoodbank.org

Greater Pittsburgh Community
Food Bank
Duquesne, PA • 412-460-3663
www.pittsburghfoodbank.org

H & J Weinberg NE PA Regional
Food Bank
Wilkes Barre, PA • 570-826-0510
www.ceopeoplehelpingpeople.org

Philabundance
Philadelphia, PA • 215-339-0900
www.philabundance.org

Second Harvest Food Bank
of Northwest Pennsylvania
Erie, PA • 814-459-3663
www.eriefoodbank.org

Second Harvest Food Bank of the Lehigh
Valley and NE Pennsylvania
Allentown, PA • 610-434-0875
www.caclv.org

Westmoreland County Food Bank
Delmont, PA • 724-468-8660
www.westmorelandfoodbank.org

Banco de Alimentos de Puerto Rico
Bayamon, PR • 787-740-3663
www.bancoalimentospr.org

Rhode Island Community Food Bank
Providence, RI • 401-942-6325
www.rifoodbank.org

Harvest Hope Food Bank
Columbia, SC • 803-254-4432
www.harvesthope.org

Lowcountry Food Bank
Charleston, SC • 843-747-8146
www.lowcountryfoodbank.org

Community Food Banks of South Dakota
Sioux Falls, SD • 605-335-0364
www.sdfoodbanks.org

Chattanooga Area Food Bank
Chattanooga, TN • 423-622-1800
www.chattfoodbank.org

Memphis Food Bank
Memphis, TN • 901-527-0841
www.memphisfoodbank.org

Second Harvest Food Bank of
East Tennessee
Knoxville, TN • 865-521-0000
www.secondharvestknox.org

Second Harvest Food Bank of
Middle Tennessee
Nashville, TN • 615-329-3491
www.secondharvestnashville.org

Second Harvest Food Bank of
Northeast Tennessee
Gray, TN • 423-477-4053
www.netfoodbank.org

Capital Area Food Bank of Texas, Inc.
Austin, TX • 512-282-2111
www.austinfoodbank.org

East Texas Food Bank
Tyler, TX • 903-597-3663
www.easttexasfoodbank.org

End Hunger Network
Houston, TX • 713-532-3663
www.endhungernetwork.org

Food Bank of Corpus Christi
Corpus Christi, TX • 361-887-6291
www.foodbankofcorpuschristi.org

FOOD BANKS

Food Bank of the Golden Crescent
Victoria, TX • 361-578-0591
www.victoriafoodbank.org

Food Bank of the Rio Grande Valley, Inc.
McAllen, TX • 956-682-8101
www.foodbankrgv.com

Food Bank of West Central Texas
Abilene, TX • 325-695-6311
www.fbwct.org

Harvest Texarkana
Texarkana, TX • 870-774-1398
www.harvesttexarkana.org

High Plains Food Bank
Amarillo, TX • 806-374-8562
www.hpfb.org

Houston Food Bank
Houston, TX • 713-223-3700
www.HoustonFoodBank.org

North Texas Food Bank
Dallas, TX • 214-330-1396
www.ntfb.org

San Antonio Food Bank
San Antonio, TX • 210-337-3663
www.safoodbank.org

South Plains Food Bank
Lubbock, TX • 806-763-3003
www.spfb.org

Southeast Texas Food Bank
Beaumont, TX • 409-839-8777
www.setxfoodbank.org

Tarrant Area Food Bank
Ft. Worth, TX • 817-332-9177
www.tafb.org

West Texas Food Bank
Odessa, TX • 432-580-6333
www.wtxfoodbank.org

Wichita Falls Area Food Bank
Wichita Falls, TX • 940-766-2322
www.WFAreafoodbank.com

Utah Food Bank Services
Salt Lake City, UT • 801-908-8660
www.utahfoodbank.org

Blue Ridge Area Food Bank, Inc.
Verona, VA • 540-248-3663
www.brafb.org

Central Virginia Foodbank, Inc.
Richmond, VA • 804-521-2500
www.cvfb.org

Foodbank of Southeastern Virginia
Norfolk, VA • 757-627-6599
www.foodbankonline.org

FoodBank of the Virginia Peninsula
Newport News, VA • 757-596-7188
www.foodbank.ws

Fredericksburg Area Food Bank
Fredericksburg, VA • 540-371-7666
www.fredfood.org

Southwestern Virginia Second
Harvest Food Bank
Salem, VA • 540-342-3011
www.swvafoodbank.org

Vermont Foodbank, Inc.
South Barre, VT • 802-476-3341
www.vtfoodbank.org

Food Lifeline
Shoreline, WA • 206-545-6600
www.foodlifeline.org

Second Harvest Inland Northwest
Spokane, WA • 509-534-6678
www.2-harvest.org

America's Second Harvest of Wisconsin
Milwaukee, WI • 414-931-7400
www.secondharvestwi.org

Second Harvest Foodbank of
Southern Wisconsin
Madison, WI • 608-223-9121
www.secondharvestmadison.org

Huntington Area Food Bank, Inc.
Huntington, WV • 304-523-6029
www.hafb.org

Mountaineer Food Bank
Gassaway, WV • 304-364-5518
www.mountaineerfoodbank.com

index of recipes

APPETIZERS

BREADS

BREAKFAST &
BRUNCH

ENTRÉES

VEGETABLES &
SIDE DISHES

SALADS

SOUPS

DESSERTS

APPETIZERS

BREADS

BREAKFAST & BRUNCH

ENTRÉES

VEGETABLES & SIDE DISHES

SALADS

SOUPS

DESSERTS

RECIPES BY SECTION

APPETIZERS

BREADS

BREAKFAST & BRUNCH

ENTRÉES

VEGETABLES & SIDE DISHES

SALADS

SOUPS

DESSERTS

APPETIZERS
BREADS
BREAKFAST & BRUNCH
ENTRÉES
VEGETABLES & SIDE DISHES
SALADS
SOUPS
DESSERTS

APPETIZERS

BREADS

BREAKFAST & BRUNCH

ENTRÉES

VEGETABLES & SIDE DISHES

SALADS

SOUPS

DESSERTS

APPETIZERS

BREADS

BREAKFAST & BRUNCH

ENTRÉES

VEGETABLES & SIDE DISHES

SALADS

SOUPS

DESSERTS

APPETIZERS

BREADS

BREAKFAST & BRUNCH

ENTRÉES

VEGETABLES & SIDE DISHES

SALADS

SOUPS

DESSERTS

RECIPES BY TITLE

APPETIZERS

BREADS

BREAKFAST & BRUNCH

ENTRÉES

VEGETABLES & SIDE DISHES

SALADS

SOUPS

DESSERTS

APPETIZERS

BREADS

BREAKFAST &
BRUNCH

ENTRÉES

VEGETABLES &
SIDE DISHES

SALADS

SOUPS

DESSERTS

APPETIZERS

BREADS

BREAKFAST & BRUNCH

ENTRÉES

VEGETABLES & SIDE DISHES

SALADS

SOUPS

DESSERTS